The
Civil War
100

The Civil War 100

A Ranking of the Most
Influential People in
the War Between the States

Robert Wooster

A CITADEL PRESS BOOK
Published by Carol Publishing Group

A Citadel Press Book
Published by Carol Publishing Group
Citadel Press is a registered trademark of Carol Communications, Inc.

Editorial, sales and distribution, and rights and permissions inquiries should be addressed to Carol Publishing Group, 120 Enterprise Avenue, Secaucus, N.J. 07094

In Canada: Canadian Manda Group, One Atlantic Avenue, Suite 105, Toronto, Ontario M6K 3E7

Carol Publishing Group books may be purchased in bulk at special discounts for sales promotion, fund-raising, or educational purposes. Special editions can be created to specifications. For details, contact: Special Sales Department, Carol Publishing Group, 120 Enterprise Avenue, Secaucus, N.J. 07094.

Manufactured in the United States of America
10 9 8 7 6 5 4 3 2 1

Library of Congress Cataloging-in-Publication Data

Wooster, Robert, 1956–
    The Civil War 100 : a ranking of the most influential people in
the War Between the States / Robert Wooster.
        p.   cm.
    "A Citadel Press book."
    Includes bibliographical references.
    ISBN 0-8065-1955-X
    1. United Sttes—History—Civil War, 1861–1865—Biography.
I. Title.   II. Title: Civil War one hundred
E467.W898   1998
973.7′092′2—dc21   98–12004
                                                              CIP

CONTENTS

PREFACE

My first real memory of anything related to the Civil War is from a family photograph taken when I was about six years old. In this picture, I am wearing canvas shoes, plaid shorts, a polo shirt, and a light blue fake German hiker's hat adorned with a white feather—my prized purchase, I believe, from the Southeast Texas State Fair. Thus nattily attired, I sit atop a cannon at some battlefield (I'm embarrassed to admit I don't remember which). My father, a distinguished historian and author of numerous works on secession and the Old South, must have noted the poignancy of his young son's appearance at a battlefield where brave American boys died. I suppose he was relieved that I wasn't complaining about something which might spoil the family vacation.

I know a little more about the Civil War now than I did then, but am still grappling to truly understand that conflict's impact on my country. From 1861 to 1865, six hundred thousand Americans died fighting for causes which they believed worth their ultimate sacrifice. Countless others were maimed physically or psychologically. Subsequent generations have fought and refought the war. Rebel battle flags still adorn automobile fenders, windshields, caps, and state flags. Some Northerners, on the other hand, still see their Southern cousins as backward and ill-disciplined country rubes who speak only a semi-comprehensible dialect.

There are millions of others doing just what I am—trying to understand this great conflict and those who fought and lived it. This enterprise is worthwhile, for although history does not necessarily repeat itself, those who do not understand the mistakes of the past are doomed to repeat them.

Fortunately, the United States is once again whole, but the fascination with the Civil War remains with us. The numbers are so staggering as to become almost incomprehensible: four times as many Americans fell casualty in a single day of fighting during the Civil War at Antietam as during the Normandy landings in World War II; eleven times more were killed from 1861 to 1865 than in our nation's decade-long involvement in Vietnam. Indeed, the conflict was conducted on such an immense scale, had such fateful consequences, and has taken on such mythic qualities that we of later generations sometimes find it difficult to think of it as real. By focusing on individuals rather than nameless statistics, however, we can often gain better insights into the triumphs and tragedies of our forebears. Perhaps, by coming to know more about the lives of the Civil War's most influential persons, modern readers will be able to see these men and women not simply as larger-than-life icons but as complex human beings, from whom we can learn and occasionally emulate.

ACKNOWLEDGMENTS

I owe this book to several people. Alan Lessoff, one of my colleagues at Texas A&M University-Corpus Christi, offered valuable insights about many aspects of the war. My father, Ralph A. Wooster, dignified and generous, installed in his only son a reverence for the past and love of the historical profession. He also took the time, as he has with all of my books, to comment on early drafts of manuscripts. My mother, Edna Wooster, loving and patient through our discussions of academe and historical minutia, somehow accepted the idiosyncracies and expectations of her two men. My wife, Catherine I. Cox, is rapidly becoming a recognized expert in the literature of two Englishmen—John Milton and William Shakespeare—whose names will long outlive those of her curmudgeonly husband. Still, she carefully edited the present volume, depriving herself of time she might otherwise have spent developing her own work to help me. Only a fellow academic truly knows how remarkably unselfish such a sacrifice was.

But it's really James Michener who made this book possible. In the early 1980s, he hired me, then a graduate student, to help with the preparation of his forthcoming novel, *Texas*. He also added to the team a recent college graduate, Lisa Kaufmann, who was looking for a career in publishing. Last year, Lisa asked if I'd be interested in writing a book about the 100 most significant persons of the Civil War. I could hardly refuse, given my own pedigree, ambitions, and interests.

In the final stages of this project, certain things changed. Lisa took a different job and Michael Lewis became my editor. I'm also in a new position as chair of the Department of Humanities at Texas A&M University–Corpus Christi in addition to my teaching responsibilities as professor of history. In the former capacity I'm ably supported by Nelda Walker-Sanford and Sonya Witherspoon. I'm not sure they'll ever understand how important it is for me to keep writing and researching while continuing to teach and handle administrative tasks; suffice it to say that I don't know how I'd function without them.

Still, I owe this book to James Michener. Whatever value this volume

has is a tribute to Jim, who convinced me that we all have a duty and obligation to share whatever knowledge and insights we might have with all of
society, not just academe. Of course, any errors in judgment or fact are mine
and mine alone.

INTRODUCTION

BACKGROUND TO THE CIVIL WAR

Slavery had long threatened the social and political harmony of the United States. The first true crisis came in 1819, when Missouri applied for admission into the Union as a slave state. This threatened the precarious balance between free and slave states, and Missouri's application sparked heated congressional debate. After two acrimonious years, a compromise was finally reached. Missouri would be allowed to enter as a slave state at the same time Maine (which had formerly been part of Massachusetts) became a free state. In an effort to forestall future controversy, Congress also divided the area acquired from France in the Louisiana Purchase. Except for Missouri, slavery would be prohibited above the 36°30′ parallel; below the line, slavery would be permitted.

The Missouri Compromise temporarily reduced political tensions, but during the 1840s, the annexation of Texas and the acquisition of the Southwest from Mexico in the Treaty of Guadalupe-Hidalgo reopened the question of slavery in the territories. After considerable wrangling, Congress passed the Compromise of 1850, which admitted California as a free state, organized the territories of Utah and New Mexico under the principle of popular sovereignty, enacted a fugitive slave law, ended the slave trade in the nation's capital, and paid Texas $10,000,000 in return for that state's cessation of its western land claims.

The recent compromise notwithstanding, contemporary observers reported vast differences between the Northern and Southern states. The life portrayed by Southern writers like WILLIAM GILMORE SIMMS [82], for example, stood in stark contrast to that described by Northerners. Simms's characters would have found the situations encountered in *Moby-Dick* (1851) by HERMAN MELVILLE [91] to be mysterious indeed. Economic differences were also obvious. Although agriculture remained dominant in both sections, the North was experiencing a far more rapid industrial development. By 1860, for example, 84 percent of the nation's investments in manufacturing were in the North, which also boasted nearly five times the South's merchant ship capacity. Northerners concluded that their better balanced economic system offered untold opportunities for free men willing to work hard. Southerners, by contrast, proudly noted the continuing demand for many of their agricultural products. Cotton alone accounted for over half the nation's total exports.

With divisions between North and South becoming increasingly apparent, the nation experienced a crisis in leadership. From 1852 to 1860, two of the most ineffective presidents in American history—FRANKLIN PIERCE [54] and JAMES BUCHANAN [26]—occupied the White House. Their inability to balance their sympathies for Southern causes with due attentiveness to Northern interests exacerbated sectional divisions. In Congress, STEPHEN DOUGLAS [11] proved a skillful political tactician in securing passage of the Kansas-Nebraska Act, which repealed the old Missouri Compromise and opened up the Kansas and Nebraska territories to slavery. Douglas, however, badly miscalculated the results of his machinations. A growing consensus in the North held that free workers could not compete successfully against slave labor; by allowing slavery to expand, Northerners believed that Douglas was limiting *their* opportunities. Many suspected that a pro-Southern conspiracy was at work.

Southerners agreed there was a conspiracy, but saw themselves as its victims. Since their major cash crops of cotton and tobacco steadily wore out the land, they needed room to expand. Naturally, they demanded that new territories be opened to slavery, so that on fresh land they could continue doing what they knew best, but they feared that the more populous North would deny them the right to take their property (i.e., slaves) to these fresh lands. Even though most white Southerners did not own slaves, they jealously defended their right to do so. Fire-eating spokesmen like EDMUND RUFFIN [72], WILLIAM YANCEY [16 (tie)], and ROBERT BARNWELL RHETT [16 (tie)], called upon the slave states to leave the Union rather than allow the sovereign rights of the states to be trampled.

Angry rhetoric was not confined to the South. Abolitionists WILLIAM LLOYD GARRISON [24] and HARRIET BEECHER STOWE [15] joined escaped slaves HARRIET TUBMAN [74], FREDERICK DOUGLASS [10], and SOJOURNER TRUTH [51] in denouncing the evils of Southern society. WILLIAM SEWARD [8] warned that he would follow "a higher law" rather than respect the federal fugitive slave law. On the floor of the United States Senate, CHARLES SUMNER [43] described slaveowners as "hirelings picked from the drunken spew of an uneasy civilization."

Two days later, Preston Brooks, a South Carolina congressman, found Sumner at his Senate desk and beat him senseless. "Towards the last, he bellowed like a calf," boasted Brooks. Maryland native ROGER B. TANEY [32], now chief justice of the Supreme Court, also was determined to strike a blow in defense of the South. In the *Dred Scott* v. *Sandford* (1857) case, Taney

ruled that blacks were not citizens and that the Missouri Compromise had
been unconstitutional, on the grounds that Congress had no right to exclude
slavery from the territories.

Useful dialogue became increasingly difficult. The Republican Party,
formed in the wake of the Kansas-Nebraska Act, drew all of its support from
the North. Southern interests, meanwhile, had become increasingly dominant within the Democratic Party. In 1856, virtual civil war erupted in Kansas
between pro- and antislavery forces. Three years later, abolitionist JOHN
BROWN [14], a veteran of the violence in Kansas, led a raid on the federal
arsenal at Harpers Ferry, Virginia, with the intention of seizing the weapons
and distributing them among the slaves to unleash a rebellion. The widespread outpouring of Northern sympathy for Brown startled Southerners,
whose long-standing fears of slave revolts now seemed to be a reality.

In 1860, Republican candidate ABRAHAM LINCOLN [1] defeated Stephen
Douglas (who represented the Democratic Party's northern wing), JOHN C.
BRECKINRIDGE [60] (the Southern Democrat), and John Bell (candidate of
the newly formed Constitutional Union Party, which pledged to avoid a war)
in the presidential election. Lincoln promised not to disturb slavery where it
already existed but vowed not to allow its expansion into any new areas. He
also supported federal initiatives which promoted greater economic opportunities, such as a transcontinental railroad and easier distribution of public
lands to private citizens. To Southerners, Lincoln seemed dangerous to liberty. The Republican programs would give the federal government too much
power; further, since slavery needed to expand in order to survive, Lincoln's
determination to limit slavery threatened their very existence.

Lincoln's election precipitated a crisis. Last-ditch efforts to craft a compromise, sponsored by Kentuckian JOHN CRITTENDEN [88], ended in failure.
Seven states in the lower South seceded from the Union, formed the Confederate States of America, and elected JEFFERSON DAVIS [5] as their president. When Lincoln made it clear that he intended to reinforce existing
Federal garrisons at Forts Pickens (Pensacola, Florida) and Sumter
(Charleston, South Carolina), Southerners acted. After a furious thirty-four
hour bombardment, the Federal garrison at Fort Sumter surrendered.

Lincoln promptly declared the South to be in a state of rebellion, called
up volunteers, and imposed a naval blockade. Upon hearing that shots had
been fired, Virginia, Tennessee, Arkansas, and North Carolina also joined the
Confederacy, but four border slave states did not follow. Delaware, where
slaves comprised only two percent of the population, never seriously considered leaving. Union troops quickly occupied Maryland, which technically
remained neutral. Missouri was also seized by force of arms. The state's governor was infuriated, and a group of secessionists formed a state government
in exile, declaring themselves to be the twelfth Confederate state. Kentucky
officially remained neutral, although a separate state convention also pledged
its loyalty to the Confederacy.

THE CIVIL WAR: DOMESTIC AND DIPLOMATIC AFFAIRS

Jefferson Davis and the new Confederate government, which had moved to Richmond with Virginia's secession, had much to do. The Confederacy, however, was grounded in the principle of states' rights, and many Southerners were reluctant to give up much authority to the central government. After all, they had left the United States to escape what they saw as the federal government's unconstitutional assumption of power. To have replaced one tyrannical government with another seemed foolish. Davis's efforts to centralize the war effort thus met stiff resistance. Vice President ALEXANDER STEPHENS [71], for example, demonstrated his opposition by staying away from Richmond for much of the war.

Lincoln, by comparison, enjoyed the benefits of a more established political system and seemed more at ease in dealing with political realities. His cabinet, for example, was excellent. In Secretary of State William Seward, Secretary of War EDWIN STANTON [9], Secretary of the Treasury SALMON P. CHASE [21], and Secretary of the Navy GIDEON WELLES [23], Lincoln could turn to men of intellect and experience. He rewarded several important politicians—JOHN C. FRÉMONT [46], darling of many Radical Republicans; BENJAMIN BUTLER [58], prominent Democrat; and NATHANIEL P. BANKS [59], former House speaker—with prestigious military appointments. Although the lives of the troops under their inept commands were endangered, these politically motivated appointments helped Lincoln to form an effective coalition of Republicans and War Democrats.

President Abraham Lincoln came to understand that the war meant more than just restoring the Union and helped to guide and shape the process of ending slavery. Before the war, he had consistently argued that the United States constitution guaranteed equality of opportunity for all men, regardless of race. Lincoln also insisted that slavery was morally wrong, even as he doubted that all races were inherently equal. As the conflict spread, however, he realized that the destruction of slavery would advance the war effort. Abolition, in addition to being morally desirable, would deprive the Confederacy of a substantial segment of its labor force and encourage hundreds of thousands of black men and women to support the Federal government. On September 22, 1862—following the Battle of Antietam, Maryland—the president issued his Emancipation Proclamation. He declared that effective January 1, 1863, all slaves in areas still under rebellion would be freed. This single act transformed the war from one simply to preserve the Union to one that would fundamentally restructure American society.

Before the Civil War, Southern and Northern Democrats had combined to block Republican legislative initiatives. Secession, by removing the Southern Democratic bloc, opened the door for the Republicans to increase the tariff, pass homestead legislation, use public lands to create land-grant colleges, and authorize construction of a transcontinental railroad. To help fund the war, Congress enacted the first income tax, introduced paper currency into circulation, and, through the marketing genius of JAY COOKE [48], sold millions of dollars in government bonds. The war also created enormous economic opportunities. PHILIP ARMOUR [97] made a fortune speculating in pork futures; GAIL BORDEN [96] found a vast new market for his condensed milk.

Frenzied diplomatic activity accompanied the American Civil War. Britain, Europe's greatest naval and economic power, was pivotal. The Confederacy pinned its hopes upon cotton, calculating that an embargo would cripple the British economy and force that nation's intervention against the North, but the Southerners failed to take into account several crucial factors. Due to European crop failures, Northern wheat and corn exports rivaled Southern cotton. In addition, English manufacturers had huge stockpiles of raw cotton on hand when the war began, and during the war would develop India and Egypt as alternate suppliers. Prime Minister Henry John Temple, the third VISCOUNT PALMERSTON [39], was a pragmatist who understood the strong working-class opposition to slavery in his country and the damage intervention would do to the lucrative trade with the United States. Finally, CHARLES FRANCIS ADAMS [67], minister to Britain, proved an adept, sensitive representative who defused several crises in U.S.-British relations.

England's neutrality meant that France, where pro-South sentiment ran strong, would also remain neutral. France's Emperor NAPOLEON III [70] did, however, hope the war would prevent the United States from stopping a French-backed coup in Mexico. Austrian Archduke Maximilian, supported by a strong French army, was temporarily ensconced as emperor of Mexico, but the Mexican people never accepted this foreign government. At the Civil War's end, the United States dispatched fifty thousand troops to the Rio Grande as a measure of its displeasure at Maximilian's continued rule. His short-lived empire collapsed soon thereafter.

THE CIVIL WAR: MILITARY AFFAIRS

In 1861, few on either side could foresee the terrible nature of the impending conflict. Naively, most believed that a quick battle or two would finish the job. Instead, it would take four long years and the lives of six hundred thousand Americans (nearly another half million would be wounded) to decide the war's outcome. Why was the war so bloody, and why did it take so long?

The answers to these questions are interconnected. American generals had no experience leading armies the size of those in the Civil War. During the war against Mexico, WINFIELD SCOTT [37] had captured Mexico City with fewer than fifteen thousand men; during the Civil War, Union armies routinely numbered between sixty thousand to one hundred twenty thousand, and with Confederate armies often exceeding sixty thousand. The logistical, organizational, and tactical skills needed to successfully lead such forces all had to be learned, often at the cost of human lives. This inexperience only compounded the "fog of war." Orders were misinterpreted or disobeyed; units got lost; men made mistakes—and soldiers died as a result.

Technical innovations also contributed to the bloodbath. Just prior to the war, firearms had undergone major changes. It had been known for years that rifled weapons (the inner barrels of which were grooved, or rifled) were far superior, in terms of both accuracy and distance, to regular smoothbores. Historically, however, these weapons had been difficult to produce and too slow to load for widespread use. Innovations, such as the Minié ball (named after Charles Minié, its French developer), now made rifling practical. As a result, muskets which had once been only marginally accurate at seventy-five yards became deadly at three hundred yards; many artillery pieces improved their accuracy to over three quarters of a mile.

Unfortunately, changes in tactics did not accompany technological advances. Most units still fought in two-deep linear formations, packed together when on the offensive to achieve sufficient mass to force a break-through. In the past, losses stemming from these tactics had been accept-able, but when facing troops equipped with the deadlier rifled weapons, Civil War assaults stood considerably less chance of success. Even when the enemy was driven from the field, casualties suffered in the process left the winners exhausted, unable to exploit their victory.

Leadership, weapons, and tactics are important elements in any war, but soldiers win or lose battles. Given the fairly lax discipline of Civil War armies, men without genuine commitment would soon refuse to expose themselves to the repeated dangers of the battlefield upon which fifteen to thirty percent of those engaged routinely fell as casualties; they would instead desert. Until the very last stages of the conflict, however, soldiers remained committed and stayed in the ranks. Only rarely did units break in battle. Belief in comrade, community, and cause overcame fear and convinced men to continually risk their lives.

The North enjoyed several military advantages at the war's outset. The Confederate navy had to be built virtually from scratch; further, the South had little of the manufacturing capacity needed to construct new ships. Although the South's navy secretary, STEPHEN MALLORY [64], utilized the resources at his disposal superbly, the Federals always enjoyed strategic naval superiority. Similarly, despite the herculean efforts of JOSIAH GORGAS [28], the South's chief of ordinance, the Confederacy's ability to equip, supply, and feed their troops in the field could never match that of the Union.

Despite these advantages, the war began badly for the North. In the east, early Union efforts centered on attempts to take Richmond. Because of pressure by the government and by politicians who believed the war could be won quickly, in July 1861, an unprepared Union Army under IRVIN McDOW-ELL [57] attacked Confederate forces under P. G. T. BEAUREGARD [35] and JOSEPH E. JOHNSTON [12] at Bull Run, Virginia, twenty-five miles southwest of Washington. Although enjoying initial success, the Federal assault floun-dered when faced with the determined resistance of THOMAS J. JACKSON [20], who would afterward be known as "Stonewall" for his stubborn defense. A Confederate counterattack routed McDowell's forces, who streamed back to Washington in disarray.

The task of revamping the Union effort in the east fell to GEORGE MCCLELLAN [7]. An able organizer and inspirational figure, McClellan was less gifted once battle had been joined. Perhaps he loved the Army of the Potomac, which he created, too much to see it bloodied in battle. In spring 1862 he landed near Yorktown, Virginia, with the intention of driving up the peninsula formed by the James and York rivers, planning to strike Richmond from the east rather than the north. Although he, in fact, enjoyed a comfortable numerical superiority over the Confederates, McClellan believed that he was outnumbered. This conviction was strengthened when reinforcements once slated for the Army of the Potomac were instead diverted to the Shenandoah Valley, Virginia, where Stonewall Jackson was in the process of embarrassing a succession of Union generals.

Rather than striking quickly at that time, McClellan, by his cautious advance up the Peninsula, gave Joe Johnston ample time to intercede. At Seven Pines, Virginia, Johnston attacked; the battle ended in a draw, but a wound Johnston suffered there forced him out of action in favor of ROBERT E. LEE [4], who would command the Army of Northern Virginia for the remainder of the war. In June, Lee wrested the initiative from McClellan, recalling Jackson from the Valley to augment his own forces, dispatching J. E. B. STUART [33] and the cavalry on a raid against McClellan's communications, and in the Seven Days Battles (Virginia) drove McClellan back down the Peninsula. With McClellan demoralized, Lee pushed north. In August, he again defeated the Federals, this time led by JOHN POPE [62], at the Second Battle of Bull Run, Virginia.

Determined to take the war out of his home state of Virginia and hoping that a victory on Northern soil might convince the Union to agree to terms or spark foreign intervention, Lee moved north. A strong Union garrison at Harpers Ferry, Virginia, was forced to surrender, but a copy of Lee's campaign plans fell into Union hands. McClellan vowed to "whip Bobbie Lee," and attacked the Army of Northern Virginia at Antietam Creek, Maryland. Although he enjoyed a two-to-one numerical advantage, McClellan failed to coordinate his assaults. At the end of the bloodiest single day in U.S. military history, Lee, though battered, remained unbroken, and fell back to Virginia in good order. The failure of Lee's invasion at least allowed Lincoln to announce his intention to free the slaves in areas still under rebellion. Lincoln was disappointed by McClellan's continued caution, and removed him in favor of AMBROSE BURNSIDE [52], who in December 1862 demonstrated his lack of military expertise by attacking prepared Confederate defenses at Fredericksburg, Virginia.

Although it was stalemated in the east, the Union enjoyed greater success in the west. A Confederate invasion of New Mexico in 1861–62 had been driven back with heavy losses. Union victories at Wilson's Creek, Missouri, and Pea Ridge, Arkansas, meant that Missouri would not fall into Confederate hands. DAVID FARRAGUT [13] led a naval assault up the Mississippi River and forced the surrender of New Orleans, the largest city in the Confederacy. Moreover, ULYSSES S. GRANT [2], who had failed at virtually everything he tried before the Civil War, had finally found his niche. In February 1862, he captured Forts Henry and Donelson in Tennessee, thus driving the Confederates from Nashville. That April, although initially surprised by Confederate general ALBERT SIDNEY JOHNSTON [79], who counterattacked at Shiloh, Tennessee, Grant recovered in time to win yet another victory.

Grant now began formulating plans against the key to the western front—Vicksburg, Mississippi, the Confederacy's major remaining citadel on the Mississippi River. The capture of Vicksburg would split the Confederacy in half. In late November, Grant began a two-pronged offensive. Part of his army, under WILLIAM T. SHERMAN [3], moved downriver and debarked just north of Vicksburg. Meanwhile, Grant marched south from Corinth, Mississippi, but enemy raids led by EARL VAN DORN [92] and NATHAN B. FORREST [44] sliced Grant's supply line and compelled the abandonment of his overland movement. Sherman's attempts to storm heavily defended Chickasaw Bluffs, Mississippi, north of Vicksburg, also failed. Further east, a bloody stalemate at Perryville, Kentucky, had forced the Confederates to abandon their invasion of that state. The year closed on a desultory note, in inconclusive fighting at Stones River, Tennessee, where WILLIAM ROSECRANS [76] and the Union Army of the Cumberland fended off the repeated attacks of BRAXTON BRAGG [30].

Grant was undeterred, and remained focused against Vicksburg. In late spring 1863, a cavalry raid through central Mississippi diverted Confederate attention even as DAVID D. PORTER [42] ran Union gunboats past the batteries of Vicksburg. In a brilliant move, Grant then divided his forces, using the protection of the gunboats to lead one wing of his army across the Mississippi south of Vicksburg, while Sherman demonstrated to the north. Grant used the confusion to get between the Vicksburg garrison of JOHN C. PEMBERTON [65] and Joe Johnston's troops at Jackson to the east. Following a six-week siege, the thirty thousand Confederates at Vicksburg surrendered in early July.

Although 1863 had begun inauspiciously, by midsummer the North also gained the upper hand in Virginia. In a brilliant maneuver, Robert E. Lee divided his army in the face of an enemy twice his size and won his most spectacular victory at Chancellorsville, Virginia, smashing Union forces now commanded by JOSEPH HOOKER [36]. In the process, however, Stonewall Jackson was accidentally shot by his own men and later died. Despite the loss of Jackson, Lee decided upon another invasion of the North. In early July, the Army of Northern Virginia and the Army of the Potomac, the latter now led by GEORGE MEADE [22], stumbled into each other at Gettysburg, Pennsylvania. After unsuccessfully battering the Union lines for three days, Lee fell back in defeat to Virginia.

Developments in Tennessee that fall also favored the North. In early September, the Union army under Rosecrans moved Braxton Bragg's Confederates out of Chattanooga, the region's transportation hub. In late September, Bragg routed the Federals under Rosecrans at Chickamauga,

Georgia, with only a determined stand by Gen. GEORGE THOMAS [29] saving the North from an even greater disaster. Bragg then laid siege to Chattanooga from Missionary Ridge, Tennessee, but the noose around the city was never fully tightened, allowing Union supplies and reinforcements, including the indomitable Grant, to trickle in. In November, Grant routed Bragg along Missionary Ridge, ending any threat to Chattanooga.

In March 1864, Lincoln appointed Grant commander of all Union armies. Grant named Sherman his successor as head of the collected armies of the Cumberland, the Ohio, and the Tennessee, and located his own head-quarters in the field in Virginia. Meade continued to command the Army of the Potomac, but Grant personally directed operations against Lee. Grant also transferred as many men as he could from rear areas to the campaigning armies and coordinated Union operations on all fronts. The South was given no time to catch its collective breath.

Still, Northern victory was not assured. Union general Nathaniel P. Banks led a campaign along the Red River designed to seize the rich cotton-producing regions of western Louisiana and eastern Texas, and was defeated by RICHARD TAYLOR [78] at the Battle of Mansfield, Louisiana. In the east, Lee parried Grant's thrusts in heavy fighting in the Wilderness, Spotsylvania, and Cold Harbor, Virginia. Grant's subsequent effort to take Petersburg, Virginia, site of the main railroad artery between Richmond and the rest of the Confederacy, also failed. Both armies dug in as Grant besieged Petersburg. The Confederates bottled up another Union army, led by Ben Butler, along the James River; further, JUBAL EARLY [81] was threatening Washington from the Shenandoah Valley. Meanwhile, in the west, Johnston's Confederates remained undefeated, although Sherman was moving against Atlanta.

In the summer of 1864, many Northerners were appalled by the mounting casualty lists and questioned the Lincoln administration's policies. It was an election year, and the Democrats had nominated ex-general George McClellan, who, despite his military failures, remained a popular figure. Lincoln might very well have lost the election had it been held that summer; it was assumed that the Democrats would negotiate an end to the war if McClellan were elected.

Troubles, however, also beset the Confederacy. Lee was pinned down at Petersburg and the trans-Mississippi supply route had been severed. Resources were strained to the limit. Jefferson Davis was upset that Sherman had reached the outskirts of Atlanta, and he replaced Johnston with JOHN BELL HOOD [38], who promised more aggressive action. Hood delivered on his word—with disastrous results. Confederate assaults squandered scarce manpower and ultimately forced Hood to abandon Atlanta. To make matters worse, Farragut's naval squadron secured control of Mobile Bay, the last major Confederate port on the upper Gulf Coast. Finally, PHILIP SHERIDAN [18] crushed Confederate resistance in the Shenandoah Valley.

Lincoln, buoyed by the recent military victories, won reelection by a comfortable margin. In the meantime, Hood had driven north, hoping either

to sever Sherman's supply lines or to force his retreat, only to be defeated by
JOHN SCHOFIELD [75] at Franklin, Tennessee, and annihilated by George
Thomas at Nashville. Rather than follow Hood, Sherman had cut loose from
his supply lines and promised to "make Georgia howl." Sherman's sixty thousand men lived off the land and encountered little organized resistance. His
army cut a sixty-mile-wide swath through the heart of the South, destroying
one of the Confederacy's major sources of supplies. Sherman then stopped
briefly to refit at Savannah before driving north into South Carolina.

With their homes in danger and the cause bleak, the Army of Northern
Virginia finally cracked. Desertion reached fifty percent among some units,
especially those from Georgia and the Carolinas. In early April 1865, in a
final attempt to salvage Confederate fortunes, Lee abandoned Petersburg
(and with it Richmond) and tried to join other Confederate forces still in the
field. Finding his escape route to the west blocked, Lee was forced to surrender to Grant at Appomattox, Virginia. Joseph Johnston, leading the remnants of the shattered Army of Tennessee, soon surrendered to Sherman.
President Davis and was captured while trying to make his way west, and
EDMUND KIRBY SMITH [56] belatedly surrendered the Trans-Mississippi
Department in June.

POSTWAR DEVELOPMENTS

Abraham Lincoln, the man most responsible for the Union victory, did not
live to see the final triumph. On April 14, 1865, JOHN WILKES BOOTH [25]
fatally shot the president at Ford's Theater, Washington. Lincoln's death
ended any hope that the shattered nation could be quickly pieced back
together, as he had so eloquently concluded near the end of his second inaugural address, "with malice toward none; with charity for all." Given the terrible losses endured on both sides, perhaps even the continued presence of
this greatest of all American presidents would not have made a difference.
Nevertheless, no other figure then alive—particularly the new president,
ANDREW JOHNSON [6]—had the experience, wisdom, and strength to match
that of Lincoln.

The slaves had secured their freedom as a result of the North's victory
and the Thirteenth Amendment. In the immediate postwar years, Congress
also enacted significant civil rights legislation. The Freedmen's Bureau,
headed by OLIVER O. HOWARD [63], provided former slaves with at least a
modicum of federal support. Serious doubts exist, however, as to whether
the majority of Northerners was ever really serious about ensuring equal
treatment for blacks. White Southerners resented what they believed to be
unwarranted federal interference, but within a dozen years Congress had
readmitted all the former Confederate states into the Union. Although slavery had been destroyed, whites again emerged as the dominant race in the
postwar South.

The war had a mixed effect upon the struggle for gender equality. ELIZ-

ABETH CADY STANTON [40 (tie)] and SUSAN B. ANTHONY [40 (tie)] led ante-bellum efforts to achieve political rights for women and had gained the support of many reformers. During the Civil War, Stanton and Anthony made abolition and black rights their top priorities. They believed that once these objectives had been achieved, they could all then concentrate on women's issues. They felt betrayed when reformers more interested in securing black rights did not honor what Stanton and Anthony believed to be this implicit quid pro quo. This lack of reciprocity helps to explain a forty-year rift between advocates of racial and gender equality. By contrast, the war at least offered women new opportunities in the public sphere. The work of MARY BICKERDYKE [90], CLARA BARTON [89], and DOROTHEA DIX [87] in nursing, for example, helped pave the way for future generations by demonstrating that women could indeed perform valuable managerial and professional duties.

The Civil War had a profound impact upon American culture. It further stimulated the expansion of mass-marketed newspapers and periodicals. The editors HORACE GREELEY [31] (*New York Tribune*) and FRANK LESLIE [85] (*Frank Leslie's Illustrated Weekly*) put many correspondents in the field to provide on-the-scene war coverage. MATHEW BRADY [34] and others recognized the public's appetite for visual images of the conflict, and dispatched teams of photographers to the battle fronts. War themes formed the subject matter for some of the greatest work of WALT WHITMAN [69] and HERMAN MELVILLE [91]; and the diaries of MARY CHESNUT [55] about wartime life in Richmond provide some of the finest insights into Southern society in existence.

Ironically, the Civil War also saw bitter fighting between the Federal government and several Indian tribes. In the Indian Territory (present-day Oklahoma) several thousand Creeks and Cherokees took up Confederate colors, although they played no significant military role. Far more momentous events occurred farther west, in part, sparked by the forced withdrawal of many regular troops from frontier duty. In New Mexico, the Navajo were defeated and driven to the Bosque Redondo Reservation. In Minnesota, a loose coalition of Dakota Sioux led by LITTLE CROW [86] also engaged in full-scale warfare. In late 1864, bitter fighting erupted on the Great Plains, where Colorado volunteers led by JOHN CHIVINGTON [100] slaughtered over one hundred and fifty Cheyenne and Arapaho Indians at Sand Creek, sparking reprisal raids from the Cheyenne, Arapaho, and Kiowa the following spring and continued intermittent hostilities until 1877.

SELECTING AND RANKING THE CIVIL WAR 100

Choosing the Civil War 100 proved a challenging intellectual puzzle. How does a historian compare, say, the relative importance of MARY TODD LIN-COLN [53], wife of the president, and DON CARLOS BUELL [95], an ineffectual Union general? The Civil War, with its mixture of military, social, economic, and cultural events, forces comparisons of persons in completely different professions from one another. If there is a systematic way to rank the men and women included in this volume, I haven't thought of it, and believe that any attempt to contrive a set formula for doing so would ring false. Perhaps that is why I see history as an art, not a science.

Decisions, however, had to be made. I found it relatively easy to choose and rank the top third of the war's most significant persons; these remained fairly stable as I edited and reedited this manuscript. The names on the latter two-thirds of my list, on the other hand, changed frequently in terms of order as well as whether or not they even merited inclusion. I also took into account the region in which an individual made his or her major contribution. Although I am a son of the South, the North's victory, combined with the fact that more than two and a half times as many people lived in the North as in the seceding states, led me to include twice as many Northerners as Southerners. Since the outbreak of the Civil War led to increased violence on the Indian frontiers, important figures from these arenas merit selection.

This book is built upon the proposition that military events decided the outcome of the Civil War. The North did enjoy tremendous material resources—two and a half times the population; three times the railroad mileage; nine times the industrial capacity; and approximately ten times the available capital. Administrators like HERMAN HAUPT [66] and MONTGOMERY MEIGS [45] ensured that the Union would be able to exploit these advantages. Some have argued that, in light of this superiority, Northern victory was inevitable, but material resources, as demonstrated during the American Revolution and the U.S. war in Vietnam, do not necessarily guarantee victory.

Another theory, especially popular in recent years, holds that the Confederates lacked (or lost) the will to fight. Had Southerners truly believed in their cause, goes this thesis, they would have more fully mobilized their resources and continued their struggle even in the face of mounting disaster. Yet this argument seems to put the cart before the horse. Southerners showed plenty of will early in the contest, volunteering in droves and fighting far afield from their homes. It was only after the Federals had by force of arms captured Atlanta and had begun to rampage through the Shenandoah Valley and Georgia that the Confederates really lost the will to resist.

Armed might thus restored the Union. As a consequence, one-half of my 100 figures either saw active military duty or were directly engaged in organizing or supplying the Union and Confederate armies and navies. I did, however, exclude military figures who did not hold significant independent command from my top 100. Thus men of mediocre records who commanded armies, like Ambrose Burnside, William Rosecrans, and Don Carlos Buell, are included, whereas more capable corps leaders, like A. P. Hill, Winfield Scott Hancock, and James B. McPherson, are relegated to the category of "Honorable Mentions."

The war's profound effect upon American life must also be recognized.

In a very real sense, Congress adopted revolutionary measures during the war. For the first time, the federal government, which had traditionally been a distant entity of little practical importance in Americans' daily affairs, assumed an active role in the lives of average citizens. To highlight these changes, which would not have occurred at the time without the Civil War, I have included a number of politicians whose chief efforts lay in the domestic, rather than the military, aspect of the conflict.

The Civil War also led to social change. The growing belief in the North that slavery was wrong and that its destruction would hurt the Confederate war effort led to Lincoln's Emancipation Proclamation and abolition. The Thirteenth, Fourteenth, and Fifteenth Amendments (which ended slavery, guaranteed black citizenship, and forbade the states from denying suffrage on the basis of race, respectively), though not always properly enforced at the time, made possible the civil rights movement of the next century. Without the war, these legal changes could not have occurred. Naturally, then, key reformers have been included.

My selections were also influenced by my belief that literature, journalism, and photography were especially influential during the war years. The mass distribution of newspapers and periodicals, many of which featured reports from correspondents in the field and the works of distinguished authors, explained the war's events and meanings to average men and women on both sides. Graphic wartime photo displays stunned the public and shaped opinion, foreshadowing the work of twentieth-century war correspondents and photographers. Popular books and periodicals fostered this sense of national involvement and participation. Americans, both north and south, were thus caught up in the war and mobilized to a degree heretofore unmatched in our history.

I have defined the American Civil War broadly to encompass not only the war itself, but the events which led to and resulted from the conflict. Because they were so important in explaining why the war began when it did, Stephen Douglas and Presidents James Buchanan and Franklin Pierce are included. So are many of Reconstruction's major figures, as these persons helped define just what the war would mean to the next generation. Whether the country would truly become a nation again, and when this reunification would occur, would be determined not by soldiers on the battlefield but by leaders of the Reconstruction period. No historical event, even one so huge as the Civil War, can be properly understood without placing it in a larger context. Thus this book is really about the characters of an entire era in American history, not just those of the war itself.

Villains also made their mark. Though their deeds were infamous, their significance must be acknowledged. The actions of Methodist elder and abolitionist John Chivington led to a major Indian war. Swiss-born HENRY WIRZ [99] was found guilty of having allowed criminally inhumane conditions at Andersonville Prison, Georgia, and was hanged. A disaffected actor, John Wilkes Booth, murdered the greatest president in American history.

Selections, as well as rankings, were based not on an individual's skill or ability, but rather their influence upon the Civil War and the way latter generations have understood that war. Stonewall Jackson was a better general than James Longstreet, Joseph E. Johnston, or George McClellan, but is ranked lower because he was less important to the war's final outcome. A person's influence also had to be focused upon some aspect of the causes, course, or results of the war. Thus Charles Minié, inventor of a new bullet which made practical the widespread use of rifled muskets, is not included, because his design was not specifically for the American Civil War. Similarly, the person had to have done some of their best work about the war. Walt Whitman, who produced some of his finest poetry about wartime subjects, is included, but my favorite late-nineteenth-century American artist, Winslow Homer, failed to survive the final cut (but is listed as an Honorable Mention). Although Homer did several Civil War paintings and was an active illustrator, these are not among the pieces for which he is most recognized today.

Final determinations on rankings also factored in the geographical regions where figures made their contributions, as well as the rich variety of military, political, social, cultural, and economic developments during the war. As such, I tried to avoid bunching too many Northerners or Southerners together. Similarly, I sought to include representatives from different occupations within a grouping of about twenty-five. For example, my twenty-fifth through forty-ninth most important persons include five Union generals, five Confederate generals, one Northern admiral, two military administrators, three Northern politicians, two social reformers, an assassin, a chief justice, a journalist, a photographer, a British prime minister, a financier, and a slave.

Ranking was based upon the cumulative importance of an individual's contribution. For instance, Confederate general Wade Hampton ranked sixty-eighth, while Confederate general Albert Sidney Johnston ranked seventy-ninth. At first glance, this might seem wrong, because Johnston once commanded the Confederacy's largest army in the west while Hampton commanded only cavalry detachments. Johnston was killed at the Battle of Shiloh (1862), however, while Hampton survived the war and became one of the South's most prominent political leaders.

A final explanation concerns nomenclature. Civil War battles often have two widely accepted names. The North generally referred to battles according to their closest river; Confederates, by contrast, usually named them after the nearest town or community. Since the Union won the war, I have adopted Northern usage throughout the text for clarity. Readers should also be aware of the maps and appendixes, which provide additional clarification about locations, names, dates, commanders, and casualties of major Civil War battles. They should be forewarned, however, that sources often differ as to numbers of troops engaged and casualties suffered.

A CIVIL WAR CHRONOLOGY

1831	William Lloyd Garrison's abolistionist paper *The Liberator* begins publication
1838	Frederick Douglass escapes from slavery
1841	Horace Greeley launches the *New York Tribune*
1846	The United States declares war on Mexico
1848	Treaty of Guadalupe-Hidalgo, ending the war with Mexico
	Seneca Falls Convention on woman's rights
	William Yancey bolts Democratic Convention
1849	Harriet Tubman escapes from slavery
1850	Compromise of 1850
	Nashville Convention contemplates secession
1851	Herman Melville publishes *Moby-Dick*
1852	Harriet Beecher Stowe publishes *Uncle Tom's Cabin*
	Election of Franklin Pierce as U.S. president
1853	Gadsden Purchase
1854	Ostend Manifesto—a secret manifesto suggesting the United States take Cuba by force if Spain wouldn't sell it. It was condemned as a scheme to extend slavery
	Kansas-Nebraska Act
1855	Walt Whitman publishes *Leaves of Grass*
	Frank Leslie's Illustrated Newspaper inaugurated
	Gail Borden receives patent for condensed milk
1856	Brooks-Sumner incident in Congress
	Sack of Lawrence, Kansas, by proslavery groups
	John Brown leads raid on Pottawatomie Creek, Kansas
	Election of James Buchanan as U.S. president
1857	Dred Scott decision by Roger Taney
	Economic Panic of 1857
1858	Lincoln-Douglas debates for Illinois senatorship
1859	John Brown's raid on Harpers Ferry, Virginia

1860		Election of Abraham Lincoln
		Secession of the lower South begins
		Southern governors demand the surrender of Federal property to the states
1861	Feb.	Formation of the Confederate States of America
		Failure of Crittenden Compromise
	Mar.	Lincoln inaugurated
		First Morrill Tariff
	Apr.	Federal commander of Fort Sumter refuses to surrender fort to South Carolina government and the Confederate army cuts off all supplies to the fort
		Fort Sumter fired upon when Lincoln declares he will resupply garrison
		Lincoln proclaims the seven seceded states to be in a state of rebellion, calls for 75,000 militiamen, and imposes naval blockade of South
	May	Secession of four states in the upper South
		Britain proclaims neutrality
	June	U.S. Sanitary Commission established
		Dorothea Dix appointed superintendent of female nurses
		First Battle of Bull Run, Virginia—Confederate victory
	Aug.	Battle of Wilson's Creek, Missouri—Union victory
		Congress passes an income tax (initially 3 percent on income over $800)
	Nov.	Battle of Belmont, Missouri—Union victory
		Trent affair threatens war between U.S. and Britain
1862	Feb.	Fall of Forts Henry and Donelson, Tennessee, to Union forces
		Battle of Valverde, New Mexico—Confederate victory
		Legal Tender Act authorizes what eventually amounts to $450 million in paper currency
	Mar.	Battle of Pea Ridge, Arkansas—Union victory
		Monitor v. *Virginia*, Hampton Roads, Virginia
		Battle of Glorieta, New Mexico—Union victory
		Jackson's Shenandoah Valley campaign begins
		McClellan's Peninsula campaign begins
	Apr.	Battle of Shiloh, Tennessee—Union victory
		Confederate Congress adopts conscription
		Fall of New Orleans, Louisiana to Union forces
	May	Battle of Seven Pines, Virginia—Confederate victory
		Homestead Act offers free public land to western settlers
	June	Lee assumes command of the Army of Northern Virginia
		Stuart's first ride around the Army of the Potomac
		Seven Days Battles, Virginia—Confederate victory
		Morrill Land-Grant College Act
	July	Pacific Railroad Act

	Aug.	Confederate invasion of Kentucky
		Alabama joins the Confederate Navy
		Sioux uprising in Minnesota
		Second Battle of Bull Run, Virginia—Confederate victory
	Sept.	Lee's first invasion of the North
		Battle of Antietam, Maryland—Union victory
		Battle of Iuka, Mississippi—Union victory
		Lincoln proclaims his intention to declare all slaves in the Confederacy free
		Battle of Wood Lake, Minnesota—Union victory against the Sioux
	Oct.	Battle of Corinth, Mississippi—Union victory
		Battle of Perryville, Kentucky—Union victory
		Jay Cooke begins bond sales campaign
		Brady's Antietam photographs exhibited in New York City
	Dec.	Raids of Forrest and Van Dorn cut Grant's supply lines near Vicksburg
		38 Sioux Indians executed at Mankato, Minnesota, for their role in the uprising
		Battle of Fredericksburg, Virginia—Confederate victory
		Battle of Chickasaw Bluffs, Mississippi—Confederate victory
		Battle of Stones River (Murfreesboro), Tennessee—draw
1863	Jan.	Emancipation Proclamation takes effect
		Battle of Sabine Pass, Texas—Confederate victory
	Feb.	National Banking Act
	Mar.	Conscription begins in the North
	Apr.	Bread riots in Richmond, Virginia
		British government seizes ships intended for Confederate use
		Union gunboats run past Vicksburg batteries
	May	Battle of Chancellorsville, Virginia—Confederate victory; Stonewall Jackson mortally wounded
		Clement Vallandigham exiled from the Union
	June	Lee's second invasion of the North
		Battle of Brandy Station, Virginia—draw
	July	Battle of Gettysburg, Pennsylvania—Union victory
		Fall of Vicksburg, Mississippi to Union forces
		Draft riots in New York City
		Attack by Robert Gould Shaw and 54th Massachusetts (colored) against Fort Wagner—Confederate victory
	Sept.	Battle of Chickamauga, Georgia—Confederate victory
	Nov.	Longstreet begins unsuccessful siege of Knoxville, Tennessee
		Battle of Missionary Ridge, Tennessee—Union victory
1864	Jan.	Navajo Indians begin surrendering, New Mexico
	Mar.	Grant appointed general in chief of the armies of the United States
	Apr.	Battle of Mansfield, Louisiana—Confederate victory

		Battle of Pleasant Hill, Louisiana—draw
		Fort Pillow, Tennessee, massacre
	May	Battle of the Wilderness, Virginia—Confederate victory
		Battle of Spotsylvania, Virginia—Confederate victory
		Battle of Cold Harbor, Virginia—Confederate victory
		Battle of Yellow Tavern, Virginia—Union victory
		Sherman's Atlanta campaign begins
		Battle of New Market, Virginia—Union victory
	June	Early's Shenandoah Valley campaign begins
		Battle of Trevilian Station, Virginia—Confederate victory
		Battle of Kennesaw Mountain, Georgia—Confederate victory
		U.S.S. *Kearsage* sinks the C.S.S. *Alabama*
		Siege of Petersburg, Virginia, by Grant begins
	July	Hood replaces Joe Johnston in Atlanta campaign
		Battles for Atlanta, Georgia—Union victories
	Aug.	Battle of Mobile Bay, Alabama—Union victory
		Confederate Gen. Price launches raid into Missouri
	Sept.	Fall of Atlanta to Union forces
	Oct.	Battle of Cedar Creek, Virginia—Union victory
		Sherman's March to the Sea begins
	Nov.	Lincoln reelected president
		Battle of Franklin, Tennessee—Union victory
	Dec.	Battle of Nashville, Tennessee—Union victory
		Sherman captures Savannah, Georgia
		Sand Creek, Colorado massacre
1865	Jan.	Fort Fisher, North Carolina, falls to Union forces
	Feb.	Freedmen's Bureau established
	Apr.	Battle of Five Forks, Virginia—Union victory
		Fall of Petersburg, Virginia, to Union forces
		Fall of Richmond to Union forces
		Lee surrenders at Appomattox, Virginia
		Lincoln assassinated by John Wilkes Booth
		Johnston surrenders all troops in the Carolinas
	May	Davis captured
	June	Confederate Gen. Kirby Smith surrenders the Trans-Mississippi Department
	Oct.	Whitman's *Drum-Taps and Sequel*
		Melville's *Battle-Pieces and Aspects of the War*
	Nov.	Wirz hanged for war crimes
	Dec.	Thirteenth Amendment ratified
1866		French withdraw troops from Mexico
		Civil Rights Act of 1866

1867   Military Reconstruction Act

            Tenure of Office Act

            U.S. purchases Alaska

            Maximilian executed

1868   Fourteenth Amendment ratified

            Johnson impeached

            Grant elected president

1869   First transcontinental railroad completed

            National Woman Suffrage Association formed

1870   Fifteenth Amendment ratified

1872   Grant reelected

1873   Economic Panic of 1873

1876   Presidential election disputed

1877   Compromise of 1877

            Hayes becomes president

            Military removed from remaining Southern states

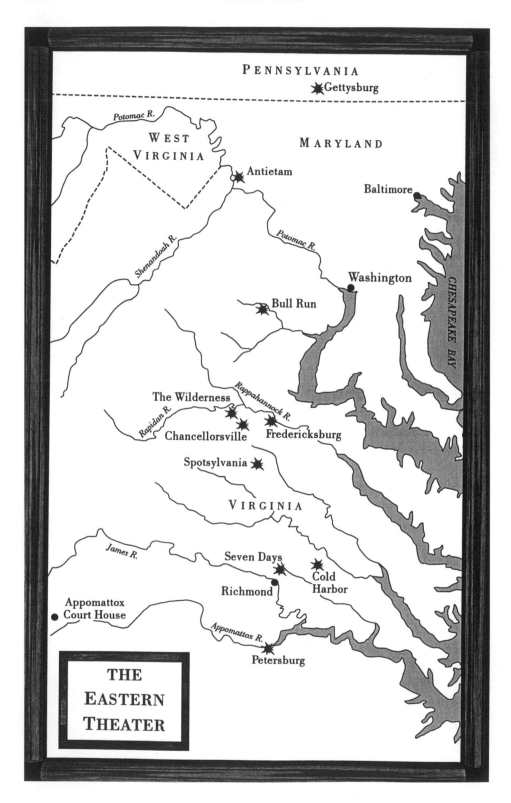

PENNSYLVANIA

Gettysburg

Potomac R.

WEST
VIRGINIA

MARYLAND

Antietam

Baltimore

Potomac R.

Shenandoah R.

Washington

Bull Run

CHESAPEAKE BAY

Rappahannock R.

The Wilderness

Rapidan R.

Chancellorsville

Fredericksburg

Spotsylvania

VIRGINIA

James R.

Seven Days

Cold
Harbor

Richmond

Appomattox
Court House

Appomattox R.

Petersburg

THE
EASTERN
THEATER

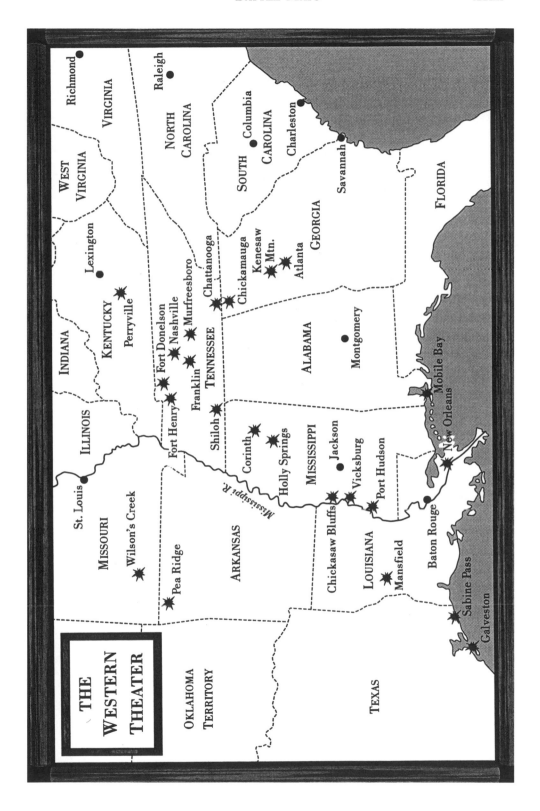

The
Civil War
100

Abraham Lincoln

(1809–1865)

Abraham Lincoln was the most significant person of the Civil War. Abraham Lincoln guided his government with a firm, active hand, and made the restoration of the Union the North's first goal; likewise, it was Lincoln who guided the transformation of the war into a moral crusade to eradicate slavery, thus profoundly changing the social and economic structure of the South.

Lincoln's rise to political power paralleled America's territorial growth and shifting political winds. He was the first president born west of the Appalachian Mountains. Of the first fifteen presidents, all save two (John Adams and his son, John Quincy Adams) had either been from the South or had been sympathetic to southern interests, states' rights, and slavery while in office. His evolution from the son of hard-working farmers to sixteenth president of the United States represents the classic realization of the American dream. His humble roots helped him understand the psyche of the average citizen, and his intellectual maturation enabled him to become a revolutionary leader. The fact that Lincoln, who opposed slavery and supported an expansion of the federal government, could become president reflected nothing less than a revolution in American politics.

Abraham was born to Thomas and Nancy Hanks Lincoln in 1809 on a small farm near Hodgenville, Kentucky. He moved with his family to southern Indiana when he was seven years old. Nancy died in 1819; Thomas soon remarried, however, and Abraham found in his stepmother, Sarah Johnston, a loving, understanding friend. He attended school only sporadically. Young Abraham (he disliked the nickname Abe) was somewhat slow to learn, nonetheless, he loved books and committed much of what he read to memory. Once he finally mastered a subject or issue, he never forgot it.

In March 1830 the Lincolns moved again, this time to Macon County, Illinois. In 1831, when he was twenty-two years old, Abraham left for New Salem, Illinois, believing his obligations to his father now completed. To his New Salem neighbors Lincoln appeared hardworking, likeable, and always ready to swap anecdotes and stories. He managed a general store and volunteered for the Black Hawk War (1832). After one electoral failure, he was elected to the state legislature in 1834. He began to study law and in 1836 received his attorney's license. Lincoln helped engineer the removal of the state capital from Vandalia to Springfield, where he, too, relocated in 1837. For the next four years, he shared a double bed with Joshua F. Speed, proprietor of the general store above which their room was located. Such an arrangement was common for the time; to save money, two other men also slept in the same room.

Lincoln was honest and courteous, despite being somewhat awkward, traits that appealed to MARY TODD [52], who married him in 1842. By 1844 they had scraped together enough money to purchase a six-room cottage. He spent much of his time following the judicial circuit, gaining a reputation for skillful oratory. In 1846, he won a single term in Congress, during which he denounced the Mexican War and the Democratic administration of James K. Polk.

In 1854, Lincoln was again elected to the state legislature and two years later helped found the state Republican Party. He was the runner-up in his party's 1856 vice-presidential nominations, and in 1858, he challenged the incumbent Democrat, STEPHEN A. DOUGLAS [11], in a hard-fought contest for the U.S. Senate. "A house divided against itself cannot stand," Lincoln had explained in his acceptance speech before his party's senatorial nominating convention. "I believe this government cannot endure, permanently half slave and half free. . . . It will become all one thing, or all the other." The two engaged in seven titanic debates, with Lincoln losing the election but enhancing his own reputation nonetheless.

Lincoln denounced slavery as a "monstrous injustice" and raised the threat that slavery might become nationalized and thus threaten the livelihood of free laborers everywhere. He also championed economic development and thus proved an ideal choice as the Republican Party's 1860 presidential nominee. While he was determined to prevent slavery from expanding into any new territories, he promised at the same time not to interfere with it where it already existed. To many Southerners who knew the limited duration of a soil's fertility, however, the inability to take their slaves west threatened the very existence of slavery. Although Lincoln won less than 40 percent of the popular vote, he won a clear electoral victory by capturing all but one free state. Ominously, however, he had not received a single popular vote in ten slave states.

Like many, Lincoln had discounted Southerners' threats to secede if he were elected president, but they did secede, precipitating a national crisis. Assassination threats forced him to enter Washington secretly, and his administration endured a shaky beginning. He eventually decided not to back down to Southern threats that they would take Federal property by force, if necessary. Lincoln's attempts to reinforce Federal garrisons at Fort Sumter, South Carolina, and Fort Pickens, Florida, forced the South into firing the war's first shots, with defense of the forts partially uniting a once-divided North in the process. His policies were also instrumental in preventing the secession of four slave states—Missouri, Delaware, Maryland, and Kentucky—thus shifting the balance of power profoundly toward the Union.

The exigencies of war reinforced Lincoln's belief in a strong executive. After the attack on Fort Sumter, he proclaimed the South to be in rebellion, declared a blockade of the Confederacy, called up the militia, spent public money, declared martial law, and suspended the writ of habeas corpus in some areas—all without congressional approval, since Congress was not in session. Patiently, Lincoln maintained an open-door policy, seeing thousands of visitors and petitioners seeking government jobs or favors, treating many to his trademark "leetle stories" as he tried to avoid taking steps that would limit his own options. He was determined to retain certain executive prerogatives to the end and later refused to allow Congress to dictate early terms of reconstruction, insisting instead that such duties properly lay with the president.

As a minority president, Lincoln understood the need to craft a coalition of Republicans, Democrats who supported the war, and border state delegates if his administration were to function. His diverse cabinet included representatives from all wings of the Republican Party; he also made sure that Democrats received several important military commands. In 1864 he accepted the political advantage of replacing his first vice president, HANNIBAL HAMLIN [94], with a War Democrat and Southerner, ANDREW JOHNSON [6], who was to strengthen Lincoln's ticket. Lincoln also proved an able party leader. Although threatened on several occasions by internal revolt, he skillfully retained a working congressional majority.

His political expediency infuriated Lincoln's many critics, who decried his often evasive responses. Especially serious were attacks by Radicals within the Republican ranks who believed he acted too slowly to abolish slavery. Labeling the institution a "monstrous injustice" and always insistent upon the inherent right of equality of opportunity for all men, Lincoln had before the war supported voluntary colonization of freed blacks to Africa as the best means of ending America's race problems. Gradually, however, he realized the flaws inherent in his earlier colonization schemes. After early attempts to convince the border states to adopt gradual emancipation came to naught, by summer 1862 Lincoln, now understanding that abolition would also hurt the Confederate war effort, determined to abolish slavery. Waiting to announce his decision until after the Union's strategic victory at Antietam, by his Emancipation Proclamation Lincoln declared an end to slavery in areas still in rebellion as of January 1, 1863. Though some criticized Lincoln's hesitancy, his decision to make the destruction of slavery his second major war aim marked a key shift in Union policy. Asking white men to die to free blacks was enormously controversial; seen in the context of the time, his Emancipation Proclamation represented an act of exceptional political courage.

Lincoln was also an effective war leader. Better than most of his military experts, he understood that in order to defeat the rebellion, the Union must defeat the Confederacy's armed forces, not simply occupy territory. Equally important, his rhetoric inspired and guided the Northern public. At the dedication of a national cemetery in Gettysburg, he explained in a mere 272 words that the war was being fought to preserve the notion that "all men are created equal" and to ensure that "government of the people, by the people, and for the people shall not perish from the earth." Lincoln's second inaugural address, delivered in March 1865, proved another of America's greatest state papers, reflecting both the president's compassion and his determination to end the war "with malice toward none; with charity for all."

Lincoln was a faithful, if an often absent-minded, husband and doting father who levied little discipline upon his children, only one of whom lived to maturity. Lincoln habitually worked long hours as president. Among the nation's youngest presidents, he aged quickly in office. His haggard face reflected the awesome burdens of his wartime presidency. Tragically, on the very eve of the victory he had done so much to achieve, an assassin's bullet struck Lincoln down on April 14, 1865, just eleven days after Union troops had captured the Confederate capital of Richmond.

2

Ulysses S. Grant

(1822–1885)

Ulysses Simpson Grant was the North's greatest military leader and later served two terms as president of the United States. This combination of military and political importance leads to his ranking behind only Lincoln. In the war's first two and a half years, Grant gained control of the Mississippi River and of the state of Tennessee for the Union. In early 1864 he took command of all Union armies and went east, where he tenaciously exploited his army's numerical superiority to grind down the Confederate Army of Northern Virginia under ROBERT E. LEE [4], forcing Lee's surrender at Appomattox, Virginia. After he was elected president in 1868, Grant's administration was plagued by corruption and political naïveté. Tragically, this great general was one of our nation's worst presidents.

Hiram Ulysses Grant was born at Point Pleasant, Ohio, in 1822. His congressman, however, upon appointing him to the U.S. Military Academy at

West Point, mistakenly listed him as Ulysses Simpson (Simpson being his mother's maiden name) and Grant kept the new name. He excelled only in horsemanship and graduated in 1843 in the middle of his class, which included thirteen future Civil War generals (on both sides). Grant was assigned to the Fourth Infantry Regiment, and won in the Mexican War two brevet promotions (an honorary appointment used to recognize conspicuous wartime service) for his role in the battles of Molino del Rey and Chapultepec.

Grant married Julia Dent in 1848 and had four children. He was assigned to the West, but the routine of frontier army life bored Grant, who took too much solace in the bottle. He was forced to resign his commission in 1854, then drifted deeply into depression, failing as a farmer, firewood salesman, real estate agent, candidate for county engineer, and customs house clerk. By 1860 he had been reduced to working as a clerk in his brothers' leather-goods store.

In August 1861, Grant was appointed brigadier general of Federal volunteers, one of four such slots parceled out to the Illinois congressional delegation. After a hard-fought skirmish at Belmont, Missouri, Grant advanced into central Tennessee. In February 1862, he captured Forts Henry and Donelson, Tennessee, winning the sobriquet "Unconditional Surrender" and forcing the Confederates to abandon Nashville. Grant now commanded the Army of the Mississippi and pushed south to Pittsburg Landing, Tennessee. There, Confederate troops launched a surprise attack at Shiloh, a two-day nightmare in which more Americans died than in all previous U.S. wars combined. Although Grant demonstrated his characteristic coolheadedness and recovered to win the battle, he had not expected the Confederate strike; rumors alleged that he had been drunk.

He was delayed for several months by the resulting controversies, but kept his command. Grant's next objective was to gain control of the Mississippi River and divide the Confederacy. The key point was heavily fortified Vicksburg, Mississippi, whose guns dominated the river traffic. Initial efforts to approach the city via the Mississippi Central Railroad and to isolate it by digging a canal through the swamps west of the river failed. In the face of mounting official and public skepticism about his ability to take Vicksburg, in late spring 1863 Grant dispatched a large cavalry force on a raid through central Mississippi and ordered his best subordinate, WILLIAM T. SHERMAN [3], to make a military demonstration of strength north of the city. With Confederate attention thus diverted, Grant daringly cut loose from his supply lines, marched part of his army west of the Mississippi River past Vicksburg, then crossed the river south of the city. Grant struck before the Confederates could react, pushed north, and laid siege to Vicksburg. On July 4, 1863, the city's garrison of thirty thousand surrendered.

Grant's next major move came in November, when he organized the relief of besieged Federal troops in Chattanooga, Tennessee. Grant routed the Confederates of BRAXTON BRAGG [30] in the Battle of Missionary Ridge, Tennessee (November 23–25, 1863), and President ABRAHAM LINCOLN [1] named Grant commander of all Union armies in March 1864. Grant went east and established his headquarters in the field with the Union Army of the Potomac. In May 1864 he marched south toward Richmond, only to suffer stinging defeats at the hands of Lee in the battles of the Wilderness, Spotsylvania, North Anna, and Cold Harbor, Virginia. Grant's attempt to cut Richmond off from the rest of the Confederacy by taking Petersburg, Virginia, was also stymied. In six weeks of fighting, Grant had suffered over fifty thousand casualties while inflicting only half that number on the Confederates. Even though Lincoln was shaken by this butcher's bill, he wisely stuck with Grant, knowing that while the Union could replace its dead, the South could not.

Grant resolved to maintain the pressure, and undertook a siege of strategic Petersburg. Meanwhile, under Grant's coordination, Union armies led by Sherman and PHILIP SHERIDAN [18] were tearing out the heart of the Confederacy, destroying supplies desperately needed by the Southern armies. Sherman captured Atlanta and began cutting through Georgia and the Carolinas virtually unopposed, while Sheridan demolished Virginia's fertile Shenandoah Valley. As Confederate supplies dwindled, desertions mounted. Lee abandoned Petersburg and tried to escape west, only to find Grant's army blocking his way.

Fierce in battle, Grant proved magnanimous in victory. On April 9, 1865, in surrender negotiations with Lee at Appomattox Court House, Virginia, he paroled Southern soldiers, guaranteed their immunity from prosecution for treason, allowed them to claim their own horses, and sent three days' rations across the lines.

Grant was lionized throughout the North and became general of the army in 1866. On the Republican ticket, he was elected president two years later, winning a second term in 1872. He proved an inept president, placing too much trust in friends who did not deserve such confidence. Ugly scandals, in which several of his appointees stole millions of dollars in public funds, scarred his two terms in office, as did the financial Panic of 1873. With interest in enforcing the Fourteenth and Fifteenth Amendments waning, Grant and the nation abandoned any pretense of significant reform, thus losing a historic opportunity to secure equality for all Americans. In 1880, the Republican Party convention rejected his bid to seek a third term.

Grant was a stubborn but genial man whose informality and imperturbability won the respect of virtually all his wartime comrades, and his genius lay in his recognition that in order to defeat the Confederacy, the Southern armies had to be beaten in battle. Without Grant, the North would not have won the war by 1865. Sadly, however, this magnificent Civil War general succeeded in little else in life. In his last days, ruined by his association with a scandal-ridden brokerage firm, dying of throat cancer, and racked with pain, he wrote his *Personal Memoirs* in a final, heroic effort to provide for his family. The enterprise was a tremendous success, providing his heirs with nearly $500,000 in royalties. In 1885, only days after finishing his manuscript, the Union's most prominent soldier died.

3

William T. Sherman

(1820–1891)

William Tecumseh Sherman's views on how best to win the Civil War differed from those of his friend ULYSSES GRANT [2]. Horrified by the bloody, often indecisive nature of the war's pitched battles, Sherman emphasized maneuver and the destruction of the enemy's ability and willingness to make war instead of slugging it out in open combat. Only after the Southern people had felt "the hard hand of war," he argued in 1864, could the terrible conflict be ended. Thus Sherman preferred raids into enemy territory, destroying supplies and transportation networks and uprooting the civilian population. The resulting impoverishment and terror crippled morale and led thousands of Confederate soldiers on other war fronts to desert. By capturing Atlanta,

Georgia, in 1864, he probably ensured the reelection of Abraham Lincoln; by marching through Georgia and the Carolinas, he helped to destroy the Confederacy's will to continue the contest.

Sherman was born in Lancaster, Ohio, in 1820, and was the sixth of eleven children. When his father died in 1829, "Cump" was raised in the home of a powerful family friend, Thomas Ewing. With Ewing's influence, Sherman secured an appointment to the U.S. Military Academy at West Point (from which he graduated sixth in his class of forty-two in 1840). Sherman later married one of Ewing's daughters. After serving in Florida, Alabama, South Carolina, Pennsylvania, and California, he won a brevet promotion in the Mexican War. Captain Sherman resigned his commission in 1853 to become a banker in San Francisco. After the bank failed, he eventually accepted the superintendency of the Louisiana Military Seminary (now Louisiana State University).

At the outset of the war, Sherman did not oppose slavery and sympathized with many of the views of his Louisiana friends, but he would not fight against the Union. With the aid of his brother, Congressman John Sherman, he secured a commission and led a brigade at First Bull Run, Virginia, July 1861, the first time he had tasted combat (he had been a recruiter and staff officer during the Mexican War). Sherman then took command of the Department of the Cumberland. Sherman, however, was overwhelmed by the real and imagined pressures of defending Kentucky. His pessimism, poor health, and generally erratic behavior soon led to his recall; many concluded that he had gone insane.

Thanks to intense lobbying by the Ewing-Sherman family, Sherman received command of the Department of Cairo, where he began organizing his own division of volunteers. With his confidence restored, in spring 1862, he joined the Army of the Mississippi commanded by U. S. Grant. ALBERT SIDNEY JOHNSTON [79] attacked at Shiloh, Tennessee, and caught Sherman, like the rest of the Union high command, completely by surprise. Though stunned, Sherman recovered quickly. He seemed to be everywhere, and had three horses shot out from under him in the two-day contest. With his confidence regained, he led a wing of Grant's army in the Vicksburg campaigns. He suffered a bloody repulse above Vicksburg at Chickasaw Bluffs, Mississippi, but performed well in semi-independent commands as Union troops besieged the city. After the successful relief of Union troops at Chattanooga, in February 1864 Sherman planned and executed a twenty-thousand-man raid from Vicksburg to Meridian, living off the land and destroying much of central Mississippi.

Sherman took command of the Military Division of the Mississippi when Grant went east to direct all Union armies. As Grant pressed the Army of Northern Virginia, under ROBERT E. LEE [4], Sherman took on the Army of Tennessee under JOSEPH E. JOHNSTON [12]. Sherman led the combined Union armies of the Cumberland, the Tennessee, and the Ohio, nearly 110,000 men, versus Johnston's 65,000. In early May 1864, Union troops pushed south from Chattanooga, Tennessee, toward Atlanta, Georgia. With the exception of a futile assault against Kennesaw Mountain, Georgia, Sherman relied on maneuver rather than frontal attacks to force Johnston's withdrawal from several excellent defensive positions. In mid-July, with the Federals now on the outskirts of Atlanta, JOHN BELL HOOD [38] replaced Johnston and launched a series of disastrous counterattacks against Sherman's forces. On September 2 Union troops occupied the city. "Atlanta is ours," Sherman proclaimed, "and fairly won."

Atlanta's fall ensured the reelection of ABRAHAM LINCOLN [1] and dealt a heavy blow to the South. Still, Sherman had failed to achieve his original objective—the defeat of the Confederate army in the field. He was appalled by the bloody nature of Civil War battles and shifted to strikes designed to break the enemy's will to fight. When Hood marched north toward Tennessee that fall, Sherman dispatched subordinates George Thomas and John Schofield to deal with Hood, while he opted instead to "make Georgia howl." After destroying everything of conceivable military use in Atlanta, he cut loose from his supply lines in mid-November, and marched toward the coast. For nearly a month his sixty thousand men cut a sixty-mile-wide swath through the heart of the Confederacy, presenting the city of Savannah "as a Christmas gift" to President Lincoln. After pausing briefly, Sherman then pushed into South Carolina. As he captured Columbia, a fire, fueled by high winds and thousands of cotton bales, destroyed the city; each side blamed the other for the disaster.

After Lee capitulated at Appomattox, Sherman's initial terms for Joe Johnston's army, granting a general amnesty to former Confederates and recognizing existing state governments in the South, reflected his view that a soft peace should follow his hard war. Washington officials, however, judged these promises too generous and directed him to dictate harsher terms; whereupon he offered Johnston the same terms as Grant had offered to Lee.

Sherman later commanded the Division of the Missouri until Grant became president, when Sherman succeeded his old comrade-in-arms as commanding general of the army. From 1874 to 1876, Sherman clashed with the secretary of war, William Belknap, over what Sherman believed to be the secretary's unnecessary meddling in army affairs. Sherman even went so far as to move his headquarters from Washington to St. Louis. He retired from military service on his sixty-fourth birthday with the rank of full general.

Representatives of both political parties frequently asked Sherman to run for president. He rejected them all, finally resorting to his often misquoted rejoinder, "I will not accept if nominated and will not serve if elected." He died in New York City in 1891. His old foe, Joe Johnston, served as one of his pallbearers and refused to wear a hat out of deference to his fallen rival. Johnston caught pneumonia and died five weeks later.

Some readers will undoubtedly question my placing Sherman ahead of Confederate general Robert E. Lee, who compiled a far superior record in battle. Had the Confederacy won, Lee would deservedly rank ahead of all others, but the Confederacy did not win, and Sherman's strikes against the

A triumphant Sherman views the breastworks at Atlanta, which his army has conquered.

enemy's will to resist had been a major factor in the Union victory. As Grant maintained his relentless pressure on Lee's army in Virginia, Sherman was marching through Mississippi, Georgia, and the Carolinas, destroying crops, industrial centers, and railroads. The combination of blows proved too much for the Confederacy to bear.

William Sherman has been vilified by Southerners and is hated even to this day. Ironically, this same man had sympathized with Southern interests before the war and went on to advocate a much more generous peace than most of his Northern contemporaries. As he explained to Grant in a letter of April 25, 1865—over three weeks before the eventual capture of the Confederate president, Jefferson Davis, "What we now want is the new form of law by which common men may regain the positions of industry, so long disturbed by the war."

4

Robert E. Lee

(1807–1870)

Robert Edward Lee was the commander of the Confederate Army of Northern Virginia from 1862 to 1865 and the best combat general of the Civil War. Lee's efforts centered upon his beloved homeland of Virginia, which was also the most populous and important Confederate state. In the face of Union numerical and industrial superiority, Lee and his army fended off Northern advances into Virginia for three long years. He was so beloved by his men and such a living symbol of Southern chivalry that he had acquired almost mythic status by the war's end. Although recent scholars have acknowledged certain flaws in his generalship, the stately Lee remains the most important figure of the Confederate war effort.

Robert E. Lee was the son of Revolutionary War hero Richard Henry "Light-Horse Harry" Lee and was born in 1807 in Virginia. In 1829, he graduated from the U.S. Military Academy second in his class of forty-six (Charles Mason of New York, who soon resigned from military duty, ranked first). Two years later, Lee married Mary Custis, heiress to a large estate at Arlington. He was assigned to the Corps of Engineers and worked on various military installations throughout the country. During the war with Mexico, Lee served on the staff of General WINFIELD SCOTT [37]. He distinguished himself for his personal courage and his reconnaissance of the terrain in the fighting at Cerro Gordo and Chapultepec. In 1852, Lee became superintendent at West Point, where he helped to implement higher academic standards and curricular reform. Three years later, he was made lieutenant colonel of the elite Second Cavalry Regiment. Normally, he was stationed in Texas with his regiment, but in 1858 he took an extended leave to care for his deceased father-in-law's estate. While still at Arlington, Lee was appointed to command the scratch force which captured JOHN BROWN [14] during the latter's abortive raid on the arsenal at Harpers Ferry, Virginia.

As secession neared, Lee agonized over his proper course of action. He had come to realize the evils of slavery. All his adult life, he had proudly worn his nation's uniform. Yet in the end, he believed his loyalty to his state, Virginia, outweighed that to his country. Thus he declined General Scott's offer of the Union field command, instead resigning his U.S. commission. Lee was soon appointed a full general in the Confederate Army, third in seniority to the former adjutant general of the U.S. Army, Samuel Cooper, and second to the highly regarded ALBERT SIDNEY JOHNSTON [79], three years his elder.

Although Lee did a good job of organizing Virginia's defenses, the war began inauspiciously. Dispatched in late 1861 to salvage Confederate efforts in western Virginia, he performed without distinction; some concluded that Lee had been overrated. Nevertheless, he retained the trust and confidence of President JEFFERSON DAVIS [5]. After his former West Point classmate JOSEPH E. JOHNSTON [12] fell wounded in the Battle of Seven Pines, Virginia, on June 1, 1862, Lee took command of what became the Army of Northern Virginia. He inherited a dangerous situation. Union troops, led by GEORGE B. MCCLELLAN [7], had advanced to within a few miles of the Confederate capital, Richmond. With Lee's encouragement, THOMAS J. "STONEWALL" JACKSON [20] had already stepped up his campaign in Virginia's Shenandoah Valley, thus diverting Union reinforcements previously bound for McClellan. Lee then launched a series of attacks, known as the Seven Days' Battles (Virginia), designed to crush McClellan's army. Despite suffering heavy casualties, Lee drove the Union forces back and saved the capital.

Lee then marched north, embarrassing Federal troops under JOHN POPE [62] at the Second Battle of Bull Run, Virginia. Eager to take the war out of Virginia and hopeful that a victory on Northern soil might bring about

British recognition of the Confederacy, Lee invaded the North. As his army pushed into Maryland, however, a set of Confederate plans fell into enemy hands, enabling McClellan to strike the scattered Southern forces in the Battle of Antietam, Maryland. Despite a two-to-one numerical disadvantage, Lee brilliantly parried the enemy's disjointed attacks. Although a strategic defeat, Antietam had been a tactical draw that allowed Lee to withdraw safely back into Virginia. In late December 1862, Lee's army won another major victory at Fredericksburg, Virginia, hurling back his attackers with heavy Union losses.

As campaigning resumed the following spring, Lee won his most spectacular success at Chancellorsville, Virginia. In an audacious move, he divided his army in the face of the enemy to deliver a flanking attack against the stunned Union troops of JOSEPH HOOKER [36]. Confederate spirits were diminished only by their heavy casualties. Undaunted, Lee swept north once more. In southern Pennsylvania in early July, he clashed again with the Army of the Potomac, now commanded by GEORGE MEADE [22]. After pounding the Union lines for three days, Lee finally fell back, defeated in the war's biggest battle. He would never fully replace the thousands lost at Gettysburg.

Both sides licked their wounds and sparred inconclusively until heavy fighting was renewed in spring 1864. ULYSSES S. GRANT [2] had moved east and now commanded the Union Army. In a series of bloody engagements in Virginia—the Wilderness, Spotsylvania, and Cold Harbor—the Army of Northern Virginia inflicted over fifty thousand Union casualties within a six-week span, suffering only about half that number in return. Grant continued his relentless pressure, moving south of Richmond against Petersburg, Virginia, through which passed the Confederate capital's major rail connection with the rest of the South. Forced to defend Petersburg, Lee could no longer afford to maneuver, thus losing what had been one of his greatest assets. During the siege, losses and desertions mounted. Finally, in April 1865, hoping to escape with the remnants of his army to the west, Lee abandoned Petersburg. He found his way blocked, and now outnumbered five to one, Lee knew the cause was lost. "I would rather die a thousand deaths," Lee declared as he surrendered his Army of Northern Virginia to Grant at Appomattox Court House.

Standing proud at an erect six feet tall, Lee cut a noble figure upon his horse, Traveller. He was pious, courteous to a fault, and self-controlled. His audacious generalship dominated the war in Virginia until summer 1864, when overwhelming Union numbers and Grant's stubborn leadership combined to claim the initiative. Certainly, Lee had his faults—always the gentleman, his orders tended to be inexact, allowing too much discretion. Sufficing for subordinates who were great military leaders in their own right, such as Stonewall Jackson, such instructions had disastrous results when given to men of mediocre ability. Lee also never fully recognized the effects of the newly introduced rifled muskets and artillery, technological advances that made firearms much more accurate and longer ranged; thus he continued

Confederate troops behind the stone wall on Marye's Heights, Fredericksburg, Virginia, May 1863

to launch costly frontal assaults such as those at Gettysburg. He sought to crush entire armies, a feat virtually impossible to achieve in light of the staggering casualties and exertions necessary simply to win a single battle. Encouraged by the prodigious feats of his army, Lee could become overly aggressive; even in his great victories in the Seven Days and at Chancellorsville, his losses were disproportionate to those inflicted on the Union. But perhaps it was Lee's gambler's instinct that the Confederacy—with its limited industrial base, shortage of capital, and inferiority in manpower—really needed if it were to have any chance of winning the Civil War.

His dark hair and beard were grayed by the long conflict's burdens, but Lee retained his dignity and graciousness in his twilight years. He preached reconciliation, and he served as president of Washington College (later renamed Washington and Lee University) before his death in 1870. Lee was buried at Lexington, Virginia.

5

Jefferson Davis

(1808–1889)

President of the Confederate States of America, Jefferson Davis was a controversial figure during his own lifetime and remains so today. He accepted the presidency reluctantly: He had hoped to lead troops in battle. Instead, Davis did what he considered to be his duty through four grueling years of war. Ill suited by nature to lead a revolutionary movement, he interfered too often in military affairs and failed to rally the political support needed to efficiently mobilize the South's limited resources. Yet, through extraordinary personal dedication and force of will, he kept the war going for four years. Captured and, for a time, manacled while awaiting trial on treason charges after the war, he symbolized the conflicts surrounding the "Lost Cause" of the South. For some, Davis is a heroic martyr of a people's attempt to maintain their freedoms; to others, he seems the misguided leader of a discredited movement that caused the deaths of six hundred thousand Americans.

Born in a log cabin in Kentucky in 1808, Jefferson Davis as a youth moved with his family to Mississippi, where he spent most of his boyhood. In 1824 he accepted an appointment to the U.S. Military Academy, from which he later graduated twenty-third in his class of thirty-two. During his four years at West Point, his fellow cadets included future Confederate generals ALBERT SIDNEY JOHNSTON [79], ROBERT E. LEE [4], and JOSEPH E. JOHNSTON [12]. Davis served in the Black Hawk War (1832) but resigned his commission in 1835.

Davis then began growing cotton below Vicksburg, Mississippi, at what became his Brierfield plantation. Prospering as a planter, he eventually acquired seventy-four slaves. His first wife, Sarah Knox Taylor, died in 1835; and he married Varina Howell ten years later. Davis was elected as a Democrat to the U.S. House of Representatives, but resigned after only a year to lead a regiment of Mississippi volunteers during the Mexican War. He demonstrated personal courage and leadership in the battles of Monterrey and Buena Vista, suffering a foot wound in the latter engagement. A U.S. senator between 1847 and 1851 and again from 1857 to 1861, Davis was secretary of war from 1853 to 1857, a post which, unlike most of his predecessors, he filled with innovativeness and effectiveness.

In February 1861 delegates from six states that had already seceded from the Union assembled at Montgomery, Alabama, where they elected Davis provisional president of the Confederacy. He was elected president for a full term later that year. His strong record of support for states' rights and slavery, as well as his considerable political, military, and administrative experience, made Davis a seemingly obvious choice. Medically, he was burdened by dyspepsia, neuralgia, and chronic eye problems, but these complaints paled in comparison to the enormous obstacles he faced in trying to create a new nation. The Confederacy had a relatively small industrial base and a population less than half that of the Union. The South's tradition of independence and states' rights made essential wartime measures such as conscription, increased taxation, and martial law difficult for the central government to implement even during times of crisis.

The Confederacy, however, did enjoy several advantages. Its large size rendered occupation by Union troops difficult. The South also boasted a number of respected military leaders, including Lee and the Johnstons. Davis recognized that the Confederacy did not necessarily have to win its freedom; rather, it had to avoid losing and outlast the North.

History also seemed to be on the Confederacy's side. Considering themselves the guardians of the revolutionary heritage of the Founding Fathers, Southerners remembered that the American colonies had overcome England's enormous material superiority to win their independence less than a century earlier. Surely, they thought, through bravery and dedication the Confederacy could win a second revolution.

Davis was six feet tall, with sunken cheeks that made him seem distant. He also was high strung, vindictive, and overly sensitive to criticism; and his pride prevented him from becoming an inspirational leader. Although frequently indecisive, once Davis made a decision he often became overly rigid. Hampered by a weak, constantly changing cabinet (he had six war secretaries in four years), he was a poor administrator obsessed with petty details. As a West Point graduate and an experienced combat veteran, he meddled too much in the affairs of his generals. Especially harmful was his tendency to award his personal favorites—BRAXTON BRAGG [30], JOHN C. PEMBERTON [65], and JOHN BELL HOOD [38]—with important commands, while allowing his antipathy for others, like Joseph Johnston and P. G. T. BEAUREGARD [35], to prevent the Confederacy from properly employing their talents.

Perhaps most damning was Davis's failure to grow in office, especially when compared with Abraham Lincoln. Since most individuals, however, would rank unfavorably when measured against Lincoln, such a comparison is probably not as illuminating as the answer to another question: Did Davis hurt or help the Confederate cause? For all his weaknesses, here the pluses outweigh the minuses. A man of impeccable personal integrity, Jefferson Davis devoted himself to the war. He formed a government and organized his nation's armies despite unrelenting wartime pressures. Loyal to his friends, his close relationship with Lee meant that "Marse Robert" could always count on the president's support. Thus, despite Davis's meddling in the west, where the South suffered repeated failures, the Confederates held their own in the east. In the face of overwhelming material disadvantages, Davis's iron-willed determination sustained the Confederate war effort for four years, a feat no other Southerner then alive could have matched.

Still stubbornly committed to the cause, Davis left the Confederate capital at Richmond in early April 1865, after it became clear the city would fall to Union forces. He tried to keep the war going but was captured near Irwinville, Georgia. After his imprisonment for nearly two years at Fortress Monroe, Virginia, Davis became president of a life insurance company and assembled his memoirs, *Rise and Fall of the Confederate Government.* An admirer provided him with a home, named Beauvoir, near Biloxi, Mississippi. He died in 1889, and his remains were eventually buried in Richmond.

6

Andrew Johnson

(1808–1875)

A proud, stubborn man, Andrew Johnson devoted his life to protecting what he believed to be the values of the United States Constitution: limited federal government, states' rights, and white male equality. He was the only representative from a Confederate state to retain his congressional seat following secession. Since he was politically valuable as a Unionist, Johnson became the running mate of ABRRAHAM LINCOLN [1] in 1864. After Lincoln's assassination, he assumed the presidency at a critical junction in his nation's history. Johnson inherited a country rent asunder by civil war, and his responsibility was to reunite the nation. It would have taken a statesman for the ages to heal its deep wounds. Lincoln might have been that person; Andrew Johnson was not. His inability to effectively reconstruct the Union makes him one of the most important and at the same time ineffective leaders of the Civil War era.

The seventeenth president of the United States was born in Raleigh, North Carolina, in 1808. His father died three years later, leaving the family impoverished. He was apprenticed to a tailor when he was fourteen years old. In 1826 Andrew moved with his family to Tennessee. He married the following year and established a tailor's shop in Greeneville. Encouraged by his wife, Eliza McCardle, he read widely in an effort to overcome the gaps left by his limited formal education.

From these humble origins, Johnson entered politics as a Jacksonian Democrat, championing a homestead law and the white yeoman farmers who populated eastern Tennessee. He held a series of offices, including alderman, mayor, state senator, governor, and finally congressman. Although in 1860 he backed JOHN C. BRECKINRIDGE [60], the Southern Democratic candidate, Johnson supported compromise efforts designed to head off secession.

A staunch Unionist, Johnson argued that wealthy slaveholders had duped the South into secession. After Federal troops occupied large parts of Tennessee in 1862, Lincoln appointed him that state's wartime governor. The president respected Johnson's Unionism; seeking to portray a bipartisan image and unimpressed by incumbent HANNIBAL HAMLIN [94], the National Union Party convention (a coalition of War Democrats and Republicans) selected Johnson for the vice-presidency on the first ballot.

The vice president–elect endured an inauspicious beginning. Exhausted by the trip to Washington and still recovering from typhoid fever, Johnson drank some whiskey to calm his nerves. Intoxicated, he delivered a rambling, semicoherent speech at the vice-presidential inauguration, which took place in the Senate chambers. "Do not let Johnson speak outside," Lincoln ordered an assistant as the presidential party proceeded to a platform outside the Capitol for his second inauguration.

After Lincoln's assassination in April 1865, Johnson was abruptly thrust into the presidency. Like his predecessor, he contended that the executive should set the standards for bringing former Confederate states back into the Union. Evincing little sympathy for the concerns of former slaves, he believed in the inherent goodness of the average white Southerner. Concili-ation, respect for states' rights, and limited federal government were the cor-nerstones of Johnson's program, which pardoned most adult white males from the former Confederate states upon their taking an oath of future alle-giance to the Union. High-ranking Confederate civil and military officers, as well as those whose property was valued at over $20,000, could make indi-vidual applications for clemency to the president. States, too, were gently treated. Once a state had nullified secession and ratified the Thirteenth Amendment, Johnson proclaimed, it could be readmitted.

Johnson sought to restore, rather than to reconstruct, the South. He granted wholesale pardons and did not object when Southerners reelected their traditional political leaders, many of whom had supported secession or the Confederacy. Every Southern state passed legal restrictions, known as the black codes, which, while acknowledging the end of slavery, sought to restore the traditional social order of the South, with whites on top and blacks at the bottom. When Congress reconvened in December 1865, Southern delegates—who included the Confederacy's former vice president, ALEXANDER STEPHENS [71], several ex-Confederate cabinet members, and a platoon of Rebel military officers—sought to take their seats, with Johnson's support.

Stunned, the Republican majority refused to seat the former Confederates, setting off a titanic struggle between the executive and legislative branches. Fearing that Johnson's lenient policies would lose the peace that military victories had won, Congress asserted its control of Reconstruction. Republicans won huge majorities in the 1866 congressional elections and passed, over Johnson's repeated vetoes, laws which laid down more stringent conditions for a state's readmission into the Union. An effort to impeach the president failed in 1867, but when Johnson tried to force Secretary of War EDWIN STANTON [9] from office in violation of the Tenure of Office Act, his critics renewed their assaults. In February 1868 the House of Representatives impeached Johnson, but in the ensuing trial, the Senate failed by a single vote to reach the two-thirds majority needed to remove him from office.

Though issues relating to Reconstruction and impeachment dominated Johnson's administrations, his presidency also saw the United States purchase Alaska and the French withdraw support from the puppet government of Emperor Maximilian in Mexico. The Tennessee state legislature elected Johnson to the Senate again in 1874. He died the next summer. Johnson was buried with a copy of the Constitution in his coffin. Courageous and uncompromising, he never understood or accommodated the Northern Unionists' determination to transform, as well as restore, Southern society in the aftermath of the Civil War. His failures meant that the nation's deep racial and sectional divisions would continue for generations to come.

7

George McClellan

(1826–1885)

"Mcclellan is to me one of the mysteries of the war," proclaimed ULYSSES S. GRANT [2] during the late 1870s. Indeed, historians remain divided in their assessments of this intriguing Union general and Democratic politician. His supporters point out that McClellan built and molded the Army of the Potomac, a great fighting force which proved a key instrument in winning the war. They also complain that, as a Democrat, McClellan was unnecessarily impeded by Republican loyalists behind his own lines. Detractors, however, emphasize McClellan's missed opportunities: his slow advance during the Peninsula campaign in Virginia in spring 1862, his inept tactics at the Battle of Antietam, Maryland, later that fall, and his failure to pursue the badly mauled Army of Northern Virginia under ROBERT E. LEE [4] in that battle's aftermath. Whatever our opinion of his abilities or shortcomings, McClellan ranks among the most important figures of the war.

George B. McClellan was bred for greatness. Born in 1826 into a prominent Philadelphia family and benefiting from a fine private school education, he entered West Point two years before the normal minimum age. A brilliant student, he graduated second in the class of 1846, easily outdistancing fellow classmates (and future Civil War generals) such as THOMAS J. "STONEWALL" JACKSON [20] and George E. Pickett. McClellan earned two brevet promotions during the war against Mexico, served a three-year stint as instructor at West Point, and acted as an American military observer to the Crimean War. He resigned his commission in 1857 to accept a post as chief engineer of the Illinois Central Railroad. Two years later, he became president of the Ohio and Mississippi Railroad.

At the beginning of the Civil War, McClellan was appointed major general of volunteers in command of the Department of the Ohio. He organized and led a successful campaign into western Virginia, doing much to facilitate the creation of the pro-Union state of West Virginia two years later. After the Union defeat at First Bull Run, Virginia, he was called to Washington, where he whipped what had been a demoralized mob into the Army of the Potomac. From November 1, 1861, to March 11, 1862, he also served as general-in-chief of all Union armies.

McClellan was handsome, erect, imposing on horseback, and immensely popular with his men. However, his Democratic inclinations and refusal to endorse measures that might have transformed Southern society, such as abolition, worried many political opponents. Perhaps his string of successes left him unprepared for the trying days to come. Under pressure from President Lincoln, McClellan finally took the offensive in spring 1862. Rather than attempt the slow overland march south from Washington to Richmond, a route which gave the Confederates several excellent defensive positions, he used his superior naval resources to land his army on the peninsula formed by the York and James Rivers. A quick strike toward Richmond, McClellan hoped, would force the Confederates to attack him on unfavorable terms.

The plan was brilliantly conceived and organized, but as was typical for McClellan, he proved too cautious to exploit his initial advantage. The siege of Yorktown, Virginia, alone lasted a month. Still, he inched forward, and in late May parried a Confederate counterattack in the Battle of Seven Pines, just four miles from Richmond. In that battle, JOSEPH E. JOHNSTON [12] was severely wounded, so command of Confederate troops in his front passed to Robert E. Lee. Convinced he was outnumbered when he in fact enjoyed a decided numerical superiority, McClellan clamored for more troops as Lee initiated a series of attacks, collectively known as the Seven Days' Battles. Although the Army of the Potomac fought Lee to a standstill, its commander seemed beaten and fell back to Harrison's Landing, Virginia. Later that summer, over McClellan's protestations, Lincoln ordered a withdrawal back to Washington.

Following the disastrous defeat of JOHN POPE [62] at the Second Battle of Bull Run, Virginia, a desperate Lincoln again turned to McClellan as Lee's veterans advanced into Maryland. "Little Mac," however, once more came up short in the Battle of Antietam, Maryland. McClellan held a two-to-one numerical advantage, but his disjointed, piecemeal attacks left Lee holding the field after the bloodiest single day of combat in the war. On November 5, infuriated by McClellan's overcaution and his nearly libelous charges that Washington officials had failed to provide him adequate support, Lincoln relieved him in favor of AMBROSE BURNSIDE [52].

In 1864, McClellan, who had opposed the Emancipation Proclamation, accepted the Democratic Party's nomination for president. He tried to distance himself from the party's official peace platform, but the Union victory at Mobile Bay, Alabama, and the capture of Atlanta by WILLIAM T. SHERMAN [3] sealed McClellan's defeat. After the war, he once again proved a successful engineer, and was twice elected governor of New Jersey. He died in 1885.

McClellan's greatest feat was his creation of the Army of the Potomac. This was his army, and would remain so, long after his departure, but, perhaps, he loved his creation too much to risk losing thousands of his soldiers in battle. He seemed unable to accept the awesome responsibility of using this great instrument to force the South to reenter the Union. It took men with more inner strength of character, such as Lincoln and Grant, to achieve this end.

McClellan's Army of the Potomac on the march during the Peninsula Campaign, 1862.

8

William Seward

(1801–1872)

Secretary of state under presidents ABRAHAM LINCOLN [1] and ANDREW JOHNSON [6], William Seward played an influential role in maintaining British neutrality during the Civil War and in purchasing Alaska from Russia in 1867. After initially mistaking Lincoln's unpretentiousness for weakness, Seward became one of the president's ablest advisers. A longtime opponent of slavery, Seward was well known for his fiery pronouncements on the evils of the peculiar institution, statements which belied his personality, which usually tended toward caution and political discretion.

William Seward was born in 1801 in Orange County, New York, and graduated from Union College in 1820. He was admitted to the bar two years later. With the support of Thurlow Weed, the powerful editor and party organizer, Seward was elected to the state senate in 1830 as an Anti-Mason. He joined the recently formed Whig Party, and also served two effective terms as governor beginning in 1838. The state legislature elected Seward to the U.S. Senate in 1848. There he became one of President Zachary Taylor's strongest political supporters. Seward denounced the Compromise of 1850, which allowed the expansion of slavery into the territories of Utah and New Mexico, as "radically wrong and essentially vicious." Suggesting that the law, if enacted, should be defied, he proclaimed that "there is a higher law than the Constitution." Although Seward had reminded his Senate colleagues that moral principle should be a factor in their vote on the Compromise, his appeal to "a higher law" of God made him odious in the eyes of many Southerners.

After winning another Senate term, Seward joined the newly formed Republican Party. He became one of the party's leading figures, denouncing the nativist tendencies of many former Whigs and promoting a program of economic growth. Positioning himself for a future presidential bid but judging that Republican chances for victory in the presidential contest of 1856 were slim, he supported the unsuccessful candidacy of JOHN C. FRÉMONT [46]. In 1858, Seward once again riled Southerners when he predicted that the collision between free- and slave-labor systems would lead to "an irrepressible conflict" that would leave the country "either entirely a slave-holding nation, or entirely a free-labor nation."

In 1860, Seward made a vigorous effort to win the Republican presidential nomination. Seen as too radical on slavery and bitterly opposed by nativists, he was passed over in favor of Lincoln. Recognizing Seward's personal talents and enormous political stature, Lincoln named him his secretary of state. Seward, who considered himself the president's intellectual superior, still believed that civil war might be averted. He hoped more time could be bought by withdrawing Federal troops from Fort Sumter, South Carolina. Lincoln rejected the secretary's somewhat impertinent plan with a firm reminder of who the commander in chief in fact was.

After this rocky beginning, Seward developed into an able secretary of state. He helped avert several diplomatic crises with Britain and helped convince Northern governors to raise Federal volunteers. Opposed to slavery but fearing that premature action might be seen as an act of desperation, in July 1862 Seward convinced Lincoln to delay issuing a proclamation of freedom until after a military victory. The president agreed, and thus waited two months until the Battle of Antietam, in Maryland, to issue the Emancipation Proclamation.

At the end of the war Seward was wounded in a botched assassination attempt the night Lincoln was shot. He recovered, remained in Johnson's cabinet, and secured three final victories. His adroit diplomacy helped convince the French to withdraw their support for Maximilian in Mexico; Seward also secured the annexation of the Midway Islands, a move which took on enormous significance during the Second World War; and finally, he negotiated the purchase of Alaska from Russia. Although denounced at the time as "Seward's folly" or "Seward's icebox," the $7.2 million acquisition proved to be a bargain in the long run.

Seward resigned from public life in 1869. He died three years later. Often known for the bombastic statements he made before the war, Seward generally espoused moderation as secretary of state. Radical Republicans branded Seward too conservative, and after the war, he supported Johnson's lenient policies toward the South. Seward mastered his presidential ambitions and contributed mightily to the Union victory.

Edwin Stanton

(1814–1869)

Secretary of war from 1862 to 1868, Edwin McMasters Stanton was second only to Seward among the most influential cabinet advisers of ABRAHAM LIN-COLN [1]. Although he could be brusque, hot-tempered, and overbearing, Stanton possessed honesty and foresight; his effective management greatly aided the development of the Union war machine. After the war, he opposed the lenient policies of ANDREW JOHNSON [6] on the restoration of the former Confederate states. Johnson's attempt to fire Stanton led the House of Representatives to impeach him.

    Born at Steubenville, Ohio, in 1814, Edwin Stanton attended Kenyon College before being admitted to the bar in 1835. Specializing in patent law, contract law, and land title issues, Stanton became a nationally known figure. During one case, he headed a team of lawyers, including Abraham Lincoln, that challenged Cyrus Hall McCormick's patent of the reaper. "Why did you bring that d———-d long-armed ape here?" wondered Stanton about the future president. "He does not know anything." Lincoln acknowledged being "roughly handled by that man Stanton." In 1859, Stanton was the first American lawyer to use successfully the defense of temporary insanity to save his client and friend, future Union general Daniel Sickles, from the charge that he had murdered his wife's lover, the son of Francis Scott Key.

In December 1860, in hopes of salvaging his tainted administration, President JAMES BUCHANAN [26] appointed Stanton his attorney general. The lame-duck Buchanan administration, beset by corruption and the threat of secession, seemed on the verge of collapse. Stanton forcefully denounced secession and helped convince Buchanan not to surrender Fort Sumter, South Carolina. Stanton's presence within the cabinet is generally credited with having helped to restore a modicum of order to the discredited administration during its last months.

With Abraham Lincoln's presidential inauguration, Stanton, a Democrat, returned to private life. He acted as legal counsel for a number of prominent Northerners, including Secretary of War Simon Cameron and Gen. GEORGE B. McCLELLAN [7], who would soon rise to command the Army of the Potomac. Chafing at the new regime's seeming inability to control events, Stanton privately lambasted "the imbecility of this administration." However, Secretary Cameron's incompetence, dubious integrity, and premature announcement of his intention to arm slaves led Lincoln to exile him to the U.S. ministry in Russia. In January 1862 the president appointed Stanton to head the War Department.

Lincoln respected Stanton's integrity and Unionism and valued the political benefits of having a Democrat in his cabinet. Stanton's energy and obvious administrative abilities paid huge dividends. The two developed a close working relationship. Although the short, secretive Stanton often clashed with other cabinet members, Lincoln felt comfortable enough with Stanton's stern management to turn his attention to affairs outside the often maddening, but essential, bureaucratic entanglements and contractual bargaining of the War Department. On most issues, such as his revision of the War Department's earlier harsh policies toward political prisoners and his opposition to McClellan's continued service, Secretary Stanton's judgment proved sound. His biggest mistake came in April 1862, when, erroneously assuming that the war would soon end, he ordered that all recruiting offices be closed. This uncharacteristic error slowed the flow of Northern recruits just as the war entered its second year.

Three years later, on the eve of the North's triumph, JOHN WILKES BOOTH [25] fatally shot President Lincoln. Stanton uttered perhaps the most memorable tribute to the murdered president. As Lincoln died, Stanton, his face covered with tears, raised his hat, briefly placed it atop his head, then removed it. "Now," mourned Stanton, "he belongs to the ages."

Stanton continued to serve as secretary of war for Andrew Johnson, but bitterly opposed what he believed to be the new president's overly lenient policies toward the former Confederate states. In early 1867 Congress attempted to protect Stanton's continued presence in the cabinet by passing the Tenure of Office Act, which prohibited the president from removing government officials appointed with the advice of the Senate without that body's consent. Johnson suspended Stanton on August 12, 1867, temporarily replacing him with Ulysses S. Grant. In December, there was a failed attempt to impeach Johnson. In January 1868, however, the Senate refused to accept the suspension, and Stanton briefly returned to office. The president then attempted to fire him, but the latter barricaded himself in his office and the House of Representatives renewed its impeachment proceedings. In the end, an implicit compromise was reached: The Senate failed by one vote to convict Johnson, and Gen. JOHN SCHOFIELD [75] replaced Stanton in the War Department.

After six and a half years in government, Stanton briefly resumed his legal practice in 1869. On December 20, the Senate confirmed his appointment to the Supreme Court, but he died three days later. Stanton's effective War Department management was crucial to the North's victory, thus meriting his high ranking in the present volume.

10

Frederick Douglass

(1817–1895)

Orator, journalist, author, and federal official, Frederick Douglass was the most important African American of the nineteenth century. An escaped slave, the self-taught Douglass became a powerful spokesman for abolition, temperance, and women's rights. During the Civil War, he also served as recruiting agent for two black regiments of Massachusetts volunteers. Rallying support for black suffrage, Douglass helped secure ratification of the Fourteenth and Fifteenth Amendments. After the war, he broke several color barriers in federal jobs and continued to press for racial equality while at the same time preaching the gospel of self-help to fellow blacks. "Learn trades or starve," he urged in one of his most famous editorials.

The exact details of Douglass's early life remain unknown. He was born Frederick Augustus Washington Bailey about 1817 in Tuckahoe, Maryland, son of Harriet Bailey and an anonymous father, possibly his master Aaron Anthony. He knew little about his mother, a field hand who died when he was eight or nine years old. Sent to Baltimore as a houseboy in 1825, he taught himself to read and worked odd jobs. After one escape attempt failed, in 1838 Frederick succeeded in fleeing with the help of Anna Murray, a free African American, and took the name Douglass. The two went north and married, eventually raising a family of five children.

Douglass found that racial discrimination prevented him from gaining steady work in his self-taught trade of ship's caulker. Moving from New York City to New Bedford, Massachusetts, to Lynn, Massachusetts, he took odd jobs and became acquainted with the abolitionist movement. An athletic six feet tall, the broadshouldered Douglass was soon pressed into service as a speaker for the Massachusetts Anti-Slavery Society. His rich baritone voice, combined with his private study and careful preparation, made him one of the reformers' most effective stump speakers. In 1845 he published the first and most important of his three autobiographies, *Narrative of the Life of Frederick Douglass*.

On the heels of this successful book, Douglass went to England, Scotland, and Ireland, hoping to spread the gospel of American abolitionism as well as to escape any attempt his former owner might make to recapture him now that he had become so easily identifiable. After a triumphant twenty-one-month tour, Douglass returned to America, relocated at Rochester, New York, and opened the first of several newspapers he would edit, *The North Star.* The Colored National Convention of 1848 selected him as its president.

During the early 1850s, he deviated slightly from the strategy advocated by his old ally WILLIAM LLOYD GARRISON [24], eschewing Garrison's withdrawal from politics to eagerly take up political activism with the Republican Party. He abandoned the possibility of achieving abolition through peaceful means and welcomed the coming of the Civil War. Impatient with Lincoln's failure to abolish slavery immediately, Douglass met the president in the White House in August 1863 and urged that black troops receive pay, supplies, and treatment equal to that accorded whites. "Though I was not entirely satisfied with his views," Douglass later wrote, "I was so well satisfied with the man and with the educating tendency of the conflict that I determined to go on with the recruiting." Still, Douglass renewed his public criticisms of the administration the following year, arguing that Lincoln should take a firmer position on black suffrage. The two held another conciliatory meeting in August 1864, at which the president outlined a scheme, never implemented, that would have had Douglass organize a group of federal agents assigned to help Southern slaves gain their freedom.

With the end of the war, Douglass supported ratification of the Fourteenth and Fifteenth Amendments. Though he had long backed woman suffrage, he accepted the exclusion of women from these amendments on the grounds that it was the black man's hour. Extending the franchise to women, he reasoned, might generate enough additional opposition to kill any guarantees for blacks. In 1877 Douglass was named marshal of the District of

Columbia, and four years later accepted another federal appointment as the capital city's recorder of deeds. A Republican Party loyalist, Douglass also received President Benjamin Harrison's appointment as minister-resident and consul-general to Haiti, and chargé d'affaires for the Dominican Republic. He resigned three years later.

Having raised himself from slavery to national prominence, Douglass had helped to secure emancipation and the passage of major civil rights legislation. He was easily the most important and effective black leader of the nineteenth century. After the war, however, some charged that he never really understood the need to ensure that blacks received equal economic opportunities, placing undue faith in self-help and self-reliance. His determination that African Americans should become amalgamated into the larger American society also drew criticism from those in the black community who urged racial separation.

In 1884, two years after his first wife's death, Douglass married Helen Pitts, a forty-five-year-old white woman who had worked for years as his secretary. The couple defied the resulting criticism about miscegenation. Douglass died in 1895.

Slaves planting fields on a plantation in Hilton Head, South Carolina.

11

Stephen A. Douglas

(1813–1861)

Often remembered as the "loser" of the Lincoln-Douglas debates, Stephen Arnold Douglas was in fact one of the most important politicians of the 1850s. Born in Brandon, Vermont, on April 23, 1813, Stephen never knew his father, who died two months after his son's birth. At age twenty, with three hundred dollars and two letters of introduction in his pocket, he set off to make his mark in the west.

Douglas settled down in Jacksonville, Illinois, and began practicing law. His real interest, however, had always been politics. A skilled debater and an organizational genius, Douglas threw himself into Democratic Party affairs. Standing just over five feet tall, Douglas was dubbed the "Little Giant" by his followers. His convivial personality, fondness for rough sports, and boundless energy seemed ideally suited to his constituents. Elected at age twenty-seven to the state supreme court, Justice Douglas's informal manners further endeared him to frontier democrats. He typically heard cases in his shirt-sleeves, leaning back in his chair with his feet placed up so as to be virtually lying on his back, and periodically leaving the bench to smoke a cigar with the lawyers.

First elected to Congress in 1843, Douglas became a prominent figure

over the next eighteen years. A Jacksonian Democrat, he distrusted banks
and paper money, hated privilege, opposed protective tariffs, denounced sectionalism, and championed national expansion. He married into a wealthy
family and began investing heavily in the booming Chicago real-estate
market. Chairing the House and Senate Committees on Territories, especially important posts given the nation's expansionist tendencies, Douglas
established himself as a Democratic Party leader. Increasing sectional divisions, however, loomed large. Fearing the North's growing population base,
most Southerners demanded federal protection for slavery in the territories,
while, in the meantime, growing numbers of Northerners sought to limit the
expansion of slavery or abolish the institution entirely. From 1849 to 1850,
legislation came to a standstill as debate raged over the question of slavery in
the lands acquired as a result of the Mexican War.

But the Compromise had not really dealt with the roots of the problem:
Believing that no issue should so divide the nation, Douglas champi-
oned compromise. After an impasse was reached over Senator Henry Clay's
"Omnibus Bill," a collection of several measures aimed at bringing together
moderates on both sides, Douglas took charge of the floor fight. He divided
the bill into separate parts and shepherded each section through Congress.
His masterful handling of the legislative package, collectively known as the
Compromise of 1850, momentarily quieted talk of secession.

But the Compromise had not really dealt with the roots of the problem:
slavery and states' rights. The New Mexico and Utah territories had been
established, but voters in each area would still need to determine the question of slavery. California's admission gave the free states a majority in the
Senate, frightening many Southerners. Ending the slave trade in the nation's
capital did not satisfy abolitionists, who wanted the institution removed
entirely. And many Northerners vowed to resist the new Fugitive Slave Law,
which to them seemed a high-handed attempt by slaveholders to round up
escaped bondsmen and freed blacks alike.

Douglas believed the cause of national development could still unite the
nation. A transcontinental railroad would link the far-flung Pacific outposts
with the rest of the country; if the route went through Illinois, it would benefit his constituents as well. But the areas west of Iowa and Missouri still had
no local government, a precondition for his planned railroad. In order to
attract the Southern support necessary to pass the legislation, Douglas crafted
a bill that effectively repealed the Missouri Compromise (which had prohibited slavery throughout the area in question) and created two territories,
Kansas and Nebraska. On the principle of popular sovereignty, voters would
determine the fate of slavery in each territory. Since slavery was impractical
this far west, Douglas contended, the Kansas-Nebraska Act did not really open
the way for its expansion. Alternately convincing, cajoling, and threatening his
colleagues, the "Little Giant" guided his measure to legislative victory.

Events proved that Douglas was, in one sense at least, correct. Slavery
never flourished in Kansas, but he had badly misjudged the Northern outrage
against what many perceived as his "sellout" to the South. He could, by his
own admission, have traveled all the way from Illinois to Washington, D.C.,

guided by the light of the fires started to burn him in effigy. Largely because of its support for Douglas's controversial bill, the Northern wing of the Democratic Party was weakened, leaving Southerners and Southern sympathizers firmly in control. Angered by the Whig Party's feeble response, many Northerners joined the newly formed Republican Party, which vowed to oppose any expansion of slavery. Although Douglas had gained territorial government for Kansas and Nebraska, his railroad bill died a quick death in a still-divided Congress.

Needing to cement his political base in Illinois, in 1858 Douglas found his Senate seat challenged by an upstart Republican, ABRAHAM LINCOLN [1]. That summer, during a series of seven afternoon debates (each three hours long), Douglas sought to portray his opponent as a "black Republican" who favored racial equality. In a somewhat tortured defense of his own positions (the so-called "Freeport Doctrine"), he also restated his support for popular sovereignty and voiced his defiance of the Supreme Court's recent DRED SCOTT [47] decision, which threatened to make it impossible for the federal government to prohibit slavery anywhere. Douglas retained his seat, but in the process completely alienated Southern Democrats, who were furious at his refusal to recognize a pro-slave government in Kansas and removed him from the chairmanship of the Committee on Territories.

By 1860, the Democratic Party was hopelessly divided, and the divisions over slavery and states' rights threatened the Union itself. Douglas won the nomination of Northern and many border-state Democrats for president, but Southerners opted instead to back JOHN C. BRECKINRIDGE [60]. In the face of additional challenges from the newly formed Constitutional Union Party and the Republicans, who nominated his old rival Abraham Lincoln, Douglas made a final effort to piece together a compromise. The only candidate that year even to attempt to secure national support, the "Little Giant" toured the country in a heroic but futile campaign. Douglas received about 30 percent of the popular vote, but was defeated by Lincoln in the electoral college.

The final irony came at Lincoln's inauguration. Douglas, sitting just behind the speaker's podium, held the new president's trademark stovepipe hat as Lincoln rose to give his inaugural address. Physically and emotionally spent by his own exertions as well as by his heavy drinking and cigar smoking, Senator Douglas pledged his full support for the Union as the war began, but he died in June 1861 of acute rheumatism, and liver and throat ailments.

A skillful politician and exuberant nationalist, Stephen Douglas unwittingly contributed much to the sectionalism that resulted in the Civil War. He opposed slavery, but never really understood the emotional reactions it engendered in both North and South. Controversy stemming from his ill-fated Kansas-Nebraska Act left Southerners firmly in control of his own Democratic Party. The act also sparked the development of the Republican Party, which, by appealing only to Northern voters, further increased sectional tensions. His unsuccessful attempt to rally voters behind his cause in the 1860 presidential election seems now a quixotic venture aimed at undoing much of the damage wrought by his own chicanery.

12

Joseph E. Johnston

(1807–1891)

One of the Confederacy's most important generals, Joseph Eggleston Johnston is also among the most controversial. After a brief stint in the eastern theater of the war, Johnston spent most of the war in the west, where he participated in the Vicksburg, Atlanta, and Carolinas campaigns. Many contemporaries saw Johnston as a defensive genius who grasped the links between military events and Northern politics; others, including Confederate president JEFFERSON DAVIS [5], criticized him as being too sensitive, overly cautious, and afraid of a fight. Whatever Johnston's abilities, he ranks second in importance only to ROBERT E. LEE [4] among Confederate military leaders.

Born in 1807 in Virginia, Joseph E. Johnston was born to a niece of Patrick Henry and a Revolutionary War veteran. He graduated from the U.S.

Military Academy in 1829, a classmate of fellow Virginian Robert E. Lee. Wounded during the Second Seminole War, Johnston suffered five more wounds during the war against Mexico. He then saw varied frontier duties in Kansas, Texas, and Utah before being appointed brigadier general in 1860.

Although personally opposed to secession, Johnston, like Lee, resigned from the U.S. Army after the Virginia secession convention voted to leave the Union. He played a leading role, along with P. G. T. BEAUREGARD [35], in leading the South to victory at First Bull Run, Virginia. Soon thereafter, however, Johnston became embroiled in controversies concerning matters of seniority. Rather than be ranked fourth in seniority among Confederate military officers, Johnston argued, he should rank first, since his U.S. Army rank had been higher than that of any other Confederate. The dispute did nothing to improve his relations with President Davis, with whom Johnston had clashed several times before the war. His arguments for high seniority were not helped by his unimpressive showings in subsequent campaigns. Commanding Confederate troops in Virginia in spring 1862, he fell back before the Union Army of the Potomac under GEORGE MCCLELLAN [7] as it advanced to the gates of Richmond. Pressured by Davis to fight, Johnston did so at last in the inconclusive Battle of Seven Pines, during which he was wounded twice.

Following a seven-month convalescence, Johnston found his place in the eastern theater of the war usurped by the brilliant Robert E. Lee. In November 1862 Davis, still hoping to exploit Johnston's experience, placed him in command of the Department of the West, where he was charged with coordinating the actions of the Army of Tennessee led by BRAXTON BRAGG [30] with the Department of Mississippi under JOHN C. PEMBERTON [65]. From this difficult position, Johnston, who argued that Confederate troops west of the Mississippi must be used to reinforce Pemberton, once again clashed with the president, who insisted that these soldiers remain in Arkansas. As the Confederates contemplated their strategic options, Union troops led by ULYSSES S. GRANT [2] moved forcefully against Vicksburg, Mississippi, the key to controlling the Mississippi River, and besieged it. Davis ordered Johnston to Mississippi, but the latter, claiming that he had arrived too late, failed to break the siege. Davis blamed Johnston for the fortress's fall and accepted his resignation.

In the wake of the debacle at the Battle of Chattanooga, Tennessee, Davis reluctantly gave Johnston the task of reorganizing and commanding the Army of Tennessee. As WILLIAM T. SHERMAN [3] began to push toward Atlanta in the spring and summer of 1864, the outnumbered Johnston slowed the Union advance, trading ground for time in the hope that cavalry reinforcements might allow him to sever Sherman's supply lines. As Union troops neared Atlanta, however, Johnston's refusal to adopt a more aggressive stance led to his dismissal on July 17, 1864.

Johnston's replacement, JOHN BELL HOOD [38], proved a disaster, and in late February 1865 Johnston resumed command of the remnants of the

The ruins of the strategic stone bridge over Bull Run, Virginia, March 1862

Army of Tennessee. By now, however, realistic chances of Confederate victory had faded; following Lee's capitulation at Appomattox, Johnston also surrendered. After the war, Johnston entered the insurance business, served in Congress, and became a railroad commissioner. He died of pneumonia in 1891 as a result of having stood hatless in a cold rain at the funeral of his old rival, Sherman.

Joseph Johnston remains an enigma. Sherman, who almost surely recognized that his own reputation would be enhanced by having beaten an enemy of high repute, always gave Johnston high marks. Many latterday historians also praise Johnston's understanding of strategic affairs, as well as his ability to avoid battle in terrain not of his choosing. Critics, however, point out that Johnston's habitual retreats placed the key Confederate cities of Richmond and Atlanta in danger. Some even suggest that Johnston's caution resulted from his belief that the Confederate cause had been hopeless from the start.

13

David Farragut

(1801–1870)

After a lifelong career in the United States Navy, David Glasgow Farragut became the Union's most successful naval officer. By capturing New Orleans and seizing control of Mobile Bay, Alabama, Farragut closed off two of the Confederacy's most valuable ports. Throughout these and other actions, Farragut's aggressiveness set an important example for other Union naval commanders.

Farragut was born in 1801 near Knoxville, Tennessee. Following his mother's death, he was raised under the tutelage of Master Commandant David Porter. With his guardian's help, at age nine Farragut accepted an appointment as midshipman. Out of gratitude, he changed his first name from James to David. The young midshipman sailed with Porter during the War of 1812. Securing promotion to lieutenant in 1825, Farragut commanded a variety of combat ships off the coasts of Brazil and Mexico. Especially significant were his observations of French naval actions against Mexican positions at Vera Cruz during the late 1830s, which convinced him that ships could overcome even the most daunting shore fortifications. He saw no important action during the Mexican War, however; he continued instead to serve in a variety of administrative positions and ship commands.

Having twice married (his first wife died in 1840) into Virginia families and himself a son of the South, Farragut nonetheless denounced secession. "Mind what I tell you," he warned those urging him to join the Confederates, "You fellows will catch the devil before you get through this business." Despite his Unionist sympathies, Farragut found it difficult to secure a Federal combat command. Quiet inquiries by naval authorities, however, suggested that he was a determined, capable professional. In January 1862 he accepted command of the West Gulf Blockading Squadron.

On April 18, Farragut launched an attack against New Orleans, the largest city in the South. Key to Confederate defenses were two forts located downriver of the city and a small flotilla that featured an ironclad ram. Initially, Farragut attempted to reduce the fortifications with his nineteen mortar schooners, but after six days of pounding, he determined on a different approach. After a daring night raid cut a narrow passage through the chain laid by the Confederates to block the Mississippi, in the early morning of April 24 seventeen Union ships steamed upriver. Shot and shell lit up the morning sky as the Union fleet ran the gauntlet of Confederate forts, fire-rafts, and rams. Thirteen Union ships succeeded; thus rendered defenseless, New Orleans was occupied the next day.

Appointed rear admiral after this brilliant victory, Farragut then moved his ships upriver, probing Confederate defenses at Port Hudson, Louisiana, and Vicksburg, Mississippi. The dramatic appearance of the enemy ironclad *Arkansas,* however, forced back Farragut's smaller ships. Ill health and failures by subordinates off the Texas coast—either to hold Galveston or to run the tiny Confederate defenses at Sabine Pass—further soured Farragut's command in 1863.

Farragut had long dreamed of cracking enemy defenses at Mobile, Alabama, the last major Confederate port in the western Gulf of Mexico east of Galveston. On August 5, 1864, with a fleet of four ironclad and fourteen wooden ships, he launched his attack. Two forts guarded the entrance to Mobile Bay. Underwater mines (then known as torpedoes) blocked the passage, save for an open channel which ran directly under the guns of one fort. An ironclad ram, the *Tennessee,* also awaited. When a lead ship struck a mine, the Union flotilla hesitated. Lashed to the rigging of his wooden flagship, *Hartford,* so that he might see the battle above the smoke, Farragut responded: "Damn the torpedoes, full speed ahead!" A melée ensued as the Union ships raced on, ramming the *Tennessee* and forcing its surrender. Now isolated, the Confederate forts followed suit within the month. Mobile Bay was effectively closed.

In recognition of his services, Farragut was appointed vice admiral in 1864 and admiral in 1866. He died of heart-related illnesses at Portsmouth Navy Yard in August 1870. Farragut outdistanced his peers by virtue of his strategic skill and aggressive combat tactics. He ranks among the giants, not only of the Civil War, but of American naval history.

14

John Brown

(1800–1859)

Ranking John Brown this high among Civil War figures will surprise many readers. How can a man who was not even alive when the war began be more influential than, for example, some of the war's most talented military leaders, such as PHILIP SHERIDAN [18] or STONEWALL JACKSON [20]?

Brown's raid against the federal arsenal at Harpers Ferry, Virginia, in October 1859 polarized a nation already rent by intense sectional divisions. Brown's action raised the specter of a slave rebellion—a prospect terrifying to Southerners. This fear was compounded by the sympathy so many otherwise respectable Northerners gave to Brown's band of terrorists. Abolitionists, concluded many Southerners, would clearly stop at nothing to destroy Southern society. For many Northerners with antislavery views, Brown became a martyr for freedom, a man whose execution merely confirmed their suspicion that violence permeated and corrupted all things associated with slavery.

Born in Torrington, Connecticut, in 1800, John Brown was one of fourteen children fathered by the twice-married Owen Brown. A pious Calvinist, Owen Brown moved from trade to trade in several Connecticut villages before resettling in Hudson, Ohio, where John spent much of his youth. John's mother, Ruth Mills Brown, died when he was only eight; she died insane, as did her mother, a sister, and five of her brothers' sons. In 1820, John Brown married Dianthe Lusk, who bore him seven children before her death in 1831. He remarried within the year, and had another thirteen children with his second wife, Mary Anne Day.

A lifelong abolitionist, John Brown ruled his household with a mixture of punishing discipline and righteous moral fervor. He stood five feet nine, and had a leathery face and glittering blue-gray eyes; one son described him as looking like a meat ax. Brown attempted, with a singular lack of success, a variety of trades, enduring fifteen business failures in four states as his debtors sought vainly to recoup their losses. Convinced that Kansas would be the site of the long-awaited struggle between freedom and tyranny, five of his sons moved there in 1855. Brown soon joined them, ostensibly as a surveyor, but bringing with him a wagonload of firearms, ammunition, and swords.

By early 1856 both sides were locked in a struggle for control of Kansas's fledgling territorial government. Seeking an Old Testament–style revenge for the destruction of the freesoil stronghold of Lawrence, during the night of May 23–24 Brown, four of his sons, and two others struck a proslavery settlement along Pottawatomie Creek. The war party butchered five men, hacking apart the bodies and limbs of several of their victims with broadswords. A week later, Brown was part of another antislavery force which ambushed a proslavery camp at Black Jack, Missouri, leaving four more dead and several wounded.

After thousands of U.S. troops were dispatched to Kansas to restore order, Brown, convinced that he was God's instrument to purge the land of slavery, resolved to take his war to the South. To his closest supporters, Brown revealed his plan. He and a "Provisional Army" would capture the federal arsenal at Harpers Ferry. The arms seized there would then be distributed to slaves, who would rise up in rebellion and establish a free state in the mountains of Maryland and Virginia.

In 1858–59 a final visit to Kansas, during which another slaveowner was killed and eleven slaves liberated, helped raise funds needed to attempt Brown's secret scheme. Prominent abolitionists also contributed to his cause. On October 16, 1859, he and twenty-one followers (sixteen whites, four free blacks, and one escaped slave) took the arsenal, grabbed several hostages, and liberated ten slaves as they awaited the arrival of reinforcements of rebellious slaves. None joined their armed cause, however, as he had made no plans for organizing such a rebellion. Instead, angry Virginia militiamen and farmers descended upon the town, determined to crush any hint of a slave insurrection.

In the resulting siege, Brown and most of his followers barricaded themselves in the armory, an adjacent rifle works, and, finally, a firehouse.

The U.S. arsenal (right) *at Harpers Ferry*

Hundreds of armed Virginians, drunk with emotion and alcohol, killed and mutilated the bodies of some of Brown's men. A company of U.S. Marines, under the temporary command of Lieutenant Colonel ROBERT E. LEE [4], home on leave at Arlington, arrived from Washington. The marines stormed the building and captured Brown thirty-six hours after the raid began. Seventeen persons—two liberated slaves who had been unable to escape once the fighting started, four civilians (including the town's mayor), one marine, and ten of Brown's recruits (including two of his sons) died at Harpers Ferry. Seven raiders were ultimately captured.

The state of Virginia tried Brown and his captured raiders ten days later. All were found guilty and hanged for conspiracy, treason, and murder. John Brown, who steadfastly refused to plead insanity, won the respect of friend and foe alike for his commitment throughout the trial to the cause of abolishing slavery. On his way to the scaffold on December 2, 1859, he handed a guard a final note that accurately predicted the war his actions had hastened: "The crimes of this guilty land will never be purged away, but with blood."

15

Harriet Beecher Stowe

(1811–1896)

Political and military figures dominated the Civil War and Reconstruction. Still, ideas had a powerful impact on the period. *Uncle Tom's Cabin* (1852), Stowe's antislavery novel and her most famous work, the stated purpose of which was "to awaken sympathy and feeling for the African race," sold 300,000 copies in its first year, a remarkable figure, considering the nation's total population was just over 23 million. In the North, *Uncle Tom's Cabin* was seen as a moral romance that depicted the evils of slavery in easily understood terms. Southerners, however, viewed Stowe's work, written by a woman and an outsider, as an unjust attack on a proud civilization. By its indictment, her book increased the sectional tensions that led to the Civil War.

Harriet Beecher was born in Litchfield, Connecticut, in 1811. Her mother, Roxanna Foote Beecher, had eight children and died when Harriet was five years old. The Reverend Lyman Beecher, Harriet's father, remarried in 1817 to Harriet Porter; he later fathered another four children. The family became prominent in Northern reform circles, with Lyman Beecher emerging as an influential Christian evangelist who advocated temperance, abolition, and the repatriation of former slaves to Africa. A brother, Henry Ward, was also one of the most influential reformers of the mid-1800s. An older sister, Catharine, an author in her own right of several widely publicized books (most important was her oft-reprinted *Treatise on Domestic Economy,* 1843), advocated the expansion of women's influence within the domestic sphere as homemakers, teachers, and guardians of society's virtue.

Harriet received an excellent education, both at home and at her sister Catharine's Hartford Female Academy. The Beecher clan moved in 1832 to Cincinnati, where the Reverend Beecher assumed the presidency of Lane Seminary. The "Queen City" of the Ohio River Valley, Cincinnati was at the time more western than eastern; its strategic position just across the river from Kentucky also offered city residents a window into the realities of slavery. The western experience profoundly influenced Harriet, who lived in Cincinnati for eighteen years. There she married Calvin Ellis Stowe, bore six of her seven children, and undertook her literary apprenticeship, writing essays for her brother's newspaper. She also wrote a successful textbook, *Primary Geography for Children,* which sold over 100,000 copies.

A successful and well-paid author, Stowe published in 1843 a collection entitled *The Mayflower; or, Sketches of Scenes and Characters.* Tragically, one of her sons died of cholera in 1849. Her husband, a professor at Lane Seminary, accepted a position at Bowdoin College the following year. Still grieving over her child's death, Stowe set up housekeeping at Brunswick, Maine. Passage of a new Fugitive Slave Act, which threatened the wholesale return of escaped slaves and free black people alike to bondage, compounded her anger over her personal loss. Stowe became determined to speak out against slavery. From June 1851 until April 1852, the *National Era,* an abolitionist newspaper, printed weekly installments of what became *Uncle Tom's Cabin, or, Life Among the Lowly.*

Published in book form in March 1852, *Uncle Tom's Cabin* sold ten thousand copies within a week. The story blends the travails of a Christian slave, Uncle Tom, with that of a family of runaways. Repeatedly sold, Uncle Tom dies under the lash of a cruel overseer, Simon Legree, for refusing to renounce God as his true master even as the runaways make their harrowing escapes. Although modern literary critics often pan the book as overly sentimental and melodramatic, it captured the mood of much of the Northern public. Southerners countered by arguing that the book was unrealistic, had been written by someone who had never lived in the South, and that its female author had dared to challenge accepted societal mores by speaking out in public. Just as controversial was Stowe's *A Key to Uncle Tom's Cabin* (1853), an assortment of legal and documentary evidence which sought to demonstrate that her original novel had accurately depicted the horrors of slavery.

Stowe then embarked on a triumphant tour of Britain, where half a million women signed antislavery petitions. She contributed generously to various abolitionist causes and continued to write, most notably *Dred: A Tale of*

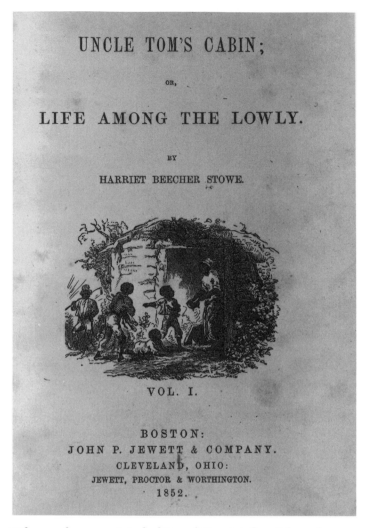

Title page from an original edition of Stowe's influential novel

the Great Dismal Swamp (1856); The Minister's Wooing (1859); The Pearl of Orr's Island (1861); and Lady Byron Vindicated (1870), the latter a sensational expose of the incestuous sexual relationships of the English romantic poet, Lord Byron.

She is profoundly important for having stimulated the vitriolic sectional debates which dominated the 1850s. Stowe's controversial writings also did much to legitimize the public role of women before her death in 1896. Family legend has it that upon meeting her in November 1862, President Lincoln proclaimed her to be "the little lady who made this big war." Although modern historians doubt the story's accuracy, few question her influence as a devastatingly effective critic of slavery.

16
(TIE)

Robert Barnwell Rhett

(1800–1876)

Sometimes dubbed the "Father of Secession," Robert Barnwell Rhett preached the virtues of secession for three decades before the Civil War. A South Carolina lawyer and rice planter who eventually owned nearly two hundred slaves, Rhett's political fortunes ebbed and flowed with the tides of the secession movement. During the war, the iconoclastic Rhett emerged as one of the leading critics of President JEFFERSON DAVIS [5]. Indeed, until his death in 1876, he fiercely opposed anything which threatened his conception of "the civilization and freedom of the Southern States."

Born Robert Barnwell Smith at Beaufort, South Carolina, in 1800, he had a somewhat sporadic education, featuring private tutors, attendance at Beaufort College, and personal reading. At the behest of his brothers, the family changed its name in 1837 to that of a more distinguished ancestor, Colonel William Rhett. Robert Rhett began practicing law, and in 1826 was elected to the state's lower house. Fiercely opposed to a protective tariff, he became a leader in the state's attempts to nullify unwelcome federal laws in 1832 and 1833.

Four years after he was elected state attorney general in 1832, Rhett purchased a plantation which he developed into a flourishing enterprise. This enabled him to enjoy the aristocratic lifestyle suitable to a Southern planter. Uncomfortable about the state's black majority and dependent upon the labor of his slaves for his livelihood, Rhett concluded that the federal government would attempt at some point to take away what he believed to be a citizen's inalienable right to own property—in Rhett's case, his slaves. His fiery eloquence led voters in his district to elect the deeply religious Rhett to the U.S. Congress from 1837 to 1849. Uncompromising in his defense of the Southern life as he knew it, Rhett eventually broke ranks even with John C. Calhoun over the latter's faith that the Constitution, if properly interpreted, would protect the South from federal intrusion. Secession, Rhett argued, was the only logical answer to the South's peculiar needs.

By forcing Congress to deal with slavery in newly acquired territory, the acquisition of Texas and the Southwest presented Rhett with the chance to widen the gap between North and South. In 1850 he replaced Calhoun in the United States Senate following the latter's death. In the same year Rhett

Contemporary sketch of the South Carolina Secession Convention, 1860

attended the Nashville Convention, the theme of which concerned the possibility of secession. Nine of the fifteen slave states were represented.

Rhett took his fight back to South Carolina, contending that the Palmetto State should secede immediately and alone, if necessary. After a special state convention failed to approve secession, Rhett resigned from the Senate in 1852.

Rhett's radicalism had seemingly been discredited, and many Southern politicians shunned him as too rash. Yet Rhett remained defiant. In 1857, his son, Robert Barnwell Rhett Jr., became editor of the Charleston *Mercury,* which had long served as the senior Rhett's mouthpiece. Buoyed by the unpopularity of the Republican Party and the outrage over the raid of JOHN BROWN [14] in the South, the elder Rhett continued to battle for control of his state's Democratic Party. Finally, in mid-1860, secessionists wrested control from the moderates. Following the election of ABRAHAM LINCOLN [1], Rhett, as a member of the South Carolina Secession Convention, helped draw up that state's ordinance of secession.

In late December 1860, Rhett proposed that a convention meet at Montgomery, Alabama, to create a new confederacy of Southern states. As a delegate to that body, he stoutly contested any efforts that he feared might reconstruct the Union. He also opposed Jefferson Davis's election as president on the grounds that the latter's commitment to secession and states' rights was insufficiently zealous. Rhett's uncompromising diatribes grew less popular as the Civil War continued, however, and in 1863 he lost his bid for election to the Confederate Congress.

Rhett's first marriage came in 1827, and he remarried in 1853 after his first wife's death. He died at one of his son's homes in Louisiana in 1876. Rhett was, along with WILLIAM YANCEY [16 (tie)], the leading firebrand champion of the South's independence. In pressing the causes of secession and states' rights to their extreme, Rhett had helped cause a civil war.

William Yancey

(1814–1863)

Orator and Confederate diplomat, William Lowndes Yancey ranks along-side his friend ROBERT BARNWELL RHETT [16 (tie)] as the most effective advocate of secession. During the war, Yancey briefly headed an unsuccessful three-man diplomatic mission to Europe to garner support, after which he returned to take a seat in the Confederate Senate. It is, however, to his prewar activities that he owes his rank among the Civil War's one hundred most influential persons. An eloquent, forceful speaker, Yancey did much to encourage the idea of a developing Southern nationalism before the Civil War, a key factor in making secession seem a practical alternative.

Yancey was born into a prominent Georgia family in 1814. His father died the following year. In 1821 his mother, Carolina, married the headmaster of a Presbyterian academy, but the marriage proved a stormy one, and his stepfather sold the family slaves, moved to New York, and became an abolitionist. Yancey's later denunciations of abolitionists undoubtedly stemmed in part from this tumultuous childhood. In 1833, Yancey left Williams College, Massachusetts, to return south, where he was admitted to the bar in 1834 and married into a wealthy slave-owning family. He moved to Alabama in 1836 and rented a plantation. Two years later, he killed his wife's uncle in a brawl. Although convicted of manslaughter, Yancey maintained that he had properly defended his honor.

He was ruined by low cotton prices and the accidental poisoning of many of his slaves, and by 1840 Yancey returned to his law practice and had taken up politics. A Democrat, he was elected to both the state house and Congress. Disavowing compromise on any issue, he resigned from Congress in 1846, but not before engaging in a duel with a fellow congressman. Their honor satisfied by the issuance and acceptance of the challenge itself, both men exchanged harmless shots.

Yancey became convinced that the federal government was bent on usurping Southern liberties by blocking the expansion of slavery into the western territories. In 1848, he walked out of the Democratic National Convention to protest the party's failure to require that its candidates oppose any attempt to exclude slavery from a territory. Initially reluctant to advocate secession, by the late 1850s Yancey was issuing calls to arms to his fellow Southerners. He argued that they must break away from the Union in order to protect their liberties, just as their forefathers had done from Great Britain during the 1770s.

Yancey also sought to promote the idea of Southern nationalism. The South, he contended, had "a unity of climate, a unity of soil, a unity of production, and a unity of social relations." The development of the concept of Southern nationalism, even in its early stages, was crucial. Previously, secession had implied that leaving the Union would force states to go it alone; Southern nationalism meant they would have a nation of like-minded states with which to join. Yancey also vigorously defended slavery, even advocating the reopening of the African slave trade. In April 1860 he led another walk-out at the Democratic National Convention, then meeting at Charleston, South Carolina, when the party refused to adopt a federal slave code. Twelve years before, only one man had followed him; this time, virtually all of the slave state delegations did so.

With the formation of the Confederacy, President JEFFERSON DAVIS [5] appointed Yancey to lead a diplomatic mission to Europe. The quick-tempered, uncompromising Yancey proved a poor diplomat, and in early 1862 returned to the South. Representing Alabama in the Confederate Senate, he frequently criticized what he believed to be the Davis administration's attempts to take away the liberties of states and individuals. A better agitator than legislator, Yancey, who had long been in poor health, died at his farm near Montgomery in 1863. Yancey's brand of southern nationalism had combined with Rhett's extreme view of states' rights to light the fires of secession.

Philip Sheridan

(1831–1888)

Philip Henry Sheridan ranks behind ULYSSES S. GRANT [2] and WILLIAM T. SHERMAN [3] as the third most effective Union general of the Civil War. Standing just five feet, five inches tall, distinguished more by his walruslike mustache than his military bearing, Sheridan compiled a fine record in the west during the war's first two and a half years. When Grant went east in spring 1864, he took Sheridan with him. After transforming the Army of the Potomac's cavalry into an effective arm, Sheridan took command of Union troops in the Shenandoah Valley, where he defeated Confederate forces and ravaged the Valley, thus eliminating a vital food source for the Army of Northern Virginia under ROBERT E. LEE [4]. Quick-tempered and relentless in his quest for victory, Sheridan combined tactical abilities with a clear vision of how the war should be won.

He listed several different accounts of his birthplace before eventually settling upon Albany, New York, where he was born in 1831. He spent most of his youth in Somerset, Ohio, before being appointed to West Point. The pugnacious lad was suspended for one year for fighting with a fellow cadet, but finally graduated in 1853, an undistinguished thirty-fourth in a class of fifty-two. After a brief stint along the Rio Grande, he was transferred to the Pacific Coast, where he fought in the Yakima and Rogue River Wars against the Indians.

Sheridan held several administrative commands in the early days of the Civil War. Thirsting for combat duty, he secured the colonelcy of a Michigan cavalry regiment and conducted a successful raid against Booneville, Mississippi, winning a promotion to brigadier general of volunteers. Sheridan was next assigned to command an infantry division in the Army of the Ohio (later redesignated the Army of the Cumberland). He distinguished himself for his tenacity in the fighting at Perryville, Kentucky, and Stones River, Tennessee, receiving his second general's star. During the second day's fighting at the Battle of Chickamauga, Tennessee, Sheridan's division broke in the face of an enemy attack. His troops redeemed themselves, however, in the fighting around Chattanooga, Tennessee. Instructed to clear Confederate skirmishers at the base of Missionary Ridge, Tennessee, they continued on, without orders, against enemy positions atop the crest. Instinctively, Sheridan joined the assault and completed the unanticipated rout of the Confederate army.

Impressed with Sheridan's aggressiveness, Grant selected him to command the Army of the Potomac's cavalry in March 1864. Sheridan promptly reorganized the corps, and, against the wishes of the army's nominal head, GEORGE MEADE [22], led his ten thousand horsemen on a raid against Richmond. Sheridan's troopers defeated the Confederate cavalry, led by the celebrated J. E. B. STUART [33], in the Battle of Yellow Tavern, Virginia (May 11, 1864). Although Sheridan shied away from Richmond itself, the fighting avenged three years of embarrassing defeats for Union cavalry in the east and left Stuart mortally wounded. At Grant's direction, Sheridan launched another diversionary raid that June, but was checked by Confederate cavalry, now commanded by WADE HAMPTON [68], at the Battle of Trevilian Station, Virginia (June 11–12, 1864).

Later that summer, hoping to threaten Washington, Lee dispatched Lieutenant General JUBAL EARLY [81] and nearly twenty thousand troops into the Shenandoah Valley, in Virginia. Grant picked Sheridan to command the newly formed Army of the Shenandoah, instructing him first to defeat Early's army, then to "eat out Virginia clear and clean as far as they go, so that crows flying over it for the balance of the season will have to carry their provender with them." In September, Sheridan bested Early in fighting at Winchester and Fisher's Hill. After receiving reinforcements the following month, Early launched a surprise attack against the Federals along Cedar Creek. Returning to rejoin his command after a Washington conference, Sheridan arrived in time to rally his defeated men and launch a counterattack which saved the day. For this he was commissioned a major general in the regular army. He then embarked upon the systematic destruction of the Valley. When Lee finally abandoned Petersburg, Virginia, Sheridan took an active role in the pursuit, blocking the Confederate escape in the Battle of Five Forks, Virginia (April 1).

Sheridan continued to render important military services following Lee's surrender at Appomattox, Virginia. As commander of the Division of the Gulf, he organized aggressive army maneuvers along the Rio Grande which helped convince NAPOLEON III [70] to withdraw French support for Maximilian's crumbling regime in Mexico. During Reconstruction, Sheridan headed the Fifth Military District (Texas and Louisiana). His strong opposition to conservative governments there, however, led President ANDREW JOHNSON [6] to transfer him west. From the Department of the Missouri, Sheridan launched offensives against the Southern Plains Indians in 1868–69. He then succeeded Sherman as head of the huge Division of the Missouri. In this capacity, Sheridan loosely oversaw the Red River (1874–75) and the Great Sioux (1876–77) wars. He also helped save Yellowstone National Park from private speculators. In 1883, Sheridan became commanding general of the United States Army. Just before his death in 1888, he was commissioned a full general, joining George Washington, Grant, and Sherman as the only Americans to hold this rank before the twentieth century.

Like Grant and Sherman, Sheridan was lucky to have begun his Civil War services in the west, where he could learn from his mistakes far from Washington's scrutiny. He enjoyed a warm relationship with Grant, under whose sponsorship he thrived. Along with the capture of Atlanta by Sherman, and the victory at Mobile Bay, Alabama, by Admiral DAVID FARRAGUT [13], Sherman's recovery at Cedar Creek helped ensure Lincoln's successful reelection bid, which made the Union's triumph only a matter of time.

19

James Longstreet

(1821–1904)

Affectionately known as the "Old War Horse" by ROBERT E. LEE [4], James "Pete" Longstreet was the Confederacy's most dependable corps commander. Yet Longstreet has often been maligned as a result of his controversial postwar politics and self-serving attempts to further his own image. Although unsuccessful in independent command, Longstreet's steadiness in combat and obvious superiority to his peers, with the exceptions of Lee and STONEWALL JACKSON [20], merit him a much higher ranking among Confederate generals than he is sometimes accorded.

Longstreet was born in South Carolina in 1821. Although he spent most of his boyhood in Georgia, he was appointed to West Point from Alabama. A mediocre student, he graduated fifty-fourth in his 1842 class of sixty-two cadets. Longstreet won acclaim for his bravery in several battles during the war against Mexico; he was severely wounded at the Battle of Chapultepec.

Longstreet served in various capacities in the frontier army before resigning his U.S. commission in 1861. Now fighting for the South, he performed well in early skirmishes in the east, but then bungled an attack at the Battle of Seven Pines, Virginia. He did much better during the Seven Days' battles, Virginia, winning Lee's confidence in the process.

In the summer of 1862, Lee made Longstreet his senior corps commander, giving him even more responsibility than Jackson. Longstreet again performed with distinction in the battles of Second Bull Run, Virginia; Antietam, Maryland; and Fredericksburg, Virginia. Following a brief stint as head of the Department of North Carolina and Southern Virginia, he returned to the Army of Northern Virginia on the eve of Lee's Gettysburg offensive.

Longstreet contended that rather than invade the North, Lee should reinforce the Confederacy's flagging efforts in the west. Overruled in that, he tried to convince Lee to maneuver his troops so as to force the Union Army of the Potomac, soon to be led by GEORGE MEADE [22], into attacking on unfavorable terms. Lee demurred, however, and launched several full-scale attacks at Gettysburg, Pennsylvania. Unsettled by Lee's orders, Longstreet, as was the case with most of the other Confederate generals during this fateful encounter, was slow and indecisive.

A long-desired transfer to the west came in September 1863. Joining the Army of Tennessee under BRAXTON BRAGG [30] only hours before the Battle of Chickamauga, Georgia, Longstreet and his corps delivered a crushing blow which broke the Union lines. Like virtually every other general who had served under Bragg, however, he then became embroiled in an ugly quarrel with his commander. By mutual agreement, Bragg detached Longstreet on an ill-fated attempt to invade eastern Tennessee.

He spent a brief time in independent command, which was marked by considerable rancor with several junior officers, and then returned to Virginia in April 1864. The reunion, however, proved short-lived, for Longstreet was accidentally wounded by his own men in the Battle of the Wilderness in Virginia. He returned for the final campaigns around Petersburg and Appomattox, Virginia.

After the war, Longstreet joined the Republican Party, worked in the cotton and insurance businesses, and held several government appointments. Censured for his attempts to accommodate federal authority and the Republican Party by other Southerners, some of whom blamed him for the Confederate failure at Gettysburg and even accused him of treason to his section, Longstreet responded by exaggerating his own importance and wisdom. He even dared criticize some decisions made by Lee, whose supporters were in the process of catapulting the great general into mythical status.

In reality, Longstreet deserved neither the credit he took in his own postwar writings nor the condemnation of his critics. He was an outstanding corps commander but proved disappointing in independent roles. Longstreet's belief in the superiority of defensive tactics and in the need to place greater emphasis on western affairs is intriguing, but had little actual impact on the course of the war. Perhaps the bitter postbellum debates about his place in history speak more to the South's celebration of the "Lost Cause" than they do about Longstreet himself. As a symbol of this phenomenon, his importance extends well beyond the wartime battlefields, placing him ahead of Jackson, his more talented colleague who died two years before the war ended.

20

Thomas J. (Stonewall) Jackson

(1824–1863)

Fearless in battle and fervent in his Presbyterian faith, Thomas J. (Stonewall) Jackson ranks second in ability only to ROBERT E. LEE [4] among Confederate generals. He gained his nickname during the First Battle of Bull Run, Virginia, when a fellow Confederate officer, Barnard E. Bee, called upon his retreating soldiers to emulate Jackson, who was "standing like a stone wall." Though it described his stubborn, secretive, self-controlled personality, as well as his magnificent defensive performances at Second Bull Run, Virginia, and Antietam, Maryland, this nickname did not reflect Jackson's penchant for the attack in battle. Jackson's death came in 1863, shortly after he was accidentally wounded by his own men in the midst of his greatest victory, the Battle of Chancellorsville, Virginia; he would never be replaced. Only his premature death explains his relatively low ranking here.

Born Thomas Jonathan Jackson at Clarksburg, Virginia, in 1824, he was orphaned at age seven by his parents' deaths from disease. Raised by a bachelor uncle, Jackson loved learning as a youth but received only a sporadic formal education. In 1842, he received an appointment to the U.S. Military Academy, but only after the original appointee had found West Point life to be intolerable and quit. The grueling academic regimen nearly overwhelmed the poorly prepared young Virginian, who barely passed his entrance exams and at the end of the first semester ranked seventy-first in his class. Though slow to learn, by hard work and prodigious study (essentially, he developed his intense powers of concentration into what amounted to a photographic memory) Jackson continually raised his standing, so that by the time of his graduation he ranked seventeenth in a class of fifty-nine.

Assigned to the artillery in the war with Mexico, the newly commissioned Jackson won promotions to regular first lieutenant and brevet major for his efforts in the campaign against Mexico City under WINFIELD SCOTT [37]. Jackson emerged a genuine war hero. When peacetime service seemed unfulfilling, he accepted a professorship in natural and experimental philosophy (physics) at Lexington's Virginia Military Institute in 1851. Jackson was gravely serious, totally dedicated to his task, and extremely demanding. His monotone classroom style hardly endeared him to his students, who often poked fun at his peculiar behavior, big feet, and awkward gait, especially during his early years in the classroom. Most observers, however, recognized in Jackson a man of immense moral courage and honesty.

Loving the Union but a firm believer in states' rights, Jackson volunteered for service with Virginia in April 1861. He led a brigade in the First Battle of Bull Run, where his cool leadership under fire played a major role in the Confederate victory. Given command of the Shenandoah Valley (Virginia) military district that fall, Jackson recaptured Romney, Virginia. Still, his refusal to accept excuses, his high expectations of his men, his quarrels with fellow officers, and his secretive demeanor led many to question his ability.

The following spring, Jackson launched his brilliant Shenandoah Valley campaign. For three months he baffled his Union foes, driving his troops on marches of epic speed up and down the Valley. Commanding fewer than twenty thousand men, he tied down sixty thousand Federals, thus preventing reinforcements for the campaign against Richmond under Gen. GEORGE MCCLELLAN [7]. In June, Lee recalled Jackson and launched a series of attacks against McClellan in the Seven Days' Battles (Virginia). Fatigued by the incessant action, Jackson displayed little of the brilliance or aggressiveness that had characterized his Valley campaign, though some of that may be attributed to his lack of experience in working with Lee. Jackson's outstanding performance at Second Bull Run, however, restored his reputation. During the subsequent invasion of Maryland, he again did well, capturing a strong Federal garrison at Harpers Ferry and holding the Confederate left at Antietam against heavy Union assaults.

Lee then reorganized the Army of Northern Virginia into two corps, giving Jackson one and JAMES LONGSTREET [19] the other. Relegated once more to the defensive in the victory at Fredericksburg, Virginia, Jackson found the fighting around Chancellorsville in May 1863 more to his liking. Though outnumbered by the Army of the Potomac, now commanded by Gen. JOSEPH HOOKER [36], Lee boldly divided his forces, giving Jackson the task of striking the exposed Union right flank. Such an assignment—a semi-autonomous operation, featuring a long march and a surprise attack—suited Jackson perfectly. After a twelve-mile march, at 5:15 on the afternoon of May 3 Jackson launched his greatest assault. Completely surprising the Federals, Jackson's men swept forward in a frenzy, routing any attempts to regroup. "I reckon the Devil himself would have run with Jackson in his rear," one Confederate remembered.

At dark, Jackson reluctantly ordered a halt to restore order to his victorious legions; as a full moon lit the cloudless night, he still hoped to complete the rout. But about 9:30 that evening, he and his staff, returning from a reconnaissance of enemy lines in a dark woods, were accidentally fired upon by their own men. A bullet struck his right hand and two others shattered his left arm. Although the arm was soon amputated, pneumonia set in, and Jackson died a week later.

To Stonewall Jackson, the Civil War had been a religious crusade against Northern aggression. Others hoped that God was on their side; Jackson truly believed it. His personal habits have become almost as legendary as the man himself. Jackson refused to drink intoxicating liquors because he enjoyed the taste too much. Following a strict diet which helped to alleviate his dyspepsia, he loved all fresh fruits, although the legend that he habitually sucked lemons seems to be apocryphal. Jackson was shy, tone-deaf, and had very weak vision (during battle he had a habit of raising his left arm, palm facing outward, toward the sky). He carried three books in his wartime haversack: a Webster's dictionary, Napoleon's *Maxims,* and the Bible. Jackson strictly observed the Sabbath, refusing even to write or post letters on Sundays. Fittingly, he died on a Sunday.

21

Salmon P. Chase

(1808–1873)

Humorless, passionate, and ambitious, Salmon P. Chase was a longtime opponent of slavery, secretary of the treasury during the Civil War, molder of national banking policy, and later chief justice of the Supreme Court. Born at Cornish, New York, in 1808, he moved with his family as a boy to Keene, New Hampshire. His father, a tavern keeper, died when Chase was nine years old. Chase was relocated to Ohio and raised by a zealous Episcopalian bishop before graduating from Dartmouth College in 1826.

Chase gained admittance to the bar in late 1829. The following year, he moved to Cincinnati and set up his legal practice, which brought him renown for his fierce defenses of fugitive slaves' claims to freedom. He entered politics as a Whig, but by 1840 Chase joined the Liberty Party. With the collapse of the latter group he advocated a pragmatic coalition between the Free Soil Party and antislavery Democrats. The move proved politically sound, and in 1849 a Democratic–Free Soil coalition in the Ohio legislature elected him to the U.S. Senate.

Zealously denouncing slavery, Chase strongly opposed both the Compromise of 1850 and the Kansas-Nebraska Act as being too generous to the South. He helped organize the Republican Party in Ohio and was elected in 1855 to the first of two terms as that state's governor. He badly wanted the presidency, but conservative and moderate Republicans saw him as too extreme, thus dooming his candidacy for the party's 1860 nomination. Still,

Chase remained a powerful force. He opposed any compromises with the secessionists on the eve of the inauguration of ABRAHAM LINCOLN [1].

Seeking to cement the support of his party's radicals, Lincoln appointed Chase his treasury secretary. Despite his lack of financial experience, Chase proved a quick learner and an able administrator. Forming a close alliance with Philadelphia financier JAY COOKE [48], Chase supported sales of government war bonds to the common man. Though inclined to back a hard-money policy, he recognized the need for flexibility during the wartime emergency and sanctioned the use of paper money as a legal substitute for gold and silver. Chase strongly backed the National Banking Act of 1863, which provided the foundation for the nation's banking system over the next half-century. In all, his policies contributed substantially to the Northern economy's continued prosperity.

Throughout his time in the cabinet, Chase faulted President Lincoln for not pursuing the war with sufficient vigor. In December 1862, with military affairs going poorly in the east, Chase backed a caucus of Republican senators which demanded the ouster of his chief cabinet rival, the more conservative WILLIAM SEWARD [8]. Lincoln, however, made it clear that if Seward went, Chase would go too. Beating an embarrassed retreat, Chase nonetheless continued to build his personal power base through Treasury Department patronage. In early 1864, his name arose as a potential challenger to Lincoln's reelection. The president, characterizing Chase's ambition as "mild insanity," also quashed this effort and eventually accepted Chase's third offer of resignation.

After the death of ROGER B. TANEY [32], Lincoln, once again hoping to conciliate Republican radicals, appointed Chase Taney's successor as chief justice of the United States. In that post, Chase presided over the Senate impeachment trial of President ANDREW JOHNSON [6]. In 1868 Chase's name again arose, this time in the Democratic convention, as a potential presidential candidate. As before, however, the Chase balloon failed to get off the ground. Two years later, Chief Justice Chase ruled that the use of paper money, which he had sponsored during the war, was unconstitutional. The court, with Chase dissenting, reversed itself in 1871. Salmon Chase died of a paralytic stroke two years later in New York.

Repeated tragedies marred Chase's personal life. Each of his three wives died at an early age, and only two of his children reached maturity. One daughter, Kate, was a leader in Washington society and did much to promote her father's unsuccessful presidential ambitions. Distinguished in bearing, strongwilled, and self-righteous, Chase devoted much of his adult life to the destruction of slavery. Though overly ambitious and too prone to ham-handed political machinations against his president, Chase, as treasury secretary, did much to keep the Union wartime economy on a sound footing.

22

George Meade

(1815–1872)

It may seem odd that George Gordon Meade, victorious commander of the Army of Potomac at Gettysburg, Pennsylvania, does not rate a higher ranking in the present work. The three days at Gettysburg certainly showed Meade at his best: He boasted an excellent eye for terrain, demonstrated a commanding physical presence, and possessed the self-confidence necessary for high command. Following his heroics at Gettysburg, however, Meade failed to attack ROBERT E. LEE [4] and his stricken army. The next six months further demonstrated Meade's caution, keeping him out of the highest echelon of Civil War military leaders.

Born in 1815 to an American citizen in Cadiz, Spain, Meade was graduated from the U.S. Military Academy in 1835, ranked nineteenth in his class of fifty-six. Meade resigned his commission the following year, but rejoined the army in 1842 as a second lieutenant in the Corps of Topographical Engineers. During the Mexican War, he served with Zachary Taylor's Army of Occupation and won a brevet at the Battle of Monterey.

Pickett's charge during the battle of Gettysburg, Pennsylvania, July 3, 1863

Backed by Governor Andrew G. Curtin of Pennsylvania, Meade won appointment to brigadier general of volunteers at the beginning of the Civil War. Severely wounded during the Seven Days' Battles, Virginia, he led a brigade at Second Bull Run, Virginia; a division at South Mountain, Virginia, Antietam, Maryland, and Fredericksburg, Virginia; and a corps at Chancellorsville, Virginia. In each case, Meade performed well, if not spectacularly so. Short on suitable replacements to lead the Army of the Potomac after the resignation of JOSEPH HOOKER [36] from that post, LINCOLN [1] and Gen. HENRY HALLECK [27] selected Meade for the command on June 28.

Meade inherited an extraordinarily difficult position. With spirits high following spectacular victories at Fredericksburg and Chancellorsville, Lee's Army of Northern Virginia had pushed into Maryland and Pennsylvania. Speculation about the new commander's appointment and ability ran rampant through the Union ranks as Meade struggled to assert his authority. On July 1, segments of the two armies collided just outside Gettysburg. After a day of hard fighting, Union troops scrambled back in some disorder south of town. Arriving that night, Meade determined that the current Union position—along Cemetery Ridge south of Gettysburg, with flanks protected by Culp's Hill and Little Round Top—was indeed a sound one. He ordered his army, some 88,000 strong, to concentrate at Gettysburg.

At Confederate field headquarters, Lee had also decided to fight. On the afternoon of July 2, the Confederates struck the Federal left flank. Meade funneled enough reinforcements to hold Little Round Top, key to the Union left. That night, in a tense council of war, he and his generals agreed to fight it out the next day. He told the commander of the Union center that "if Lee attacks tomorrow, it will be in *your front.*" Meade's prediction proved accurate, and on the afternoon of July 3, George Pickett spearheaded a massive Confederate assault against Union positions along Cemetery Ridge. The Southern attack was turned back with heavy casualties.

Having lost twenty-eight thousand troops in the three-day slugfest, Lee quietly began to withdraw back to Virginia. Understandably stunned by his own twenty-three thousand casualties, Meade followed discreetly. Told of President Lincoln's displeasure with his failure to pursue more vigorously, Meade offered his resignation, which was promptly rejected. For the remainder of the year, Meade probed cautiously against Lee, allowing his enemy enough time not only to recoup some of his Gettysburg losses but to temporarily detach almost an entire corps to bolster the Confederacy's sagging fortunes in the west.

On March 10, 1864, ULYSSES S. GRANT [2] was given command of the armies of the United States. Grant set up his field headquarters with the Army of the Potomac, still nominally under Meade's command. The ensuing relationship, fraught with potential disasters, speaks well to the personal strength of both men, who worked out an arrangement whereby Grant provided strategic direction and Meade handled the administrative details of running the army. Meade performed this role well, although his irascibility and short temper, exacerbated by his awesome responsibilities, made him a difficult man to work for.

After the war, Meade commanded the military Departments of the East and, later, of the South. During Congressional Reconstruction, he headed the Third Military District, which included Alabama, Georgia, and Florida. He was appointed to command the Division of the Atlantic in 1869, but he died three years later of pneumonia, possibly stemming from complications from an old Civil War wound. Though not a great general, Meade was certainly a good one: Lee ranked him with Grant and MCCLELLAN [7] as his most able opponents. Most telling perhaps was Meade's steady performance at Gettysburg; when his nation needed him most, Meade was at his best.

23

Gideon Welles

(1802–1878)

As secretary of the navy during the ABRAHAM LINCOLN [1] and ANDREW JOHNSON [6] administrations, Gideon Welles oversaw the navy's massive wartime expansion and difficult postwar reduction. Competent rather than brilliant, the steady Welles proved one of Lincoln's most loyal cabinet officials. His detailed diary and various works for publication also offer superb insights into the inner workings of the Lincoln and Johnson administrations.

Born in Glastonbury, Connecticut, in 1802, to a prosperous Yankee family, Welles attended a private academy that ultimately became Norwich University. After dabbling in legal studies and toiling as a wholesale merchant, he became part owner and editor of the *Hartford Times*. Fascinated by journalism and politics, Welles was elected to the state assembly in 1825 and emerged as a leader among Jacksonian Democrats in Connecticut. Having enjoyed only mixed success in subsequent runs for elective office, in 1846 Welles accepted President James K. Polk's appointment as chief of the Naval

Bureau of Provisions and Clothing. After his 1850 defeat in a bid for the Senate, he broke with the Democrats over slavery and in 1856 ran unsuccessfully for governor of Connecticut as an antislavery Republican. Welles also established the *Hartford Evening Press,* which became one of the leading Republican journals in New England.

Welles headed the Connecticut delegation to the 1860 Republican national convention. Strongly opposed to the candidacy of WILLIAM SEWARD [8], he backed SALMON P. CHASE [21] in an unsuccessful presidential bid against Lincoln. Nevertheless, Welles liked and respected Lincoln, who, with an eye to placing a New Englander in his cabinet, included Welles in a list of eight key advisers compiled the night after his election.

Welles's previous naval experience made him a logical choice for the Navy Department. He took over a disintegrating fleet that numbered only forty-two commissioned ships. Ably served by Assistant Secretary of the Navy Gustavus V. Fox, Welles helped manage the fleet's wartime growth with a minimum of scandal and corruption. During his administration, the navy laid keels for over two hundred new ships and purchased four hundred more. Naval manpower increased from 7,600 to 51,500. By 1862, this powerful force had grown to four squadrons—two in the Gulf of Mexico and two in the Atlantic Ocean. Additional flotilla commands were established on the Potomac and Mississippi rivers. Though plagued by difficulties of communication and supply and by enemy raiders, Welles and the navy established an effective blockade of the Confederacy. Federal ships also conducted several amphibious operations, most notably those against New Orleans (1862) and Mobile Bay (1864).

The Civil War also saw the first widespread use of ironclad warships. Under congressional pressure to develop prototype ironclads, Welles overrode criticism from many naval officers and backed a radical design crafted by naval engineer John Ericsson. With Welles's help, Ericsson's ingenious little vessel, the *Monitor,* was rushed to completion in late January 1862. Five weeks later the *Monitor* forced the Confederate ironclad *Virginia* to withdraw, thus saving the Union fleet at Hampton Roads, Virginia, and ensuring that the Virginia Peninsula campaign of GEORGE MCCLELLAN [7] could continue. In all, the North would go on to construct fifty-eight ironclads during the war.

Welles was married and had nine children. He was a devout Episcopalian, and usually wore an ill-fitting wig and sported a long gray beard, leading Lincoln to dub him "Father Neptune." A capable administrator, he rarely allowed personal ambitions or petty jealousies to sway him from his loyalty to Lincoln. After the latter's death, Welles remained in the cabinet and generally backed the conservative restoration policies of Andrew Johnson. He also supported Johnson through the impeachment crisis before rejoining the Democratic Party in 1868. After the election that year of ULYSSES S. GRANT [2], Welles resigned his cabinet post. He was among the country's best naval secretaries. Welles died at Hartford, Connecticut, in 1878.

24

William Lloyd Garrison
(1805–1879)

William Lloyd Garrison was the preeminent reformer of the antebellum United States. He advocated nonviolent resistance, Christian perfectionism, and political equality for women, while denouncing capital punishment, the use of tobacco and alcohol, and the traditional clergy. Garrison's most important contribution was by way of his militant abolitionism. He demanded an immediate end to slavery; the motto of his weekly newspaper, the *Liberator,* captured the intensity of his beliefs: "I am in earnest—I will not equivocate—I will not excuse—I will not retreat a single inch—and *I will be heard.*"

Garrison was born in Newburyport, Massachusetts, in 1805. His father, a hard-drinking seaman, deserted his family while William was still a young boy. Brought up by a local deacon, Garrison learned the basics of printing and journalism during an apprenticeship to a newspaper editor before taking over another local paper, the *Free Press,* in 1826. There he published some of the earliest poems of John Greenleaf Whittier, with whom he formed a lifelong friendship. Garrison then moved to Boston, where he met Benjamin Lundy, an inspirational Quaker abolitionist. The two men relocated to Baltimore and jointly edited the weekly *Genius of Universal Emancipation* until Garrison was found guilty of libeling a slave trader.

Unable to pay his fine, Garrison spent seven weeks in the Baltimore jail. Released in mid-1830, he and a partner, Isaac Knapp, published the first issue of their new weekly, the *Liberator,* on January 1, 1831. Garrison spent the next thirty years censuring not only slaveholders, but all who failed to denounce slavery. In 1833 he founded the American Anti-Slavery Society, which demanded immediate emancipation while eschewing the use of violence. He also formed an alliance with fellow abolitionists in Great Britain. Garrison's inflammatory language was a matter of concern for many of his less zealous supporters. Religious groups that did not condemn slavery, for example, he labeled "cages of unclean birds, Augean stables of pollution." More serious divisions, however, stemmed from Garrison's insistence that women receive equal treatment. Some abolitionists formed separate organizations rather than recognize women's roles. By the early 1840s, he was calling upon free states to leave the Union, which he concluded was under the domination of a proslavery conspiracy. Garrison later publicly burned the Constitution.

In staking out such uncompromising positions, Garrison endured years of verbal and physical abuse. Southerners often removed his antislavery literature from the mails; the state of Georgia set up a $5,000 reward for his arrest and conviction. On one occasion, an angry Boston crowd dragged him through the streets and nearly lynched him.

Despite such vilification, Garrison remained unmoved. The Civil War, however, severely tested his idealistic perfectionism. Initially cool to Abraham Lincoln, Garrison nonetheless refused to sanction criticism of the president by fellow abolitionists and eventually came to understand the important practical benefits of the Emancipation Proclamation. In early 1865, Garrison refused to accept a twenty-third term as president of the American Anti-Slavery Society. Soon after passage of the Thirteenth Amendment, which formally abolished slavery, he published the last issue of the *Liberator,* in late December 1865.

Garrison stood just under six feet tall. His eyeglasses gave him the appearance of a mild-mannered academician, which he decidedly was not. He married in 1834 and fathered seven children, two of whom died in infancy. Garrison continued to crusade for various causes, especially woman suffrage, prohibition, and reform of the government's Indian policy, as long as his health allowed. He died in New York in 1879.

William Lloyd Garrison's influence on the Civil War comes chiefly through the emotions he stirred, rather than the number of persons who agreed with his uncompromising philosophy. He was a poor administrator and difficult to get along with; circulation of his famous (or, to many, infamous) *Liberator* probably never exceeded 3,000. Courageously principled and unhesitatingly critical of all who failed to meet his high moral standards, Garrison ranks as the age's purest reformer.

25

John Wilkes Booth

(1838–1865)

John Wilkes Booth was an actor and the assassin of President ABRAHAM LIN-COLN [1]. Booth was born in 1838 at Bel Air, Maryland, and raised at his family's farm. He was the second to last of ten children, and his mother's favorite. His formal schooling was erratic, and he seemed destined to join his family on the stage: his father, Junius Brutus Booth, and brother, Edwin, were both great actors; another brother, Junius Jr., was a noted producer. Booth, with his black hair and mustache, black eyes, and five foot, eight inch bearing, cut a handsome figure on and off the stage. His horsemanship, generosity, gaiety, and marksmanship with a pistol only added to his heroic demeanor.

Though audiences initially hissed his failure to properly learn his lines, Booth developed quickly as an actor. He overcame his somewhat sloppy preparation with flamboyant stage feats and passionate character portrayals. In 1860 and 1861, Booth conducted a successful tour playing a variety of Shakespearean roles, then considered the real test of an actor's ability. Reputedly involved in several failed romances, he was stabbed in May 1861 by an actress, Henrietta Irving, who then tried to take her own life.

Southern audiences were especially appreciative of Booth's theatrical talents. In return, he idealized the Southern lifestyle. Slavery, he maintained, was "one of the greatest blessings . . . that God ever bestowed upon a favored nation." Though he decided not to join the Confederate army (claiming that he was keeping a promise to his mother to stay out of the conflict), Booth developed a passionate hatred of President Lincoln. By 1863 chronic trouble with his throat and voice threatened Booth's stage career; failing investments in Pennsylvania oil fields further upset his tenuous mental balance.

The growing certainty of Lincoln's reelection in 1864 spurred Booth into action. After contacting Confederate agents in Maryland, Boston, and Canada, Booth dreamed of kidnapping the president and smuggling him to the South, where Lincoln would be held as hostage against the release of Southern prisoners of war. It is not known who in the Confederate government knew of Booth's scheme, although a similar plan to kidnap the president had been authorized in fall 1864. Recruiting a motley collection of six conspirators, Booth and his team organized at the Washington and Maryland properties owned by Mary Surratt, mother of one of the group, who may or may not have known the details of their operation.

Masterminded by Booth, in early 1865 the conspirators' plans were thwarted on two occasions by the president's failure to appear as scheduled: on January 18 at Ford's Theater, and on March 17 at a site en route to a performance at Campbell Hospital. Frustrated, Booth drank more heavily and found it increasingly difficult to distinguish his previous theatrical roles from reality. On April 11, he was among a crowd which heard Lincoln recommend limited suffrage for blacks. "Now, by God, I'll put him through. That is the last speech he will ever make," Booth vowed.

About midday on April 14, Booth learned that Lincoln was scheduled to attend a lighthearted comedy, *Our American Cousin,* at Ford's Theater. With Richmond in Union hands and the Confederacy collapsing, Booth determined upon more decisive measures. The team would assassinate not only Lincoln, but also Vice President ANDREW JOHNSON [6] and Secretary of State WILLIAM SEWARD [8]. In the ensuing disorder, Booth fantasized, the Confederacy might recover. Although half his group had by now backed out, Booth still had his three most loyal followers. Prussian-born George A. Atzerodt was ordered to kill Johnson; guided to the Secretary of State's home by a druggist's clerk, David E. Herold, burly Lewis Paine would take care of Seward; Booth took upon himself the task of murdering the president. The attacks were to take place at 10:15 that night.

Atzerodt decided not to carry out his assignment. Paine, however, entered Seward's house and nearly killed his target, wounding three others who attempted to block his escape. Booth, well-known to workers at Ford's Theater (he had performed there as recently as March 18), easily gained admittance to the presidential box. At about 10:13 that evening, he moved stealthily to within a couple of feet behind Lincoln, aimed his derringer at the back of the president's head, and fired at point-blank range. The assassin then stabbed one of Lincoln's companions, Civil War veteran Major Henry R. Rathbone, with a hunting knife, before vaulting onto the stage and breaking his ankle in the process. Shouting out "Sic semper tyrannis" ("Thus always to tyrants"), Booth hobbled out of the theater. He was cornered on April 26 at a northern Virginia farm, where he was shot and killed.

Federal authorities accused nine people of participating in a plot by JEFFERSON DAVIS [5] and Confederate officials in Canada to assassinate Lincoln. After clumsy, irregular trials, four persons (Herold, Paine, Atzerodt, and Mrs. Surratt) were hanged on July 7. Four others were imprisoned and one, Mrs. Surratt's son John, an original member of Booth's conspiracy who had departed for Canada, was eventually acquitted.

It had been relatively easy to kill Lincoln. The single policeman assigned to protect the president in the passageway leading to his theatre box had left his post, and the executive office footman had allowed Booth to enter upon receiving the noted actor's calling card. Although it is clear that Booth had contacts with Confederate agents and that the South's secret service had considered a variety of plots to kidnap President Lincoln, no credible evidence linking the Confederate government to the assassination has to date emerged. Attempts by present-day conspiracy theorists to link Secretary of War EDWIN STANTON [9] to the president's murder are even less convincing. By murdering Lincoln, Booth had killed the nation's last best hope for smooth reunification.

James Buchanan

(1791–1868)

James Buchanan was a mediocre president in a time when his nation needed a great statesman. His unimaginative leadership intensified the growing split between North and South during the late 1850s. Scandal and corruption marred his administration, and he proved unwilling to support Northern-sponsored legislation in response to the depression of 1857. A Pennsylvania Democrat, Buchanan sympathized with Southern demands that slavery be allowed to expand into new territories, a stance which badly weakened his party in the North. These failures contributed to the onset of war, and rendered him one of the conflict's most significant figures.

Born in 1791 to a prosperous Pennsylvania family, Buchanan graduated from Dickinson College, became a lawyer, and was elected to Congress as a Federalist in 1820. Following that party's demise he became a Democrat and remained a loyal party functionary for the rest of his political life. In 1834 he was elected to the U.S. Senate, where he served for a decade. In return for his help in delivering Pennsylvania to the Democratic fold in 1844, President James K. Polk named Buchanan his secretary of state. Though Polk set policy, Buchanan proved an able assistant in the Texas, Oregon, and Mexican controversies, which increased the national domain by one-third.

Buchanan sought the Democratic Party's presidential nomination in 1848 and again in 1852. Defeated in these quests, he accepted an appointment as minister to Great Britain. In this capacity, Buchanan, having long backed the U.S. acquisition of Cuba, supported the Ostend Manifesto. Signed by Buchanan at the behest of the Southern-born American ministers to France and Spain, this declaration asserted that if Spain refused offers to purchase Cuba, the U.S. would be justified in taking the island by force. The ill-timed manifesto did much to equate, in the minds of many Americans, the formerly unifying cause of Manifest Destiny with the naked expansion of slavery.

Despite the controversies surrounding the Ostend Manifesto, Buchanan at least had the foresight to dissociate himself from the even more contentious Kansas-Nebraska Act (1854). Calling in all his chits from a lifetime of politics, the "Old Public Functionary," as Buchanan called himself, secured the Democratic nomination in 1856 on the seventeenth ballot. In the presidential race he combined the support of the solidly Democratic South with that of five border states to secure a comfortable electoral victory over JOHN C. FRÉMONT [46] (Republican) and Millard Fillmore (American). Having won only 45 percent of the popular vote in the three-cornered contest, however, Buchanan was a minority president—a fact that boded ill for the future of his presidency.

At age sixty-five he was the oldest man to assume office to that date and the nation's only bachelor president. Buchanan failed on virtually every score: In the face of every indication that a majority of the territory's legal voters opposed the measure, he resolutely endorsed admission of Kansas as a slave state under the Lecompton Constitution; blocked on that score by the House of Representatives, the president supported the Supreme Court's outrageous *Dred Scott* v. *Sandford* decision, which declared that blacks were not citizens and denied Congress the right to outlaw slavery in the territories; and widespread corruption in the War, Navy, and Postmaster departments further weakened the administration's credibility.

The 1860 presidential victory of ABRAHAM LINCOLN [1] sparked the quick secession of seven states from the lower South. As lame-duck president, Buchanan declared secession illegal but believed the Constitution forbade him from coercing the states back into the Union. His calls for the Republicans to make further compromises in favor of Southern interests went unheeded. Determined to avoid precipitating open warfare until he left office, Buchanan, buoyed by the eleventh-hour addition of several Unionists to his cabinet, nonetheless refused to give up the remaining federal properties in the deep South, Forts Pickens (Pensacola Bay, Florida) and Sumter (Charleston Harbor,

James Buchanan and his Cabinet: (from left to right), *Jacob Thompson, Lewis Cass, John B. Floyd, Buchanan, Howell Cobb, Issac Toucey, Joseph Holt, and Jeremiah Black*

South Carolina). In January 1861 he authorized an ill-fated attempt to reinforce Sumter. Two months later, Buchanan thankfully turned over the crisis to Lincoln. He retired from political life, and died in 1868.

A dour Presbyterian, the colorless Buchanan entered office with a wealth of political and diplomatic experience. Inheriting a difficult situation, Buchanan's actions only made matters worse. His pro-Southern positions infuriated most Northerners and helped exacerbate the nation's sectional tensions. Many historians now rate Buchanan the second-worst president in American history, above only Warren G. Harding. Unfortunately, the circumstances he encountered required a genius far exceeding Buchanan's capacities.

27

Henry Halleck

(1815–1872)

Dubbed "Old Brains" by his soldiers for his high forehead, large eyes, and intellectual proclivities, Henry Wager Halleck served first as general in chief and later as chief of staff of Union armies from 1862 to 1865. Although lacking strategic vision and possessing an annoying tendency to evade responsibility for controversial decisions, he proved an excellent administrator. This latter service, combined with his influential prewar military scholarship and his preservation of the Confederate archives, makes Halleck one of the most significant figures of the American Civil War.

    Born in Oneida County, New York, in 1815, Halleck left his family farm to pursue studies at the Hudson Academy and Union College before entering the U.S. Military Academy. In 1839, he graduated third in his class of thirty-one. In the process, he earned the respect of West Point's most influential professor, Dennis Hart Mahan. As an army engineer, Halleck worked on Atlantic seaboard defensive fortifications until 1844, when he toured European military sites. Returning to the United States the following year, he delivered a series of lectures before the Lowell Institute of Boston which were published in 1846 as *Elements of Military Art and Science.* The first truly American contribution to military scholarship, the book became a standard text at the Military Academy and would later be read by President ABRAHAM LINCOLN [1]. It emphasized conventional operations, concentration of forces, and the occupation of key strategic points.

Although Halleck missed most of the fighting during the Mexican War, he acted as secretary of state to the military governor of California and helped draft that state's constitution. He then held various staff posts in California until 1854, when he resigned his commission to take up a full-time legal practice. A respected jurist, by 1861 Halleck had served on the boards of several companies, was part owner of a large mercury mine, and had an estate valued at $500,000.

In August 1861 Lincoln appointed Halleck a major general in the regular army. Halleck took command of the Department of the Missouri three months later, restoring order to a region left in administrative chaos by its former commander, JOHN CHARLES FRÉMONT [46]. His subordinates, ULYSSES S. GRANT [2] and JOHN POPE [62], won important victories—Grant at Fort Donelson and Shiloh, Tennessee, Pope in capturing Island No. 10 on the Mississippi River. Concerned by reports about Grant's drinking and anxious to elevate his own reputation, Halleck assumed field command, bent on taking Corinth, a strategic railroad junction in northeastern Mississippi. Corinth fell to Union troops in mid-June, but it had taken them two months to advance twenty-five miles.

Despite the slow progress, Union successes in Halleck's command—now expanded to the Department of the Mississippi—far exceeded progress else-

A photograph taken of Corinth, Mississippi, before the battle.

where. On July 11, 1862, Lincoln appointed him general in chief. In this capacity, Halleck moved to Washington, but confined himself to serving as liaison between civilians and officers in the field and as military adviser to Lincoln and Secretary of War EDWIN M. STANTON [9]. He felt more at ease dealing with Washington political intrigues, shifting about reinforcements, and overseeing reforms in army regulations than in taking responsibility for field operations. As he explained, "I have always, whenever it was possible, avoided giving positive instructions to the commanding generals . . . leaving them the exercise of their own judgment, while giving them my opinion and advice."

But Lincoln had hoped Halleck would supply strategic direction and command rather than merely "opinion and advice." On March 9, 1864, Ulysses S. Grant was promoted to lieutenant general and named general in chief; Halleck willingly relinquished the post in favor of a new position as chief of staff. The shift in titles meant little real change. Grant made his field headquarters with the Army of the Potomac while Halleck remained in Washington, essentially carrying out the same functions he had for the previous two years. The new establishment clearly suited the strengths of both Halleck and Grant.

With the end of the war, Halleck intervened to save much of the Confederate war archives, which otherwise would have been destroyed. The eighty-one boxes of documents he salvaged later provided the bulk of Southern correspondence in the government-sponsored *War of the Rebellion, the Official Records of the Union and Confederate Armies*, a one hundred twenty-eight-volume set that remains the essential primary source for Civil War scholarship. By this work alone, he left a permanent imprint on future generations. During Reconstruction, Halleck, whose administrative talents had helped win the war for the Union, commanded the military divisions of the James, the Pacific, and the South. He died in January 1872.

Josiah Gorgas

(1818–1883)

Many readers may be unfamiliar with Josiah Gorgas. With the unpretentious title of chief of ordnance, Confederate States of America, Gorgas was responsible for meeting the South's huge wartime needs for arms and ammunition. Given the Confederacy's material disadvantages in industry, transportation, and finances, his ability to satisfy the South's armaments requirements was remarkable. At the outset of the war, the seceding states produced only a tenth of the total value of United States manufactured products, had just over a third of its railroad mileage, and boasted only a tenth of its total capital. Still, by combining blockade running, battlefield capture, home production, and innovation, Gorgas's Ordnance Department kept the Confederate ground forces adequately armed. Though Southern troops ran dangerously low on

79

munitions on several occasions, only in the war's final months, when the South's major ports and much of its territory had fallen under Federal control, could defeat on the battlefield be fairly attributed to inadequate ordnance.

Born one of ten children in 1818 at Running Pumps, Pennsylvania, the hardworking, intelligent Gorgas was appointed to the U.S. Military Academy, from which he graduated sixth in his class in 1841. He demonstrated his organizational skills during the Mexican War, in which, based at Vera Cruz, he helped supply the army of WINFIELD SCOTT [37] as it captured Mexico City. Subsequently stationed at Mount Vernon Barracks, Alabama, in 1853 Gorgas married Amelia Gayle, daughter of one of that state's former governors. For the remainder of the decade, he worked on seaboard fortification sites in several Atlantic and Gulf coast locations, and in ordnance testing.

With the secession of the South in 1860–61, Gorgas found his loyalties divided between the Pennsylvania of his birth and Alabama, where he had married into a prominent family. Initially, he rejected a commission as a major in the Confederate artillery, apparently hoping for personal and professional advancement with the North. After failing to secure a satisfactory posting in the Union army, however, Gorgas accepted a new offer to become chief of Confederate ordnance.

One of very few men at the South's disposal with the experience and talent to handle the complex task of scraping together the millions of rifles and muskets, thousands of artillery pieces, and tons of ammunition required to fight the war, Gorgas found his element. With a steady, penetrating eye and a knack for projecting future needs as well as selecting able subordinates, he oversaw not only the strategy for purchasing war materials abroad, but the establishment of a large domestic production base. The latter task proved especially demanding. His attempts to maximize efficiency were slowed by the insistence of certain governors, such as Georgia's Joseph Brown, on maintaining local control over ordnance, and, as the war continued, by the Union occupation of ever-larger amounts of Confederate territory. Despite such hurdles, Gorgas managed the complex procurement of suitable raw materials, guided new research efforts designed to overcome material shortages, secured skilled labor, organized and built manufacturing plants, and moved armaments to armies in the field. In order to do so, he established a virtual dictatorship over Southern industry.

After the war Gorgas found enough financial backing to purchase an iron works at Brierfield, Alabama. Beset by inadequate capital, uncooperative railroad officials, and low iron prices, the plant operated only sporadically until finally closing in 1869. Anticipating this failure, Gorgas had already accepted a position at the University of the South (Sewanee, Tennessee). He helped build that institution into one of the region's finest before becoming president of the University of Alabama in 1878. Illness forced him into retirement the following year, and he died in 1883. One of his sons, William, became a U.S. Army surgeon and helped find the means of eradicating yellow fever, thus allowing completion of the Panama Canal.

29

George Thomas

(1816–1870)

During his thirty-year military career, George Henry Thomas acquired a set of nicknames almost as formidable as his army record. Known variously as "Old Tom" as a West Point cadet, "Slow Trot" as a Military Academy instructor, "Old Pap" by the adoring men of his Army of the Cumberland, and "the Rock of Chickamauga" for having held the left wing of an endangered Union army during the latter battle, Thomas was one of the steadiest Federal generals of the Civil War. Yet despite winning the intense loyalty of those who served under him, he was also continually embroiled in controversies with his fellow generals.

Born in Southampton County, Virginia, in 1816, George Thomas graduated from the U.S. Military Academy in 1840, twelfth in a class of forty. He fought with distinction in the Second Seminole War and the war against Mexico. After a stint as artillery and cavalry instructor at West Point, Thomas survived an arrow wound while fighting the Comanche Indians in 1860.

Though a Virginian by birth, he remained loyal to the Union upon the secession of his native state the following year. His sisters promptly disowned him. Though Thomas never fully explained the rationale for his decision, undoubtedly he counted his lifetime of service to the Union as more significant than the loyalty he owed his state.

Relegated to a series of minor commands during the first year of the war, Thomas finally secured a major generalship and fought well at the Battle of Shiloh, Tennessee, and during the Union advance upon Corinth, Mississippi. In the following campaigns, he refused to take charge of the Army of the Cumberland, contending that War Department interference had ruined the chances of its commander, DON CARLOS BUELL [95]. Thomas fought at the bloody but inconclusive battles of Perryville, Kentucky, and Stones River, Tennessee, but it was at the Battle of Chickamauga, Georgia (Sept. 19–20, 1863), where he made his biggest mark. During the second day of the fighting, WILLIAM S. ROSECRANS [76], commanding the army, mistakenly pulled a Union division from his lines. By coincidence, a Confederate assault spearheaded by JAMES LONGSTREET [19] struck the hole in the Federal positions. Longstreet's veterans rolled up the Union right flank, and it seemed as if the entire Army of the Cumberland was in danger of collapsing. Coolly, however, Thomas maintained a position atop Snodgrass Hill, which allowed the rest of the army to escape back to Chattanooga, Tennessee.

Thomas received command of the Army of the Cumberland for his heroic stand at Chickamauga. Under the direction of ULYSSES S. GRANT [2], Thomas's men broke the Confederate siege of Chattanooga by taking Missionary Ridge, Tennessee, in perhaps the war's most spectacular charge. When Grant went east, Thomas was once again superseded for overall command of Union field armies in the west, this time by WILLIAM T. SHERMAN [3]. Thomas did acceptably well during the Atlanta campaign, although Sherman complained about what he believed to be Thomas's overly deliberate movements.

After the Union capture of Atlanta, Thomas returned to consolidate the Union hold over middle Tennessee. He soon found himself confronted with a major Confederate offensive, as JOHN BELL HOOD [38] drove north. Though his attack against JOHN SCHOFIELD [75] at Franklin, Tennessee, had severely weakened his army, the aggressive Hood nonetheless pushed to the outskirts of Nashville. Ironically, Thomas had been Hood's instructor of artillery and cavalry tactics at West Point (he had ranked his charge in the bottom quartile of a class of fifty-two students). In the Battle of Nashville, Thomas demonstrated the accuracy of his early judgment, annihilating Hood's army.

Thomas remained in the regular army until his death in 1870. Although usually not ranked among the "great captains" of the war, his combat performance places him high in the second tier. At six feet and 220 pounds, with his handsome beard turning white, Thomas offered a steadying, fatherly figure to those who served under his command. In turn, they fiercely defended his

General George Thomas on the battlefield at Chickamauga, Georgia,
September 20, 1863

reputation in the postwar squabbling among former generals. On the other
hand, his fastidious speech and mannerisms often irritated his peers and
superiors. Indeed, he never got along well with Grant, who shared Sherman's
belief that Thomas was too slow. Just before the Battle of Nashville, Grant,
frustrated that Thomas had delayed so long before attacking, decided to
replace him, initially with Schofield, later with John A. Logan. Of course,
after Thomas's victory at Nashville, the order was returned, undelivered, to
the secretary of war.

30

Braxton Bragg

(1817–1876)

Even though some recent historians have attempted to defend him, Braxton Bragg continues to be one of the most criticized of all Confederate generals. In part, disapproval of Bragg stems from his close wartime association with the equally controversial Confederate president, JEFFERSON DAVIS [5]. Perhaps, however, it also arises from the belief that although Bragg possessed many of the qualities essential to a successful military leader, he never reached his full potential. As a consequence, the cause of the Confederacy was severely hurt, and the lives of thousands of soldiers squandered to little purpose.

He was born in North Carolina in 1817. After graduating from West Point fifth in his class of 1837, Bragg soon became legendary among fellow officers for his quarrelsome nature. ULYSSES S. GRANT [2] recorded the following whimsical story in his *Memoirs*:

As commander of the company he [Bragg] made a requisition upon the quartermaster—himself—for something he wanted. As quartermaster he declined to fill the requisition, and endorsed on the back his reasons for so doing. As company commander he responded to this, urging that his requisition called for nothing but what he was entitled to, and that it was the duty of the quartermaster to fill it. As quartermaster he still persisted that he was right.

Still, most observers saw in Bragg enormous potential, a perception borne out by his outstanding performance during the Mexican War. Following that conflict, he engaged in a bitter dispute over the effectiveness of artillery on the western frontiers with the secretary of war, Jefferson Davis (his future patron). Protesting that his honor had been violated, in 1856 Captain Bragg resigned from the army to manage a Louisiana sugar plantation, purchased with his wife's money. By 1860 he owned 109 slaves.

Fervently supporting the South, Bragg initially oversaw Gulf Coast defenses between Mobile, Alabama, and Pensacola, Florida. In spring 1862, as a corps commander in the army under ALBERT SIDNEY JOHNSTON [79], he launched a successful assault on Grant's army during the first day of the Battle of Shiloh, Tennessee. Bragg was later appointed commander of the Army of Tennessee and led a strike into Kentucky, hoping to bring that state into the Confederacy. He missed the opportunity to exploit the initial success stemming from this bold campaign and was fought to a draw at the Battle of Perryville, Kentucky. Falling back into Tennessee, Bragg counterattacked a Union army led by WILLIAM S. ROSECRANS [76] at the Battle of Stones River, Tennessee. Bragg's withdrawal, after an indecisive slugfest fought over three days that cost him a third of his thirty-five thousand troops, drew sharp criticism from many subordinates. President Davis, however, who had come to admire Bragg's abilities as a disciplinarian and had praised his Kentucky offensive, now firmly supported his old antagonist.

The struggle for Tennessee consumed most of Bragg's energies through 1863. Maneuvered out of strategic Chattanooga, Tennessee, in early September by Rosecrans, Bragg, now reinforced by a corps under JAMES LONGSTREET [19] (on loan from the Army of Northern Virginia), counterattacked at the Battle of Chickamauga, Georgia. Here Bragg won his greatest victory, driving back the Federals in disarray to Chattanooga. Rather than pressing home his advantage, he settled in for a siege, thus allowing the Union time to regroup and receive reinforcements. Despite holding the high ground atop Missionary Ridge, Tennessee, Bragg's Army of Tennessee suffered a major defeat during the subsequent Battle of Chattanooga.

Bragg had long been criticized by his corps commanders, and perhaps one of the reasons for the stunning Confederate loss was the demoralization resulting from the constant backbiting among general officers in the Army of Tennessee. His resignation from command of that army was immediately accepted. Still a Davis favorite, Bragg served as military adviser to the Confederate president in 1864. In the last months of the war he held several minor commands in the west. After Appomattox, he served as a commissioner of public works in Alabama and a railroad engineer in Texas.

Intelligent, a solid administrator, and a strict disciplinarian, Bragg saw to it that troops under his command were invariably better supplied and equipped than comparable Confederate forces. But he owed his comparatively long stead as commander of the Army of Tennessee to the support of Davis—who valued Bragg's devotion to the Confederacy—rather than to success on the battlefield. Plagued by chronically poor health and emotional instability, Bragg antagonized virtually everyone who served under him by his contentious behavior and general irritability. Indecision often paralyzed him in combat. In terms of casualties per troops engaged, Bragg commanded in some of the war's bloodiest battles—Perryville, Stones River, and Chickamauga—without achieving the strategic success that the Confederacy so desperately needed. Heavily outnumbered from the outset, the South could not afford to lose so many of its sons so pointlessly.

The Battle of Missionary Ridge, Chattanooga, Tennessee, November 24–25, 1863.

31

Horace Greeley

(1811–1872)

Editor of the *Weekly Tribune* and the daily *New York Tribune* from 1841 to 1872, Horace Greeley was the most influential newspaper editor of the Civil War era. In clearly written, forceful editorials he promoted land grants to prospective western settlers, emancipation, labor unions, free speech, temperance, rights for women, and government aid to railroads. In 1872 Greeley gave up his editorial duties to make an unsuccessful bid for the presidency. Nominated by the Liberal Republican and Democratic parties to challenge ULYSSES S. GRANT [2], Greeley received 44 percent of the popular vote to Grant's 56 percent.

Born in 1811 into an impoverished family in Amherst, New Hampshire, Horace Greeley had little formal schooling. Largely self-educated, he was apprenticed to a newspaper editor at age fourteen and developed a lifelong passion for journalism. He landed a job in New York City in 1831 and worked on various publications, gaining the attention of Whig leaders such as WILLIAM H. SEWARD [8]. In 1841, Greeley launched the daily *New York Tribune,* a penny paper, and later the accompanying *Weekly Tribune,* meant for national circulation.

Greeley's papers featured some of the period's best intellects, including contributions from Margaret Fuller and Karl Marx. Influential fellow editors like Charles A. Dana, editor of the *New York Sun,* and Henry Raymond, founder of the *New York Times,* worked on Greeley's staff before branching out on their own. Although less overtly partisan than many contemporary journals, Greeley's publications nonetheless reflected his philosophy of self-reliance, nationalism, justice for the common man, and westward expansion. Popularizing a phrase first used in an Indiana editorial, Greeley urged, "Go West, young man!" He opposed slavery and argued against the fugitive slave law, the Kansas-Nebraska Act, and the Dred Scott decision. Even after its price increased to four cents, total circulation of his paper surpassed 250,000, making the *Tribune* one of the most influential pro-Republican papers in the country.

During the Civil War, Greeley sometimes appeared to vacillate. He joined many Republicans in doubting whether Southerners would carry though with their threat to secede, arguing that "they simply mean to bully the Free States into concessions." Thus, shortly after the election of LINCOLN [1], Greeley suggested that the South be allowed to go in peace, but with the formation of the Confederacy, he urged decisive military action. "Forward to Richmond! Forward to Richmond!" blared the *Tribune's* July 20, 1861, headline. An editorial entitled, "The Prayer of Twenty Millions" (the approximate population of the non-slave states) climaxed Greeley's campaign to pressure Lincoln into ending slavery. In mid-1864, despairing that the war could not be won, Greeley sent out peace feelers to Southern agents and only belatedly endorsed Lincoln's reelection.

Following the war, Greeley supported ratification of the Fourteenth and Fifteenth Amendments and the impeachment of ANDREW JOHNSON [6], while at the same time advocating a general amnesty for all former Confederates, including JEFFERSON DAVIS [5]. Although he initially backed Ulysses S. Grant, Greeley broke with him over Grant's failure to promote civil service reform and his inability to curb corruption within his administration. Nominated to oppose Grant by the Democratic Party and a splinter group, the Liberal Republicans, Greeley was pilloried by most of the press for deserting the president.

With a shambling gait, clothes which never seemed to fit, and throat-whiskers, rounded out by a squeaky, high-pitched voice, Greeley was often lampooned and caricatured. His final days represented a tragic end to a life devoted to reform and education. Less than two weeks before his 1872 defeat at the hands of Grant, Greeley's wife died. When he attempted to return from the campaign to his beloved *Tribune,* he found that control of the paper had passed to a longtime assistant, Whitelaw Reid. Physically and emotionally broken, Greeley died within a few weeks. Only with his funeral procession down New York City's Fifth Avenue, attended by the president, vice president, several governors, and a huge crowd, did he receive the belated tribute his long public influence had merited. Many of his causes—land grants to western settlers, emancipation, and federal assistance to railroads—were now part of American life.

32

Roger B. Taney

(1777–1864)

Roger B. Taney served as chief justice of the U.S. Supreme Court from 1835 to 1864. During this long tenure, he wrote his most important decision in the much-disputed *Dred Scott* v. *Sandford* (1857) case. In this ruling, a court majority supported Taney's assertions that blacks were not citizens and that Congress could not exclude slavery from the territories. Though the controversial judgment seemed to have changed few political allegiances, it intensified and cemented the resolve of the pro- and antislavery factions. By finalizing the sectional schism within the Democratic Party and reinforcing Republican fears that a slave-power conspiracy would force slavery upon the free states, Taney unwittingly contributed to the presidential election of ABRAHAM LINCOLN [1] and the secession of the South.

Born the second son of a Maryland tobacco planter in 1777, Taney graduated from Dickinson College in 1795 and soon gained admission to the bar. He entered politics as a Federalist and was by 1820 a powerful state figure. Following the demise of his old party, Taney became a Jacksonian Democrat. In 1831 he joined Andrew Jackson's cabinet as attorney general. Convinced that the Second Bank of the United States had become too powerful, he supported the president's determination to destroy that institution. In 1833, Taney accepted Jackson's offer to become treasury secretary and promptly announced that the government would no longer use the bank as its depository. Though the Senate refused to confirm Taney's appointment, the bank had been permanently weakened.

Following the death of Chief Justice John Marshall, in 1836 Jackson named his loyal supporter chief justice. Taney stood about six feet tall and was soft-spoken. He developed a reputation for writing clear, pointed judicial opinions, and his most important early decision came in the *Charles River Bridge* v. *Warren Bridge* case (1837), in which the court ruled that a state could change or revoke a contract if such an action advanced the well-being of the larger community. Since government functioned to promote happiness and prosperity, reasoned Taney, that object took precedence over the property rights of a single corporation. Over the years, his tenure also saw the enlargement of the power of federal courts over local and state governments.

Plagued by chronic ill-health, Taney was struck by personal tragedy in 1855, when yellow fever claimed his wife and daughter. The loss apparently robbed Taney of his remaining emotional and intellectual balance. Though he had freed his own slaves nearly four decades earlier, he had come to idealize the Southern way of life, which was heavily dependent upon the "peculiar institution." Angered by what he saw to be unjustified and sanctimonious attacks on his beloved homeland, the chief justice, now eighty years old, took the DRED SCOTT [47] case as an opportunity to end such blasphemies by judicial decree.

The slave of an army surgeon, Dred Scott had sued for his freedom on the grounds that he had for several years lived in free states and territories. The court included five Southern justices, who all used the opportunity offered by Scott's suit to make a broad decision protecting slavery. Joined by a single northern jurist from Pennsylvania, who had been improperly pressured by President-elect JAMES BUCHANAN [26], the majority supported Taney's fifty-five pages of labored, tortuous logic. Taney ruled that Scott, as a black man, was not a citizen, had no right to sue, and thus must remain a slave. He also decreed that the Missouri Compromise had been unconstitutional, because Congress had no right to prohibit slavery in the territories. Such a prohibition, he argued, was a violation of the Fifth Amendment, which protected individuals from being deprived of property (slaves) without due process of law.

In the years which followed, Taney was a stubborn opponent of President Abraham Lincoln. Privately supporting secession, the chief justice tried to strike down the president's wartime suspension of habeas corpus in *Ex parte Merryman*. Taney also believed the Emancipation Proclamation, conscription, and the Legal Tender Act all to be unconstitutional, but in the absence of cases on these issues had no chance to formalize his opinions. He died in 1864. Though jurists still respect many of his decisions, his polemical *Dred Scott* opinion continues to draw sharp criticism.

33

J. E. B. Stuart

(1833–1864)

Born in Patrick County, Virginia, in 1833, James Ewell Brown Stuart was the Civil War's most celebrated cavalry leader. He was audacious, dedicated to his cause, and had a knack for the spectacular in dress as well as in deed. Stuart took command of the cavalry of the Army of Northern Virginia under ROBERT E. LEE [4] in early 1862. He infused his own high spirits and aggressiveness into his cavalrymen, traits which helped his mounted forces dominate their Northern counterparts through the early war years. As the fighting continued, however, the Union cavalry improved, and Stuart's efforts to match his earlier exploits often came at the expense of the more mundane assignments of reconnaissance. Whatever his faults, Stuart's death from a battle wound in 1864 was a serious blow to the Confederacy.

The son of a prominent Virginia family, Stuart attended Emory and

Henry College before securing an appointment to the U.S. Military Academy. In 1854, he graduated from West Point thirteenth in his class of thirty-six cadets. Stuart received a much-coveted appointment to mounted service and spent most of his pre-Civil War career in Kansas with the First Cavalry Regiment. There he helped keep the peace between pro- and antislavery factions as well as along the Indian frontier. Wounded by the Cheyennes during the Battle of Solomon Fork, Kansas, on July 29, 1857, he secured a six-month leave of absence in late 1859 so that he could patent his designs for a new sabre-hanger for cavalrymen. While on leave, he helped Lt. Col. Robert E. Lee capture JOHN BROWN [14] and his followers during their abortive raid on the federal arsenal at Harpers Ferry, Virginia.

Stuart followed his state when Virginia seceded from the Union, resigning his U.S. commission in favor of a colonelcy of state troops. He distinguished himself throughout the First Bull Run campaign in Virginia. Promoted to brigadier general in September 1861, Stuart established his reputation just before the Seven Days' Battles, Virginia. Given the task of obtaining information about the right flank of the Army of the Potomac under Gen. GEORGE B. MCCLELLAN [7], Stuart led his twelve hundred cavalryman on a spectacular three-day ride (June 12–15, 1862) completely around the Union army. Celebrated throughout the Confederacy, Stuart's ride left the Union command baffled and the enemy's supply lines badly mangled.

With a knack for securing reliable information about the enemy while at the same time effectively screening his own infantry, Stuart was promoted to major general and given command of a cavalry division. He did well at both Second Bull Run, Virginia, and Antietam, Maryland. Following the latter battle, he led a diversionary raid on Chambersburg, Pennsylvania, in another ride completely around the Union army. His repeated skirmishes with the Union cavalry marked the winter months of 1862–63. After both STONEWALL JACKSON [20] and Ambrose P. Hill fell wounded during the Battle of Chancellorsville, Virginia, Stuart took command of Jackson's corps and drove back the Federal infantry, helping to complete the Confederate victory there.

On June 9, 1863, Federal cavalry surprised Stuart's troopers at Brandy Station, Virginia. Though Stuart recovered and regained the field, his reputation was badly damaged. Seeking to restore his prestige, he launched another raid behind enemy lines as Lee moved north into Maryland and Pennsylvania. While Stuart was away, Lee fought blindly during the first two days at Gettysburg, Pennsylvania. Although Stuart exhausted horsemen rejoined Lee in time to participate in the third day of fighting there, his absence was a major factor in the Confederate defeat.

After Gettysburg, shortages in horses and proper weapons reduced the effectiveness of his own forces, while the Union cavalry began to dramatically improve. On May 11, 1864, attempting to parry a mounted thrust by PHILIP SHERIDAN [18] toward Richmond, Stuart, outnumbered two to one, was decisively defeated at the Battle of Yellow Tavern, Virginia. Badly wounded during the fighting, he died the next evening.

Two of J. E. B. Stuart's adversaries at the Battle of Brandy Station: Captain George Armstrong Custer (left) and General Alfred Pleasonton (right)

Handsome, ornately uniformed, and dashing in combat, Stuart came to symbolize the bold Southern cavalier. He was lionized throughout the South before his thirtieth birthday. In camp he assembled a circus-like retinue of aides and followers which included at various times a giant, several minstrels, a pet raccoon, and a Prussian soldier of fortune. Though his failures during the Gettysburg campaign and his defeat at Yellow Tavern tarnished his image, in his earlier days Stuart was a splendid cavalryman—energizing his men, confusing his Northern counterparts, and providing timely and reliable intelligence about enemy dispositions.

34

Mathew Brady

(1823–1896)

Mathew Brady owned the most prestigious photographic studio in the country during the 1850s. Understanding the camera's value in recording the Civil War, Brady secured the government's permission for his photographers to accompany Federal armies in the field. His studio acquired negatives and displayed numerous images before the Northern public, providing more realistic glimpses of war than had ever before been possible. In the process, Brady permanently changed the American public's perception of war.

Born in Warren County, New York, in 1823, Mathew Brady had only a meager formal education. He opened a New York City daguerreotype studio in 1844. During the early 1850s, he mastered the wet plate process, which allowed for faster and cheaper developing. Wearing his trademark broad-brimmed hat and linen duster, the genial Brady earned celebrity status for his fashionable studio, where the nation's elite gathered to take advantage of the novelty and have their photographs taken.

With the outbreak of war, photographers flocked to the training camps which began to dot the countryside. The cumbersome techniques of the time—which required the photographer or an assistant to develop plates in a darkroom almost immediately after an exposure was taken—made campaign or battle scenes difficult to capture. Brady claimed that he accompanied the Federal army to the Battle of First Bull Run, Virginia, but if he did, none of his prints or negatives from that excursion have been located. Severely near-sighted, and busy with his New York and Washington studios, he typically dispatched teams of photographers and assistants with a wagon full of equipment rather than going to the field himself. One of his employees, Timothy O'Sullivan, accompanied a Union amphibious expedition to South Carolina in late 1861. But most of the shots seemed static and lifeless, and the resulting photographic display generated little interest.

While teams of Brady workers busily documented behind-the-lines scenes during the subsequent campaigns, the war itself took an increasingly high toll of American lives. The conflict's bloodiest single day came on September 17, 1862, near the quiet Maryland village of Sharpsburg. Along the meandering Antietam Creek, nearly 5,000 young men died. Unlike other encounters in the east to that date, Union troops occupied the ground imme-

A representative shot from the war's noted photographer

diately after the battle. Confederate photographers rarely had the resources to go into the field as Brady's men could do. Only two days after the battle, one of Brady's crack photographers, Alexander Gardner, began taking the first of what eventually came to be ninety-five different photographic negatives of the battlefield.

One of Gardner's images, that of Confederate bodies strewn near the battle-scarred Dunker Church, accompanies this essay. Brady's gallery began displaying the photographs in mid-October under the title, "The Dead of Antietam." An anonymous reporter for the *New York Times* understood the public's morbid fascination with the often gruesome exhibit when he wrote: "Mr. Brady has done something to bring home the terrible reality and earnestness of war. . . . These pictures have a terrible distinctness." Other contemporary periodicals give testimony to the interest aroused by Brady's display of Antietam. The general public, not reading the fine print and influenced by Brady's name and self-publicity, assumed that the owner himself had done the photography. Furious at Brady's shamelessness in this regard, Alexander Gardner and James F. Gibson, who had assisted in the work at Antietam, started up their own firm in 1863.

Still, Brady's Antietam exhibition was a tremendous financial success. Understanding the public's appetite for gory details, competing companies raced to the scene of future battles. Famous images of dead soldiers at Chancellorsville and Gettysburg would alternately shock and fascinate civilians. Brady, however, hurt by the defection of so many good employees during the war, never regained his dominance. Ruined by the Panic of 1873, he sold over five thousand negatives still in his possession to the federal government for $25,000 in 1875; many of the photographs in this book are from Brady's collection now housed in the Library of Congress.

Brady's wife, Julia Handy, died in 1887. Brady died impoverished in New York eight-and-a-half years later.

35

P. G. T. Beauregard

(1818–1893)

Proud, flamboyant, and quixotic, Pierre Gustave Toutant Beauregard oversaw the South's bombardment of Fort Sumter, South Carolina, and, with JOSEPH E. JOHNSTON [12], led Confederate troops to victory in the First Battle of Bull Run, Virginia. He held several wartime commands; perhaps most notable was his able defense of the strategic railroad junction of Petersburg, Virginia, in mid-June 1864 against attacks by numerically superior Union forces. A fierce critic of President JEFFERSON DAVIS [5], Beauregard advocated the concentration of scattered Confederate armies and a greater emphasis on western affairs.

Born in 1818 to a prominent Louisiana Delta family, Beauregard received a strong private education which equipped him to handle the academic rigors of West Point, from which he graduated in 1838 second in his class. As a staff officer in the Mexican War, he distinguished himself throughout the WINFIELD SCOTT [37] campaign from Vera Cruz to Mexico City. Twice wounded, Beauregard earned brevet appointments to captain and major. He spent most of the 1850s in Louisiana supervising military engineering projects. Named superintendent of West Point in early 1861, his prosecession stance led to his almost immediate replacement.

A handsome man of olive complexion, medium build, neatly trimmed mustache, and considerable intelligence, Beauregard had married the daughter of a prominent Louisiana politician. He was appointed the Confederacy's first brigadier general and organized the siege of Fort Sumter. In early June 1861, Beauregard took command of the largest Confederate army in Virginia, winning, with the assistance of reinforcements led by Johnston, the First Battle of Bull Run. His unrealistically optimistic plans, political machinations, and uncooperative behavior, however, worried President Jefferson Davis, who in early 1862 transferred him west as second in command to ALBERT SIDNEY JOHNSTON [79]. There Beauregard outlined an ambitious, if overly complex, counteroffensive which ended in the Battle of Shiloh, Tennessee. When Johnston fell mortally wounded during the first day's fighting, Beauregard assumed command. Although he reported to Richmond officials a great victory, Beauregard, battered by Union counterattacks the second day, retreated back to Corinth, Mississippi. In chronic ill-health, he took an unauthorized leave of absence from his military duties in mid-June 1862. Furious, Davis relieved Beauregard in favor of BRAXTON BRAGG [30].

The Louisianan never forgave Davis. Future references to his president usually referred to "that living specimen of gall and hatred," or, more simply, "that Individual." Now relegated to command the Department of South Carolina, Georgia, and Florida, Beauregard ably defended Charleston, South Carolina, from Union attack and busily plotted to change Confederate strategy. Here he seemed in his real element: drawing up imaginative plans far removed from the reaches of any battlefield. In late April 1864 he received command of the Department of North Carolina and Southern Virginia. Although unable to destroy the Army of the James under BENJAMIN BUTLER [58], Beauregard bottled up this enemy threat south of Richmond. That summer, he brilliantly managed the defense of Petersburg, holding off Union forces long enough to allow the Army of Northern Virginia under ROBERT E. LEE [4] time to fall back and continue the war.

After the fall of Atlanta, Davis overcame his personal prejudices and selected Beauregard to head the Military Department of the West. The new post, however, brought little real authority, as Beauregard had little influence over JOHN BELL HOOD [38], commander of the largest army in his department. On February 22, 1865, Beauregard resigned this final command and returned to New Orleans.

A prolific writer and imaginative strategist, Beauregard published his *Principles and Maxims of the Art of War* in 1863. In this, as well as in his other voluminous plans and recommendations, he stressed the importance of concentrating the South's forces. Such reminders, combined with the emphasis he gave to affairs outside the Virginia front, had the potential to provide valuable input to Confederate planning, which was sometimes focused too narrowly on the Old Dominion. However, his behind-the-scenes denunciations of Davis and fanciful, complex plans—often based upon overly optimistic assumptions—discredited the more constructive elements of his counsel. Finally, when in actual command of real troops, Beauregard demonstrated the flair that characterized his paper schemes only at Petersburg.

After the war he became president of two railroads, adjutant general of the Louisiana militia, and supervisor of drawings for the Louisiana Lottery Company. He died in 1893.

A casement at Fort Sumter during the bombardment ordered by General Beauregard.

36

Joseph Hooker

(1814–1879)

J oseph Hooker's spectacularly unsuccessful foray as commander of the Union Army of the Potomac during the Battle of Chancellorsville, Virginia, stands in stark contrast to his fine wartime performance in positions of lesser responsibility. His long record of military service in both eastern and western theaters merits his high ranking among Civil War figures. Born at Hadley, Massachusetts, in 1814, Hooker graduated twenty-ninth out of a class of fifty from the U.S. Military Academy in 1837. He fought in the Second Seminole and Mexican wars, winning three brevet promotions. Frustrated by the lack of regular army promotion, he resigned his commission in 1853.

Upon the outbreak of the Civil War, Hooker offered his services to Union authorities in Washington. Despite his excellent combat record, he was at first received coolly, probably snubbed by commanding general WIN-FIELD SCOTT [37] for Hooker's having testified in favor of one of the latter's rivals years earlier. Following the Battle of First Bull Run, Virginia, Hooker gained an interview with President ABRAHAM LINCOLN [1], boasting that he was "a damned sight better" than any Federal general on the field. Lincoln, undoubtedly impressed by Hooker's handsome, soldierly bearing, liked his confident attitude, and Hooker soon secured an appointment as brigadier general of volunteers.

As division commander, Hooker performed well in the Peninsula campaign, the Seven Days' battles, and the Battle of Second Bull Run, all fought in Virginia. Citing Hooker's bravery and magnetism, one reporter sent back a story headlined, "Fighting—Joe Hooker." Newspapers, however, seized upon the simpler and more dashing "Fighting Joe Hooker," a sobriquet the general disliked. Wounded in the foot while serving as a corps commander during the Battle of Antietam, Maryland, Hooker returned to active duty in time for the Battle of Fredericksburg, Virginia. He vocally opposed the strategy of Gen. AMBROSE E. BURNSIDE [52] who used futile frontal assaults there.

In January 1863 Lincoln named Hooker, who made no secret of his belief that a military dictatorship might be useful, to command the Army of the Potomac. In his remarkable letter of appointment, the president noted Hooker's impolitic pronouncements. "Of course it is not for this," wrote Lincoln, "but in spite of it that I have given you the command. Only those generals who gain successes, can set up dictators. What I now ask of you is military success, and I will risk the dictatorship." Temporarily chastened, Hooker enjoyed an auspicious beginning in his new command, reorganizing the army, improving its health services, and securing fresh bread and back pay for the troops. By late March, his self-confidence had returned: "My plans are perfect . . . may God have mercy on General Lee, for I will have none."

The following month, Hooker set his army, some 130,000 strong, into motion. In a masterfully executed maneuver, he swung west with his main body of ninety thousand, crossed the Rappahannock and Rapidan rivers, and threatened to outflank sixty thousand Confederates under ROBERT E. LEE [4] at Fredericksburg. But Hooker mysteriously slowed, allowing Lee to regain the initiative. On May 2, Lee struck Hooker's exposed right flank, as the Battle of Chancellorsville began. Hooker was surprised by the fierce Confederate onslaught and was nearly decapitated by a stray rebel cannonball the following day; shaken, he was later quoted as saying that "I lost confidence in Joe Hooker." With the Union commander emotionally paralyzed, Lee won his most remarkable victory.

Hooker's request that he be relieved as commander of the Army of the Potomac was accepted on the eve of the Battle of Gettysburg. He was transferred west as a corps commander, once again demonstrating a flair for this position, under ULYSSES S. GRANT [2] in the fighting around Chattanooga, Tennessee, and under WILLIAM T. SHERMAN [3] during the Atlanta campaign. When a junior officer, OLIVER O. HOWARD [63], was appointed to a vacant position as head of one of the armies under Sherman's command, however, Hooker angrily demanded a transfer. He served the remainder of the war at

Couch's troops covering the retreat of XI Corps, Chancellorsville, Virginia, May 2, 1863.

Cincinnati as head of the quiet Northern Department. He retired from the army as a major general in 1868 and died eleven years later.

Tales of Hooker's personal life, especially the wild parties thrown by his staff and close friends, abound. One theory even holds that Hooker, noted as a heavy drinker, gave up alcohol upon taking command of the Army of the Potomac and that what he really needed at Chancellorsville was a stiff drink to bolster his self-confidence. Hooker and his friends, though, always disclaimed the lurid tales of his personal behavior. Whatever the case, his disastrous failure at Chancellorsville undoubtedly lengthened the war, overshadowing what would otherwise be considered a successful Civil War career.

37

Winfield Scott

(1786–1866)

One of the greatest soldiers in American military history, Winfield Scott, aged seventy-five when the war began, made two important contributions to the Civil War. His Mexican War campaigns had been directly observed or studied by many future Civil War officers on both sides. In addition, his "Anaconda Plan" for conducting the war, proposed shortly after secession, accurately foretold many of the steps needed to defeat the Confederacy.

A native of Virginia, Winfield Scott had an antebellum career marked by successful field operations and unseemly public bouts with his civil and military subordinates, peers, and superiors. He joined the army in 1807, and distinguished himself fighting against the British at the Battles of Chippewa and Lundy's Lane during the War of 1812. His successful diplomacy during the nullification crisis of 1832 and in several Canadian border disputes later in the decade helped avert needless bloodshed. Further, Scott's writings on infantry tactics influenced the American army for generations. As commanding general during the war against Mexico, his brilliant campaign that resulted in the capture of Mexico City remains a classic in the annals of military history.

Tempering these triumphs were problems stemming largely from his vain, contentious personality. Among those with whom Scott clashed were Presidents Andrew Jackson and James K. Polk, Secretary of War JEFFERSON DAVIS [5], and Senator Henry Clay, as well as innumerable fellow officers. Indeed, his seeming inability to get along with anyone left him virtually isolated on the eve of the Civil War, despite his post as commanding general of the United States Army.

ABRAHAM LINCOLN [1], whose military experience was limited to a brief stint in the Illinois militia during the Black Hawk War, turned to Scott for advice. Most Northerners expected a short war. After a battle or two, the enemy capital could be occupied and the war ended. Scott, however, recognized the difficulties of defeating such a large and powerful enemy as the Confederacy. Military means must be used to help achieve political ends. Rather than an immediate offensive, Scott proposed a slower, more deliberate strangulation of the enemy. Union forces, he argued, must establish a naval blockade and seize control of the Mississippi River. With vital imports denied and the Confederacy cut in half, the South would be forced to come to terms and costlier military campaigns avoided.

The aging Scott's deteriorating physical condition and unimpressive appearance (he suffered from intense vertigo and was too fat to mount a horse) made it impossible for him to effectively promote his plan before the general public, which demanded more decisive steps. Skeptical newspapers soon dubbed Scott's strategy the Anaconda Plan, after the snake that slowly squeezes the life out of its prey. He took some part in planning the war's opening campaigns, but resigned from active duty in November 1861 with the accession of GEORGE MCCLELLAN [7].

True to form, the egotistical Scott took two volumes to write his memoirs. He died in 1866 and was buried with honors at West Point. Though largely dismissed at the time by the public, Scott understood better than most the difficulties of defeating the Confederacy. Too, he predicted that the war would produce heavy casualties on both sides. On the other hand, Scott's belief that a naval blockade, combined with Union control of the Mississippi River, would convince the South to come to terms was inaccurate. His prediction that the war would require three hundred thousand soldiers and two or three years to win also proved to be overly optimistic. Scott, of course, would undoubtedly have blamed the failure of his predictions to be fulfilled on inadequate Union leadership.

38

John Bell Hood

(1831–1879)

Aggressive, courageous, and loyal to his Southern cause, John Bell Hood ranks among the best combat leaders of brigade- and division-level forces in the Civil War. Yet his impatience, overoptimism, limited intellect, and refusal (or inability) to master administrative details also made him one of the war's worst army commanders. Indeed, he holds the dubious distinction of being the only general on either side to see an entire army dissolve around him on the battlefield.

Born in Kentucky in 1831 to a prosperous slaveholding doctor, Hood entered the U.S. Military Academy at age eighteen. A physically imposing six feet, two inches tall, the blond, broad-shouldered Hood became a favorite of his fellow cadets but struggled with his studies. West Point library records indicate that he checked out only two books—both tales of Scottish romanticism—during his four-year tenure there. He graduated in 1853, an undistinguished forty-fourth in a class of fifty-two.

Hood remained in the army, serving for most of the late 1850s in Texas. In minor actions, he demonstrated superb combat leadership of small commands along with great personal courage. For example, in an 1857 engagement against a group of Comanche Indians, when wounded in the hand by an arrow, he broke off the shaft and remained in the fight. Hood resigned his U.S. commission with the outbreak of the Civil War. When Kentucky failed to secede from the Union, he declared Texas to be his adopted state and joined the Confederate army.

By early 1862, Hood commanded three regiments from Texas and one from Georgia, a unit which came to be known as "Hood's Texas Brigade." As part of the Army of Northern Virginia under ROBERT E. LEE [4], Hood's troops soon gained a reputation as one of the finest combat commands in the eastern theater. The brigade spearheaded a successful assault against prepared Union defenses at Gaines' Mill, Virginia, a battle which ensured that the Union would not quickly seize the Confederate capital at Richmond. STONEWALL JACKSON [20] characterized the action as having been a "rapid and almost matchless display of daring and valor." Hood and his men won further accolades during the Battle of Second Bull Run, Virginia; their ferocious counterattack at the Battle of Antietam, Maryland, probably saved Lee's army.

Upon the recommendations of Lee and Jackson, Hood was promoted to major general, but luck now seemed to have deserted him. Early on the second day of fighting at Gettysburg, Pennsylvania, an exploding shell left fragments in his left hand and wrist, leaving his hand virtually paralyzed. At the Battle of Chickamauga, Tennessee, a Yankee bullet tore into his right leg just as Hood's division had shattered the Union line, forcing surgeons to amputate only a few inches below the hip. But "the Gallant Hood" still yearned for combat, and during his convalescence he was appointed lieutenant general.

Having earned the confidence of President JEFFERSON DAVIS [5], Hood returned to active duty in late February 1864 as a corps commander in the Army of Tennessee under JOSEPH E. JOHNSTON [12]. Like Davis, the impatient Hood grew increasingly critical of Johnston's refusal to attack the enemy as the Confederates fell back in the face of the Union advance under WILLIAM T. SHERMAN [3] toward Atlanta. On July 17, with Federal troops on the outskirts of that heavily fortified city, Davis removed Johnston in favor of Hood. The latter promptly launched a series of unsuccessful assaults just outside the city. In danger of being surrounded, Hood evacuated Atlanta on September 1.

Severely outnumbered, Hood now moved his men north toward Nashville, Tennessee, hoping to cut Sherman's supply lines. But in a campaign plagued by carelessness and inattention to detail, Hood's Confederates were defeated at the Battle of Franklin, Tennessee, and annihilated by a Union counteroffensive at Nashville. In the meantime, Sherman had marched virtually unopposed through central Georgia, wreaking havoc throughout his "March to the Sea." Hood stepped down from army command at his own request, and surrendered to Federal officials while en route back to Texas.

Only thirty-three years old when the war ended, Hood eventually settled in New Orleans, where he worked as a cotton trader before entering the insurance business. He married in 1868 and fathered eleven children. Like many of his peers, Hood vigorously defended his wartime record in the years which followed. He, his wife, and eldest daughter died from yellow fever in 1879, a tragic ending to the life of one of the South's romantic cavaliers.

The battle of Chickamauga, Georgia, September 19–20, 1863.

Viscount Palmerston

(1784–1865)

Henry John Temple, the third Viscount Palmerston, was British prime minister during the American Civil War. As leader of the world's most important economic and naval power, Palmerston, through his government's policies, greatly affected the outcome of the American conflict. French assistance had been crucial to the colonies' success during the American Revolution, and the South hoped to attain similar help from Europe. By remaining neutral, Britain ensured that no major power would come to the Confederacy's defense, thus removing any possibility that the conditions that had helped guarantee U.S. independence in 1783 would be repeated.

Born into an aristocratic family in 1784 in Broadlands, Hampshire, Henry John Temple received an excellent education in Edinburgh and at Cambridge. In 1807 he entered Parliament from the Isle of Wight, nominated by a fellow aristocrat on the condition that Temple would never actually visit the region while holding its seat. Good-humored, self-confident, and bearing a patriotic righteousness of purpose, Palmerston went on to serve in every government except two from 1809 until his death. As secretary of state for foreign affairs from 1830 to 1841 and again from 1846 to 1851, he gained considerable international experience. Tenacious in his view that what was good for England was good for the world, Palmerston helped to mediate several European disputes and expand his nation's involvement in China. "We have no eternal allies and we have no perpetual enemies," he told the House of Commons in 1848. "Our interests are eternal and perpetual, and these interests it is our duty to follow." He culminated his long public career as prime minister in the mid-1850s and from 1859 until his death in late 1865.

In May 1861 Queen Victoria proclaimed British neutrality in the American Civil War. This accorded the Confederacy belligerent status but fell short of granting it recognition. The carefully considered position reflected British ambiguity as well as self-interest. A divided United States would reduce a potential rival's power and influence. Crucial to the British economy were its massive textile mills, which had depended upon the South for two-thirds of their prewar supply of raw cotton. Southerners sought to parlay this into a diplomatic advantage, embargoing cotton exports until Europe recognized their independence. Citing the ineffectiveness of the Northern blockade in the war's early stages, the Confederates further argued that it violated international law and the British navy must protect freedom of trade and the seas.

Yet other factors counterbalanced any decisive action in favor of the South. As Palmerston noted in 1861, those nations that meddle in the conflicts of others "will often get a bloody nose." Further, if England accepted the South's contention that the Federal blockade was illegal, it would set a dangerous precedent that might make it more difficult for Britain to establish future blockades. Unfortunately for the South, British companies held huge inventories of raw cotton; making matters even worse, the market for cloth was poor. By the summer of 1862, when fears of a cotton famine might have become more real, imports from India and Egypt seemed a good bet for England's future needs. Also, poor harvests in much of Europe increased demand for Northern foodstuffs. Corn and wheat, not cotton, seemed king.

A nineteenth-century liberal, Palmerston disliked slavery and had read *Uncle Tom's Cabin* three times. He was more realist than ideologue; Britain must "know that their [the South's] separate independence is a truth and a fact" before granting the Confederacy official recognition. In late summer 1862 military conditions seemed to approach Palmerston's requirement. Union offensives had stalled in the west; in the east, the Army of Northern Virginia under ROBERT E. LEE [4] won a smashing victory at the Second Battle of Bull Run, Virginia, and was marching triumphantly north into Maryland. Although cautious in his public pronouncements, in private Palmerston gave careful consideration to the idea of international mediation of the American conflict.

The bloody fight at Antietam, Maryland, after which Lee retreated into Virginia, drew Palmerston back from the brink. As U.S. Minister CHARLES FRANCIS ADAMS [67] wrote from England, it had "done a good deal to restore our drooping credit here." Lincoln's later Emancipation Proclamation seemed to confirm the decision to stay out. U.S.-British relations subsequently deteriorated over the thorny issue of reparations due American merchants whose property had been destroyed by English-built ships sold to the Confederacy. Despite these tensions, Palmerston's Britain remained neutral.

Elizabeth Cady Stanton

(1815–1902)

Elizabeth Cady Stanton's importance to the Civil War era lies chiefly in her support for abolition, expanded roles for women, and woman suffrage. Understanding that the time was ripe for reform, Stanton did as much as any other individual to make it easier for women to enter public life and was a notable figure within the abolitionist movement. Despite her best efforts, however, an opportunity to gain the vote for women in the heady days of Reconstruction, when reformers passed the Civil Rights Act of 1866 and the Thirteenth, Fourteenth, and Fifteenth Amendments, was lost. Women, whose support for black rights had been invaluable and who had made enormous contributions to the war effort, would continue to be denied the vote at the federal level for another half-century.

The leading women's rights advocate of the mid-nineteenth century,

Elizabeth Cady was born in 1815 at Johnstown, New York. Daughter of an attorney, she attended Emma Willard's famous Troy Female Seminary. Elizabeth married a dashing abolitionist, Henry B. Stanton, in 1840; at her insistence, the word "obey" was omitted from their marriage vows. They spent their honeymoon in London, where Henry was a delegate to the World Anti-Slavery Convention. There she also met Lucretia Mott, who had been refused official recognition by the group because of her gender.

The Stantons moved in 1847 to Seneca Falls. Disenchanted by her husband's frequent absences on political and professional assignments and disheartened by the lack of opportunities outside the home, in 1848 she, together with Mott, helped to organize the nation's first women's rights convention. There Stanton presented her "Declaration of Sentiments." Modeled upon the Declaration of Independence, she asserted "that all men and women are created equal." Over Mott's reluctance, she also insisted that woman suffrage be included in the group's resolutions. Exercising the franchise, concluded Stanton, was the only means by which women could truly protect their liberties.

As the mother of five sons and two daughters, Stanton faced domestic burdens common to most nineteenth-century women. Fortunately, in 1851 she met SUSAN B. ANTHONY [40 (tie)], who became her closest friend. The two formed a dynamic partnership: Stanton, the charismatic speaker, writer, and philosopher; Anthony, the organizer, tactician, and soulmate who frequently helped with the household chores. They initially threw their efforts into the New York State temperance movement, but Stanton's assertion that drunkenness should be recognized as a legitimate cause for divorce and her unconventional bloomer attire alienated many prohibitionists. Shifting their focus more specifically to women's issues in New York, by the time of the Civil War Stanton and Anthony had persuaded the state legislature to pass laws extending property rights and equal claims to guardianship of their children to married women. Suffrage, however, remained unrealized.

During the war, Stanton and Anthony formed the National Women's Loyal League to press for a constitutional amendment abolishing slavery; they gathered nearly four hundred thousand signatures on their petitions. Dissatisfied with Lincoln's slow pace on racial matters, Stanton backed JOHN C. FRÉMONT [46] in his abortive 1864 bid for the Republican presidential nomination.

After holding women's issues in temporary abeyance during the war, Stanton hoped the reformers' alliance might finally turn toward gender issues after Appomattox. The Republican-sponsored Fourteenth Amendment, however, extended citizenship rights specifically to "males," the first time that term had been used in the Constitution. Convinced their former allies had betrayed them, Stanton and Anthony broke with other reformers such as FREDERICK DOUGLASS [10], who argued that "this hour belongs to the negro." To press their own agenda, in 1869 Stanton and Anthony established the National Woman Suffrage Association, which resolved to support the Fifteenth Amendment (granting black males the vote) only if it also enfranchised women.

Stanton frequently differed with mainstream women's groups. Her call for liberalized divorce laws always evoked a good deal of controversy. She also urged women to demand "the right to self-sovereignty" by asserting their reproductive self-determination. Critical of organized religion, she frequently clashed with the Women's Christian Temperance Union, an increasingly powerful force in Gilded Age America.

In 1890, the long-divided factions of the women's movements merged into the National American Woman Suffrage Association, which elected Stanton its first president. She died in 1902. Her ultimate goal—women's suffrage—was finally realized at the national level in 1920, with ratification of the Nineteenth Amendment. On a more immediate level, however, Stanton and Anthony had helped make it possible for women, through their work in hospitals, in factories, on farms, and doing piecework at home, to more effectively assist the Union war effort.

Susan B. Anthony

(1820–1906)

Susan B. Anthony is inextricably linked with her close friend and ally, ELIZ-ABETH CADY STANTON [40 (tie)]. Like Stanton, Anthony was a key figure in the women's rights movement in New York State during the 1850s and a faithful abolitionist during the Civil War. Like Stanton, Anthony felt betrayed when the Fourteenth and Fifteenth Amendments excluded women from their guarantees of equal rights. This reflected the painful reality that the Civil War period would not bring legal equality for women despite their contributions to the Union victory.

Anthony was born in 1820, the second of eight children, of a Quaker father and a Baptist mother. Her father, Daniel Anthony, owned a small cotton mill in Adams, Massachusetts. Quaker doctrine held that education should be egalitarian; when a male teacher at the district school refused to instruct Susan in long division because she was a girl, Anthony organized a home school for his children. He enrolled Susan for the 1837–38 term at Deborah Moulson's Female Seminary, a Quaker boarding school in Hamilton, Pennsylvania.

The Panic of 1837 left the Anthonys virtually bankrupt. Suddenly required to be self-sufficient, Susan took an assignment as assistant teacher at a Quaker school in New Rochelle, New York. In 1846, she became head-mistress of the female department of the Canajoharie Academy, built along the Mohawk River. There she joined a local temperance organization and made her first public speech, which called upon women to save society's flag-ging moral virtues. Tired of teaching, she briefly returned to live with her parents, but soon immersed herself in the temperance and abolitionist crusades.

Anthony met Stanton at Seneca Falls in 1851. The two women became devoted friends and allies, with Stanton the better speaker and writer, Anthony the more capable critic and organizer. They gained control of the Woman's New York State Temperance Society, and Anthony energetically took the field, lecturing, organizing, petitioning, and fundraising. Instead of merely reforming drunks, Anthony argued, women needed to gain the ballot and strike at the very root of the evil, the traffic in alcohol. More conserva-tive elements within the temperance movement rejected the Stanton-Anthony radicalism.

By 1854 the two women were devoting themselves exclusively to women's issues. They formed an effective team, with Anthony often helping Stanton—who was married and had seven children—with domestic chores, while at the same time prodding her friend to take a more active public role in the movement. In 1860 their efforts paid off with the New York legisla-ture's passage of the Married Women's Property Act, which granted married women the right to own separate property, enter into contracts and take legal action in their own name, and be joint guardians of their children.

With the outbreak of the Civil War, Anthony and Stanton concentrated their efforts on securing immediate abolition. With the pressure from women's rights supporters now off, in 1862 New York repealed most of the provisions of the Married Women's Property Act. Still, black freedom remained an important goal, so they organized the Woman's National Loyal League to lobby for the complete abolition of slavery. Having spent much of the war traveling, lecturing, petitioning, and organizing on behalf of black rights, Anthony was devastated when the Fourteenth and Fifteenth Amend-ments granted suffrage exclusively to males. The acts seemed to both Anthony and Stanton to be a clear betrayal. In response, they formed the National Woman Suffrage Association, the goal of which was woman suffrage at the federal level. Rivals organized the American Woman Suffrage Associ-ation, which supported the Fifteenth Amendment as it was proposed and called for a state-by-state approach to woman suffrage.

For the remainder of the century the intense, independent, self-disciplined Anthony carried on the crusade. Unlike Stanton, Anthony forged an alliance with Frances Willard, head of the Women's Christian Temperance Union, and was a leader in efforts to reunify the suffrage movement during the late 1880s. She succeeded Stanton in 1892 as president of a coalition group, the National American Woman Suffrage Association. Anthony resigned the presidency in 1900 and died six years later, having late in life probably surpassed Stanton as the nation's preeminent suffragist. Both at least lived long enough to see women gain the vote in several western states. And the crowning jewel—what eventually became the Nineteenth Amendment—was at least on the national horizon. In the meantime, their visibility during and after the Civil War had opened up new arenas in the public sphere for women.

42

David Dixon Porter

(1813–1891)

Admiral David Dixon Porter ranks behind only his adopted brother DAVID FARRAGUT [13] and Navy Secretary GIDEON WELLES [23] as an important Union naval leader. Following a long and undistinguished prewar naval career, Porter blossomed during the war between North and South. His audacious use of his Mississippi River gunboat fleet was instrumental in the capture of Vicksburg, Mississippi. Later, Porter's amphibious attack on Fort Fisher, North Carolina, helped reduce the Confederacy's last major Atlantic fortress.

   David Dixon Porter was born in 1813 at Chester, Pennsylvania, the third of Commodore David Porter's ten children. As did his adopted brother, Farragut, David D. Porter took to sea with only a minimal formal education. He was made a lieutenant in 1841, serving in various missions in the Mediterranean, the South Atlantic, and the Caribbean, as well as with the U.S. Coastal Survey. He spent most of the war against Mexico performing administrative tasks, but played a daring role in the capture of the Mexican port of Tabasco. Despite his pedigree and excellent war record, Porter, like so many naval officers, had by 1860 nearly given up the service because of the lack of opportunity for promotion. By then he had spent twenty of his thirty-two years in the navy at the rank of lieutenant, and had during the early 1850s taken a six-year leave of absence.

Intelligent, imaginative, restless, and critical of his superiors, Porter had decided to leave the navy once again, but the outbreak of the Civil War led him to reconsider. After seeing blockade duty, he proved an effective subordinate in Farragut's capture of New Orleans. In October 1862, Porter, now a commander, was promoted over eighty senior officers to acting rear admiral and given charge of the Mississippi Squadron. His river gunboats aggressively supported the army's operations during the Vicksburg campaign, winning the appreciation of GRANT [2] and SHERMAN [3].

Appointed to rear admiral effective July 4, 1863, Porter found cause to call upon his administrative talents during the months after Vicksburg's fall. Commanding over eighty fighting ships and overseeing operations along the entire Mississippi River and its tributaries—waterways which totaled over three thousand miles in length—he organized his command into eight districts and continued the development of the naval yards at Cairo, Illinois. Porter led the naval squadron that accompanied NATHANIEL P. BANKS [59] on his ill-fated Red River, Louisiana, campaign in 1864, extricating his ships just in time to escape being stranded by the river's falling waters.

Transferred to the North Atlantic Blockading Squadron, Porter now set his sights on Fort Fisher, which held the key to the defense of Wilmington, North Carolina. After one attempt failed, he returned in January 1865 with a fleet of sixty ships, the strongest ever assembled to date under an American flag. Some 8,000 troops, led by Major General Alfred H. Terry, accompanied the flotilla. Under cover of a heavy naval bombardment, Terry's infantrymen charged across a narrow peninsula while two thousand marines and sailors launched an amphibious attack against the works facing the sea. The naval forces suffered the brunt of the casualties (which numbered over a thousand), but Terry's soldiers captured the fort and thus opened Wilmington to Federal occupation.

Porter boasts three congressional votes of thanks, and later became superintendent of the Naval Academy. Upon the death of Farragut in 1870 he was appointed admiral, but due to the Navy Department's convoluted administrative structure he had little authority over practical operations. Porter watched in pain as the mighty navy which had helped to win America's greatest war deteriorated through lack of funding, national interest, and energy. An 1889 study ranked the United States Navy the world's twelfth most powerful, below China and Turkey and just above Austria-Hungary. Turning largely to writing in his postwar years (he published three historical works and several novels), Porter lived quietly until his death in 1891. His adroit administration and combat leadership during the Vicksburg, Red River, and Fort Fisher campaigns had been an important factor in the Union victory.

43

Charles Sumner

(1811–1874)

Charles Sumner, an antislavery senator from Massachusetts, launched some of the most vitriolic public attacks of the entire Civil War generation on slavery and Southerners. His verbal onslaughts, along with the response against him, greatly exacerbated the sectional bitterness of the 1850s. After the war, he was a vocal advocate of congressional Reconstruction, arguing that only a strong federal presence could ensure the protection of black rights and prevent the return of secessionists to power in the South. An idealistic, driven man, he championed emancipation and black rights in the face of spirited opposition and served as the uncompromising conscience of his Republican Party.

Born a year before the War of 1812, Charles Sumner came from a distinguished Boston family. He graduated from Harvard Law School in 1833. Though admitted to the Massachusetts bar, he grew bored with the routine of a daily legal practice. Standing six feet, two inches tall and possessing a deep bass voice, Sumner found politics and public speaking more to his liking. After declining a Whig nomination to Congress in 1846, he became a leader in the upstart Free Soil Party two years later.

Sumner was swept into the Senate in 1851 by a coalition of antislavery

A somewhat sensationalized contemporary portrayal of the 1856 attack on Sumner

Democrats and Free-Soilers in the Massachusetts state assembly. He would remain a senator for the rest of his life. An outspoken crusader for emancipation, Sumner became a Republican when that party was formed after the passage of the Kansas-Nebraska Act. From the Senate floor on May 19 and 20, 1856, Sumner launched into a particularly vitriolic harangue against what he labeled the "Crime Against Kansas." Proslavery raiders from Missouri, whom he described as "hirelings picked from the drunken spew and vomit of an uneasy civilization," had laid waste to Free-Soilers in Kansas. Sumner then directed his invective against South Carolina's Andrew P. Butler, characterizing his fellow senator as "a Don Quixote who had chosen a mistress to whom he has made his vows . . . the harlot, Slavery."

Butler's cousin and fellow South Carolinian, Congressman Preston Brooks, retaliated two days later. Finding Sumner alone at his Senate desk after that body had adjourned for the day, Brooks rained down blow after blow upon Sumner with his walking cane, leaving his victim a bloody pulp. Brooks paid a three hundred dollar fine and resigned his House seat, returning triumphantly to Washington after voters in his district reelected him without opposition. Well-wishers sent him dozens of souvenir canes. Traumatized by the incident, Sumner spent most of the next two-and-a-half years recovering his mental and physical well-being.

With his party suddenly thrust into power with the 1860 presidential victory of ABRAHAM LINCOLN [1], Sumner became chairman of the Senate Committee on Foreign Relations. His influence was especially strong early in the conflict, when Secretary of State WILLIAM SEWARD [8] had not yet recognized President Lincoln's abilities as a statesman. Although Sumner and Lincoln differed radically in background and temperament, they came to respect and like each other. Sumner urged Lincoln to emancipate the slaves quickly, reasoning that such an action, in addition to being morally correct, would destroy all Confederate hopes for recognition from England. The senator's proposals that blacks be granted full equality, however, went largely unheeded.

Sumner believed that by seceding, Southern states had committed "state suicide," and thus had few if any constitutional rights after the Civil War. Seeking to protect blacks, Northerners, and Unionists in the former Confederacy, Sumner adhered to the radical wing of the Republican Party and soon broke with President ANDREW JOHNSON [6] over what he believed were his overly lenient policies toward the South. The senator strongly backed conviction of Johnson following his impeachment by the House of Representatives. Later, however, Sumner's repeated denunciations of Britain's wartime assistance to the South and vigorous opposition to President ULYSSES S. GRANT [2] in his efforts to annex Santo Domingo (today's Dominican Republic) led to his ouster from the Foreign Relations Committee chairmanship.

Because he was permanently shaken by the Brooks assault of 1856, Charles Sumner considered himself a martyr for the cause of liberty. This lonely, outspoken civil rights champion married in 1866, but was separated within a year and later divorced. Uncompromising to the end, he died in Washington in 1874, and was interred at Cambridge, Massachusetts. Sumner's presence had helped blacks gain at least some federal protection during the Civil War and Reconstruction.

44

Nathan Bedford Forrest

(1821–1877)

Nathan Bedford Forrest was the war's foremost cavalry raider and was associated with some of the sectional conflict's ugliest racial incidents. Forrest's brilliant mounted operations were among the Confederacy's few bright spots in the west, where his troops bedeviled Union leaders for the last three years of the war. Forrest, a master of psychological warfare, deception, and sudden attack, nevertheless epitomized the racial hatred and bitterness which marked nineteenth-century America. In 1864, his command massacred several dozen black Union soldiers following an engagement at Fort Pillow, Tennessee. After the war, he became grand wizard of the newly formed Ku Klux Klan, a secret organization which often resorted to violence and intimidation in order to restore white rule in the South.

Born in Chapel Hill, Tennessee, in 1821, Forrest's early life was dominated by his struggles against the hardships of the Southern backcountry. On his father's death sixteen-year-old Nathan assumed responsibility for supporting his family, despite having less than a year of formal schooling. He later married and fathered two children and, after several moves, had by the early 1850s relocated to Memphis. There Forrest founded a thriving real estate and slave-trading business, establishing in the process a sizeable Mississippi plantation. He accumulated an estate valued at a quarter of a million dollars by the end of the decade; he also held several elected positions in local government.

After Tennessee's secession, Forrest, a son, and his youngest brother volunteered for the state militia as privates. Soon afterward, the governor commissioned Forrest to raise a mounted regiment. In February 1862, he distinguished himself during the Fort Donelson campaign in Tennessee, when, refusing to surrender with the rest of the garrison, he and his men cut their way through Union lines to safety. Wounded during the Battle of Shiloh, Tennessee, Forrest recovered in time to lead a cavalry raid which destroyed the strategic Federal depot at Murfreesboro, Tennessee, and disrupted the enemy's attempted summertime advance against Chattanooga, Tennessee. Commissioned a brigadier general, his performance during the offensive into Kentucky led by BRAXTON BRAGG [30] that fall was uncharacteristically lackluster.

Forrest soon recovered from this temporary malaise. In December 1862, his raids against Union communications helped to stall ULYSSES S. GRANT [2] in his early advances against Vicksburg, Mississippi. In the autumn of 1863, furious with Bragg's failure to vigorously pursue the beaten Federals following Chickamauga, Georgia, Forrest called his superior "a coward" and "a damned scoundrel," refused to obey any more of his orders, and threatened to kill him if he interfered with his request for a transfer. Forrest received his sought-after independent command, raised a new cavalry force, and over the next year raided the Federals in Alabama, Tennessee, and Mississippi. During one of these actions, his troops overran Union-held Fort Pillow, Tennessee, and murdered dozens of black troops after they had surrendered. In late fall 1864 he linked up with JOHN BELL HOOD [38] and the Army of Tennessee as it moved north following the surrender of Atlanta. In the wake of the disastrous Battle of Nashville, Tennessee, Forrest's supervision of the Confederate rearguard saved what little was left of Hood's command. In May 1865, by now a lieutenant general, Forrest surrendered at Gainesville, Alabama. He had suffered four wounds and claimed to have had twenty-nine horses shot out from under him and to have killed thirty enemy soldiers in close combat.

Profane, nearly illiterate, and fond of gambling, Forrest hoped to restore white supremacy to the South after the war. He was a principal figure in early Ku Klux Klan activities. Later, however, he repudiated some of his most virulent racist statements and actions. He died at Memphis in 1877, having never fully recovered his antebellum fortune.

Over six feet tall and 180 pounds, Forrest used his imposing physical presence to defy all challengers, Union and Confederate alike. His military success stemmed from his intuitive sense of tactics and his audacious attacks in the face of numerically superior enemy forces. WILLIAM T. SHERMAN [3] once described him as a "devil," who must "be hunted down and killed if it costs 10,000 lives and bankrupts the treasury." He used his influence to help restore whites to political dominance in the postwar South.

45

Montgomery Meigs

(1816–1892)

Popular histories of the Civil War have largely ignored Montgomery C. Meigs, for thirty-one years quartermaster general of the United States Army. Though he never saw combat, Meigs proved invaluable to the Union effort. Under his direction the Quartermaster Department spent over one billion dollars between 1861 and 1865. Though fraud and waste were unavoidable in such a massive operation, Meigs kept such excesses to a tolerable minimum. His department also did an outstanding job of supplying the Union armies. Separate from his wartime service were his many contributions to the Washington landscape; he either directed construction for or designed several of the city's major landmarks, including the Washington Aqueduct, the Capitol Dome, the National Museum, and the Pension Office building.

Born in Augusta, Georgia, in 1816, Montgomery Meigs moved with his family to Philadelphia as a child. He studied at the University of Pennsylvania before entering the U.S. Military Academy. Meigs graduated in 1836, fifth in his class of forty-nine. After a short stint with the artillery, he entered the Corps of Engineers and worked on a series of projects that included navigational improvements to the Mississippi River and Atlantic seaboard and Great Lakes fortifications.

In 1852 Meigs was charged with bringing a dependable water supply to the District of Columbia. His oversight of that project, which included the immediate need for a reliable water source and the construction of the Capitol Dome were soon added to his portfolio. In the process, Meigs occasionally allowed his pride to get the best of him, adorning the project with numerous plaques and memorials to himself and the Corps of Engineers. Meigs clashed with Secretary of War John Floyd over the latter's determination to undermine efficient construction in the interest of providing political patronage. This led to Meigs's banishment to the Dry Tortugas, where he supervised work on military fortifications.

Floyd's resignation in 1860 allowed Meigs to return to Washington. Upon the request of President ABRAHAM LINCOLN [1] and Secretary of State WILLIAM SEWARD [8], Meigs oversaw the successful relief of the Federal position at Fort Pickens, Florida. In May 1861 he was appointed quartermaster general. From this post Meigs met the massive logistical needs of the North's

The U.S. Capitol, one of Meigs's projects, under construction at Lincoln's 1861 inauguration

armies. Virtually everything except food, weapons, and ammunition came under the quartermaster's purview, including uniforms, overcoats, shoes, packs, canteens, mess gear, blankets, tents, horses, mules, forage, harness gear, horseshoes, wagons, and fuel. Wise in the ways of Washington, he used competitive bidding, rather than the more expensive cost-plus system, to fill the army's requirements.

Because of the massive purchases needed to keep the war going, Meigs left his imprint on American life in a number of ways. The concept of sizing in men's civilian clothes, for example, stemmed from his department's huge orders of uniforms in graduated standard measurements. To meet the army's enormous need for shoes—over three million pairs a year—Meigs also encouraged the large-scale mechanization of the American shoe industry.

Ironically, Meigs also demonstrated a good deal of strategic ability. He devised the blueprint for Gen. JOSEPH HOOKER [36] in his Chancellorsville, Virginia, campaign, an effort lost not because of its design but because of the inability of its executor. Meigs was also one of the first Washington officials to recognize the war's totality. As early as January 1863 he concluded that the war was "gradually assuming the aspect of a long one, to be settled by exhaustion." This could be achieved, argued Meigs, not only by encouraging Union armies to forage more liberally while in enemy territory, but also by denying such produce to the Confederates.

After the war, Meigs remained an active figure in Washington. His 1867–68 blueprints for the city's street remodeling projects, based on similar projects in Berlin and Paris, helped create magnificent thoroughfares lined with trees and gravel promenades. He demonstrated less interest, however, in continuing to reform and modernize the quartermaster bureau to fit the army's postwar needs. Married in 1841, he and his wife had seven children, four of whom lived to maturity. Meigs retired in 1882 and died ten years later.

46

John C. Frémont

(1813–1890)

Army officer, explorer, and Republican presidential candidate, John C. Frémont for a time ranked among the most prominent Americans of the mid-nineteenth century. During the 1840s he conducted several spectacular scientific explorations of the far West and played a major role in wresting California from Mexican control. His well-publicized western surveys earned him the appellation "Pathfinder." Though he lost to Democrat JAMES BUCHANAN [26] in his 1856 presidential bid, Frémont's impressive showing helped pave the way for the election of ABRAHAM LINCOLN [1] four years later. While instrumental in helping the Republican Party to achieve early political respectability, Frémont's Civil War career was largely anticlimactic. He served ineffectually as commander of troops in Missouri and the Shenandoah Valley, Virginia, and made a disastrously unsuccessful bid to challenge Lincoln's 1864 renomination.

Born in 1813 in Savannah, Georgia, Frémont as a young man came to the attention of Joel R. Poinsett, who as secretary of war secured his commission in the Corps of Topographical Engineers. Leading several surveying teams, Frémont helped open the west to the popular American imagination. He joined California's Bear Flag Revolt, remaining in public view despite a court-martial, serving as U.S. Senator from California, and leading two more surveying expeditions. In 1856 Republican elders, realizing their party had little chance of immediate victory but hoping to lay the foundation for future races, found in the handsome, youthful, Frémont an ideal presidential candidate. Somewhat surprisingly, the results demonstrated that the Republicans, by winning eleven of the sixteen free states, were already a force with which to reckon.

Frémont remained the darling of many antislavery Republicans. Upon the Civil War's outbreak he rushed home from Europe to accept a commission as major general of volunteers and commander of the Western Department, with headquarters at St. Louis. Inheriting a complex situation that would confound Union commanders for four years, Frémont found the mix of strong Southern sentiment, guerrilla warfare, and fierce political factionalism in Missouri far beyond his abilities. With military affairs deteriorating, he unilaterally declared martial law in Missouri on August 30, 1861, threatening guerrillas with the death penalty and Confederate sympathizers with confiscation of their property. Fearing that Frémont's policy was premature and would push the slave states of Missouri and Kentucky into secession, Lincoln suggested that his headstrong general soften the announcement. Frémont responded by sending his wife, Jessie, to visit the president. The move backfired; soon afterward Lincoln removed Frémont from command.

Despite the Missouri debacle, Frémont retained some political strength, so in spring 1862 Lincoln created a new military department in western Virginia for him. Once again, the Pathfinder was somewhat unlucky, for there, in the Shenandoah, he faced the brilliant STONEWALL JACKSON [20]. Outgeneraled and embarrassed, Frémont soon resigned his command. In May 1864 a splinter group of German-Americans and abolitionists, calling themselves the Radical Democrats, named him their presidential candidate, but they eventually withdrew his nomination in exchange for the resignation of the conservative postmaster general, Montgomery Blair.

Throughout his life, Frémont's greatest champion was his wife Jessie (daughter of the formidable Senator Thomas Hart Benton). Both, however, had ambitions that far outreached their abilities. Frémont was governor of the Arizona Territory between 1878 and 1881, but was unsuccessful in several speculative ventures. He died in 1890. Jessie, whose published works often supported the couple through the lean postwar years, died twelve years later.

47

Dred Scott

(1795–1858)

On April 6, 1846, Dred Scott and his wife, Harriet, filed suit in the Missouri circuit court in St. Louis, contending that they had been beaten and falsely imprisoned by Mrs. Irene Emerson. Asserting that they were free persons of color, each claimed damages of ten dollars. The suits sparked an eleven-year saga of legal challenges, resulting in Supreme Court Chief Justice ROGER B. TANEY [32] handing down the *Dred Scott* v. *Sandford* (sic) decision. The ruling that the Scotts were not citizens and could not sue inflamed and intensified the debate over slavery in the territories, helping to lead to the outbreak of war.

Dred Scott's origins remain unclear. Probably born in Southampton County, Virginia, about the turn of the century, at a young age he came to be one of Peter Blow's six slaves. Blow died in St. Louis in 1832; Scott, who

126

some contend had previously used the name of Sam, was purchased by Dr. John Emerson about the same time. Upon receiving an army appointment as assistant surgeon, Emerson took Scott with him to Fort Armstrong, Illinois, in late 1833. In 1836, Emerson was transferred to Fort Snelling, Wisconsin Territory, where Scott married Harriet Robinson.

Emerson also married and, after several transfers, returned to Fort Snelling. Upon his appointment to Florida, the doctor's wife and slaves settled down in St. Louis. Emerson died in late 1843, naming his wife's brother, John F. A. Sanford, as one of the executors of his will. By this time, Dred Scott had been assigned to work for Mrs. Emerson's brother-in-law, Captain Henry Bainbridge. After brief sojourns in Louisiana and Texas with Bainbridge, Scott returned to St. Louis in 1846. Mrs. Emerson's rejection of Dred's offer to purchase his family's freedom led the Scotts to take their case to court.

Like so much about the personal histories of Dred and Harriet Scott, the exact origins of the lawsuit remain cloudy. Dred had clearly resumed his relationship with his former owners, the Blows; Taylor Blow, who had been about twelve years old when Scott had left the family, proved an especially loyal supporter and benefactor in the latter's quest for freedom. Over the years, several lawyers represented the Scotts; their services were probably donated or given for reduced fees. There is little good evidence to support subsequent allegations that antislavery elements hoped, from the outset, to use this as a test case.

The Scotts based their assertions on the fact that they, by virtue of their stays at Forts Armstrong and Snelling, had prolonged residences in areas in which slavery was prohibited. Missouri courts had previously ruled that a slave who was taken by a master to reside in a free state or territory was thereby emancipated. Debate about the "peculiar institution" had intensified, however, and proslavery forces did not want to allow this opportunity for freedom to remain open. After losing initial cases on legal technicalities, the Scotts each won 1850 retrials in a St. Louis county court. By a two-to-one vote, however, the state supreme court overturned these decisions and remanded the Scotts to slavery. The court acknowledged earlier precedents to the contrary, but reasoned that since abolitionist attacks now posed a threat to state government, "it does not behoove the State of Missouri to show the least countenance to any measure which might gratify this spirit."

Effective control over the Scotts had by this time devolved to John Sanford, former executor of the Emerson estate. Scott's lawyers now took the case to federal district court. Judge Robert W. Wells acknowledged that Scott was a citizen and thus able to file suit, but ruled in favor of the defense. Scott's backers, now including Montgomery Blair, scion of a powerful Missouri family, appealed to the U.S. Supreme Court. Though the official Supreme Court report misspelled the defendant's name, its opinion, written by Chief Justice Taney and issued in February 1857, left no doubt as to its author's intent. As a black, Taney claimed, Scott was not a citizen and thus ineligible to file suit. Taney further ruled that the Missouri Compromise had been unconstitutional

Montgomery Blair, Scott's able attorney

and that Congress had no right to exclude slavery from the territories.

After the decision, the owners of the Scotts transferred the family to the Blows, who promptly freed them. They remained in St. Louis, where Harriet took work as a laundress and Dred as a hotel porter. Dred Scott died in September 1858. He and his wife had four children, two of whom died in infancy. Although Scott had lived just sixteen months as a free man, his long quest for liberty was an important rallying point for those who opposed slavery. Likewise, Scott's threat solidified proslavery demands that the federal government protect the institution in the territories. Since his case served as a rallying point for extremists on both sides, Dred Scott deserves recognition as one of the most important figures of the period.

48

Jay Cooke

(1821–1905)

An innovative promoter whose agents sold over a billion dollars in federal government bonds during the Civil War, Jay Cooke is often forgotten amidst the war's military drama. Yet without Cooke, the North would have suffered devastating wartime inflation. By mounting effective advertising and public relations campaigns, Cooke made government bonds attractive investments for average Americans for the first time. Indeed, largely through his vision, over six hundred thousand citizens helped to finance the war by purchasing bonds.

Born at Sandusky, Ohio, in 1821, Jay Cooke was the son of a prominent local figure and one-term congressman. Always restless, Jay left school to seek employment at age fourteen. He moved to St. Louis and became a clerk but lost his job in the Panic of 1837. Resettling in Philadelphia, where he married in 1844, Cooke handled advertising and publicity for a transportation and shipping company. He soon entered a Philadelphia banking house, eventually becoming a partner. In the wake of the Panic of 1857 he left the firm to become a venture capitalist, concentrating on canal and railroad projects.

On January 1, 1861, the Jay Cooke and Company banking house opened its doors in Philadelphia. As manager, Cooke held a two-thirds interest; a brother-in-law owned the remaining shares. Although possessing relatively small capital (actual cash reserves were probably less than $10,000), Jay Cooke and Company was uniquely positioned to take advantage of wartime economic opportunities. Its manager boasted not only a variety of financial experiences and an ambitious, confident personality, but also an important personal advantage: Cooke's brother Henry, owner and editor of the leading Republican newspaper in Ohio, was a close political associate of the new treasury secretary, SALMON P. CHASE [21]. The government's early efforts to raise money failed, but Jay Cooke stepped in and sold over $50,000,000 in three-year treasury notes in the wake of the First Battle of Bull Run, Virginia. In 1862, recognizing that the war opened lucrative possibilities in government finance, Cooke mounted a massive public relations campaign, selling another $500,000,000 worth of bonds at six percent interest. Continuing financial shortfalls in 1865 led Chase's successor as treasury secretary, William Fessenden, to appoint Cooke "fiscal agent." In less than six months, Cooke sold another $600,000,000 in three-year notes.

During the war, Jay Cooke and Company's profits totaled over $1.6 million, the vast majority of which came from its government business. The firm continued to expand after the war, opening new branch offices in New York and London. Now the country's best-known banker, Cooke remained active in both private and government financial ventures. He was especially interested in securing funding for the Northern Pacific Railroad, which would link the Great Lakes to the Pacific Ocean. But Cooke failed to foresee either the project's huge costs or the public's increasing reluctance to speculate in railroad bonds. Beset by staggering debts and unable to raise more money, Jay Cooke and Company closed its doors on September 13, 1873, precipitating a four-year-long national depression.

Eventually, the Northern Pacific Railroad was completed and Cooke recovered some of his personal fortune, emerging from bankruptcy after several lucrative western mining investments. He died in 1905.

A better promoter than investment banker, Cooke's optimism blinded him to the oncoming financial crisis of 1873. Yet his campaign to sell bonds, conducted with an evangelical fervor, gave huge numbers of investors a direct stake in the Civil War's outcome. The fact that bond sales funded two-thirds of the North's wartime costs, thus significantly reducing the dependence upon inflationary paper currency, serves as a remarkable tribute to Cooke's significance.

49

Benjamin Wade

(1800–1878)

Longtime leader of Republican Party radicals Benjamin F. Wade served eighteen tumultuous years in the United States Senate. During this time he championed abolition, the Homestead Act, and black suffrage. As chairman of the Joint Committee on the Conduct of the War and the Senate Committee on the Territories, Wade demanded that the Lincoln administration prosecute the war more vigorously and act more swiftly to end slavery. In insisting that LINCOLN [1] move to the left, Wade served as a counterweight to those on the opposite end of the political spectrum who believed the president was moving too quickly.

Benjamin Wade was born the tenth of eleven children in 1800 at Feeding Hills, Massachusetts. Although his mother introduced him to books and learning, he received little formal education as his family struggled to maintain their farm. He and his parents moved in 1821 to Andover, Ohio, where Benjamin worked as a farmer, cattle drover, and occasional schoolteacher. Admitted to the Ohio state bar in 1828, he took up residence in Jefferson and teamed up with a more prosperous partner, Joshua Giddings, to carve out a solid reputation throughout northeastern Ohio.

A frank, well-built man with intent, jet-black eyes, the pugnacious Wade became a forceful advocate for the underdog. Strongly opposed to slavery and the state's black codes, which specifically denied certain rights and liberties to black residents, he held various elected and appointed positions in Ohio until 1851, when the legislature elected him to the Senate. A Whig, Wade maintained his strident opposition to slavery, denouncing the federal fugitive slave law, passed as part of the Compromise of 1850, and the Kansas-Nebraska Act. He eagerly joined the new Republican Party, denouncing his enemies as pawns of a slaveholding conspiracy. During the secession crisis, Wade sat on the Senate Committee of Thirteen, established to investigate the possibility of some last-ditch compromise. Like President-elect Lincoln, however, Wade rejected such proposals.

In the wake of early military reversals, Congress formed the Joint Committee on the Conduct of the War, with Wade as chairman. The committee focused most of its attention on military affairs in the east, where the Army of Northern Virginia under ROBERT E. LEE [4] repeatedly bested the Army of the Potomac. Often mixing politics and the war effort, the Committee was most critical of political conservatives such as GEORGE McCLELLAN [7]. Disappointed by his own failure to win the Republican nomination in 1860, Wade never hesitated to censure the administration's policies. In one meeting with Lincoln, for example, Wade accused the president, who he believed was not prosecuting the war with sufficient vigor, of "murdering the country by inches."

Wade and Lincoln also clashed over the management and philosophy of Reconstruction. In 1864, Lincoln pocket-vetoed a measure sponsored by Wade and Congressman Henry Winter Davis that asserted congressional control over the process. Reconstruction policy was still unresolved when ANDREW JOHNSON [6] assumed the presidency. Though Johnson's verbal threats to punish all traitors initially pleased Wade, the new president's conservative policies and refusal to protect the rights of either freedmen or Unionists in the South ended the uneasy partnership. Wade supported Johnson's impeachment and conviction. Elected president pro tempore of the Senate following the landslide Republican congressional victories of 1866, Wade would have become president had Johnson been removed from office. But Wade's long public record and blunt outspokenness had made him many enemies; several contemporary observers linked the failure to convict Andrew Johnson to the fact that Benjamin Wade would have been his successor.

After three tumultuous terms in the Senate, Wade returned to his private legal practice in 1869, serving for several years as general counsel for the Northern Pacific Railroad. He died in Jefferson, Ohio, in 1878, survived by his wife and two sons. As chair of the Joint Committee on the Conduct of the War and a key figure in early Reconstruction planning, Benjamin Wade had been one of the Civil War era's most influential legislators.

50

Lyman Trumbull

(1813–1896)

Chairman of the Senate Judiciary Committee during the Civil War and Reconstruction, Lyman Trumbull sponsored the Thirteenth Amendment and the Civil Rights Act of 1866. Although Lincoln's Emancipation Proclamation declared an end to slavery in areas not yet under Union control as of January 1, 1863, the Thirteenth Amendment completed the process by abolishing slavery throughout the United States. Further, Trumbull's Civil Rights Act of 1866 conferred citizenship on blacks and guaranteed their civil rights. Often flouted for nearly a century after its passage, it nonetheless emerged as the cornerstone of numerous Supreme Court decisions in 1960s and 1970s civil rights cases.

Born in 1813 at Colchester, Connecticut, Lyman Trumbull was the seventh son of parents of moderate means. At age twenty, he became headmaster of a school in Greenville, Georgia. Like many ambitious young men of the period, Trumbull used his spare time to read law and in 1836 was admitted to the bar. He moved to Bellevue, Illinois, to begin his law practice. Among his cases were those that helped eradicate slavery in Illinois. In 1843 he married Julia Jayne, who had been a bridesmaid at the wedding of MARY TODD [53] and ABRAHAM LINCOLN [1].

Entering politics as a Democrat, Trumbull was elected to the Illinois Supreme Court in 1848. Six years later, the state legislature elected Trumbull to the U.S. Senate when his associate, Lincoln, withdrew in order to prevent the election of a Democrat who supported STEPHEN A. DOUGLAS [11] in his controversial Kansas-Nebraska Act. With Southern interests increasingly dominant within the Democratic Party, Trumbull became a Republican. Like Lincoln, Trumbull vowed to prohibit the expansion of slavery and did not advocate abolishing the institution where it already existed. Again mirroring Lincoln's position, Trumbull did not yet accept the notion of black equality, suggesting instead that colonization offered the ultimate answer to the nation's racial divisions.

Senator Trumbull often broke with President Lincoln, however, during the Civil War. Trumbull was irked by what he believed to be the president's failure to supply him with sufficient patronage-related jobs and benefits. In addition, Trumbull equated secession with treason and criticized the administration for not conducting a harsher war against the Confederacy. Over Lincoln's objections, Trumbull also championed strong confiscation measures that legalized the seizure of Confederate property, including slaves. While maintaining that the administration was not prosecuting the war with sufficient vigor, Trumbull nonetheless sought to maintain legal principle despite the urgencies of war. Thus he contested the president's use of arbitrary arrest and sought to limit suspensions of the writ of habeas corpus and opposed the legalization of Lincoln's emergency proclamations issued while Congress was in recess.

Tall, evenly proportioned, and a keen debater, Trumbull made his most lasting contributions during Reconstruction. In addition to his work in support of the Thirteenth Amendment and the Civil Rights Act of 1866, he sponsored the postwar extension of the Freedmen's Bureau, which provided schools, a separate justice system, and aid in developing employment contracts to former slaves. Angered by ANDREW JOHNSON [6] because he vetoed the latter two measures, Trumbull nonetheless sought to chart a moderate course between the president's leniency and the harsher measures advocated by congressional radicals. Believing impeachment of Johnson unfounded on legal grounds, he was among seven Republican senators who voted against the president's conviction. Shorn of his leadership role by his party and critical of the corruption within the administration of President ULYSSES S. GRANT [2], in 1872 Trumbull backed HORACE GREELEY [31] and the unsuccessful Liberal Republican revolt.

Following three tumultuous senate terms, Trumbull retired to practice law and teach part-time at the Union College Law School. He reemerged as legal counsel for Samuel J. Tilden and the Democratic Party in the disputed 1876 presidential contest and again as an unsuccessful Democratic candidate for the Illinois governorship in 1880. He died in 1896, survived by his second wife but by only one of his seven children. Lyman Trumbull's work on behalf of the Thirteenth Amendment, the Civil Rights Act of 1866, and the Freedmen's Bureau ensured that the Civil War ended slavery in the United States.

Sojourner Truth

(1797–1883)

One of the nineteenth century's most remarkable figures, an illiterate former slave, Sojourner Truth became a powerful voice for the rights of blacks and women. Standing nearly six feet tall, she proved an extraordinarily effective speaker, mixing oratorical polish with a deep voice and powerful singing as she proclaimed the virtues of evangelical Christianity and denounced the evils of slavery, alcohol, and barriers to women's rights. Though only partially successful in achieving these goals during her lifetime, her example has inspired countless thousands to speak out against inequality of both race and gender.

The woman we now call Sojourner Truth was born Isabella in Ulster County, New York, in the late 1790s. As the owners of her parents spoke Dutch, it became Isabella's native tongue. English-speaking owners who bought her when she was nine equated her inability to understand their commands with stupidity or defiance and frequently beat her. Resold twice more before she was thirteen, Isabella wound up in the hands of John and Sally Dumont. Although she was beaten by John, her later narrative reflects a certain attachment to him; by contrast, recent scholars have suggested that

Sally Dumont sexually abused her. Isabella bore five children between about 1815 and 1826, at least four to fellow slave Thomas, whom her master seems to have selected as her husband.

Slated for emancipation under New York State law in 1818, Isabella later recalled that the voice of God instructed her to seek her freedom two years early. Carrying a baby and a small cache of food and clothing, she took up residence with a family of Dutch abolitionists who paid Dumont twenty-five dollars for her services and set her free. In gratitude, Isabella adopted their last name, Van Wagenen. Here she also experienced a religious conversion and, with the financial assistance of some local Quakers, sued for the freedom of one of her sons, who had been illegally sold. Though four of her children remained indentured to the Dumonts in accord with New York law, about 1828 Isabella Van Wagenen left Ulster County for New York City, where she worked as a domestic servant. Increasingly convinced that she had a special personal relationship with God, she participated in the revivalist camp meetings that swept the country and became something of a mystic.

Certain that she had to flee the sins of New York City, on June 1, 1843, she declared herself to be Sojourner Truth and became an itinerant preacher. On her journeys she met WILLIAM LLOYD GARRISON [24] and other abolitionists, and helped support herself with sales of her *Narrative of Sojourner Truth* (1850), ghostwritten for her by Olive Gilbert. In addition to speaking out against slavery, Truth also took up the cause of women's rights. In 1851—just three years after ELIZABETH STANTON [40] had helped to organize the first woman's rights convention at Seneca Falls, New York—Truth gave her most famous address, before the Ohio Woman's Rights Conference meeting at Akron. Mixing humor with biting sarcasm, she demanded equal rights for women of all races.

By now a featured speaker throughout New England and the Midwest, Truth alternately shocked and inspired her listeners. In another famous incident, when opponents asserted that she was really a man in disguise, she defiantly bared a breast before the audience "in vindication of her truthfulness," as she later explained. Truth maintained an exhausting pace throughout the Civil War, going on the stump to raise money and supplies for black troops and meeting with President ABRAHAM LINCOLN [1] in August 1864. From 1864 to 1868, she worked in various refugee camps sponsored by the National Freedmen's Relief Association and the Freedmen's Bureau, urging ex-slaves to secure jobs and become independent of government support.

After the Civil War, Truth devoted herself to women's rights and to settling former slaves on free western land. Like her comrades in the woman's movement, she was stunned when the Fourteenth Amendment excluded women, and she opposed ratification of the Fifteenth Amendment because it failed to extend the suffrage to women. In 1880, she finally retired from public life to her home at Battle Creek, Michigan. As a symbol of hope and inspiration to so many blacks throughout the period, Sojourner Truth merits a place among the most influential leaders of the Civil War.

52

Ambrose Burnside

(1824–1881)

A better man than military officer, Ambrose Everett Burnside was one of the most spectacularly unsuccessful Union generals of the Civil War. A genial, personable figure who carved out an impressive career in business and politics after the war, Burnside's poor leadership squandered the lives of thousands of troops and helped extend the war, but his significance far transcends his military abilities.

Born in Indiana in 1824, Burnside secured through his father's influence an appointment to the U.S. Military Academy, from which he graduated in the middle of his class in 1847. He joined his artillery unit too late to see action in the Mexican War. He resigned his commission in 1853 after inventing a breech-loading rifle. Failing to make money with his new firearm, Burnside secured a job with the Illinois Central Railroad from an old army friend, GEORGE MCCLELLAN [7]. At the outset of the Civil War, Burnside organized a Rhode Island regiment; his early arrival in Washington and pleasing personality soon won the friendship of President ABRAHAM LINCOLN [1].

Unfortunately, in this case Lincoln's judgment proved poor. Troops under Burnside's command were dismal at the Battle of First Bull Run, Virginia, during which he was spotted riding at breakneck speed toward the rear—to secure reinforcements, he maintained. Still, he was commissioned a brigadier general and charged with launching an amphibious strike against several Confederate posts along the North Carolina coast, a task that he performed well. Winning general public acclaim for these achievements, Burnside was promoted to major general and dispatched to join the Army of the Potomac, where he took command of the army's right wing. Again, he performed poorly. At the Battle of Antietam, Maryland, Burnside's disjointed afternoon attacks against the Confederate flank gave the enemy time to bring up reinforcements and thus stave off disaster. The narrow Antietam Creek bridge across which his troops attacked is now known as "Burnside's Bridge."

Disappointed with General McClellan's failure to pursue the wounded army of ROBERT E. LEE [4] after Antietam, Lincoln turned to Burnside, who had rejected earlier offers of command. Saying "[I am] not fit for so big a command," Burnside accepted this latest assignment with great reluctance. His inept leadership during the Battle of Fredericksburg, Virginia, promptly proved the accuracy of his words. After several futile frontal assaults against prepared Confederate positions, the Union army broke off the action, having suffered nearly thirteen thousand casualties. Denounced by several prominent subordinates, Burnside demanded either their dismissal or his own replacement. In January 1863, Lincoln removed his old friend.

After a short leave of absence, in March Burnside assumed command of the Department of the Ohio. Here he arrested the North's most prominent opponent of the war, former congressman CLEMENT VALLANDIGHAM [73]. Burnside later successfully defended Knoxville, Tennessee, against Confederate siege. He returned to the Army of the Potomac in spring 1864 as a corps commander. Once again, he did poorly. During the siege of Petersburg, Virginia, Union miners blew a huge hole under Confederate defenses facing Burnside's lines. The attempted breakthrough at "the Crater," however, proved a disaster, for which a court of inquiry held Burnside responsible. He resigned his commission just before the war's end.

An honest man who recognized his own shortcomings, Burnside was an unimaginative, inflexible leader. His failures wasted the lives of thousands of Union soldiers. The missed opportunity to coordinate timely attacks against Lee at Antietam, for which Burnside shared responsibility with McClellan, stands as a classic example of inept generalship. In derision of his bushy facial hair and mustache, troops dubbed him "Sideburns," a term that gained popular usage. To Burnside's credit, he became a railroad president, governor of Rhode Island, and United States senator after the war, and in those capacities served his nation well.

53

Mary Todd Lincoln

(1818–1882)

Early biographers of ABRAHAM LINCOLN [1] tended to portray his wife Mary Todd as an ineffectual shrew whose Southern background blinded her to the evils of slavery and who detracted from rather than complemented her husband, but more recent accounts suggest something quite different. Though troubled late in her life by the cumulative effects of the premature deaths of her mother, father, three of four sons, and husband, Mary Todd Lincoln emerges as an enormous asset to Abraham Lincoln's rise from country lawyer to president. Indeed, newspapers coined the term, "First Lady," to describe her unusually public role during her husband's early years in the White House.

Born in Kentucky, in 1818, Mary Ann Todd descended from one of Lexington's leading families. Her mother died when Mary was only six years old; her father remarried two years later. Mary never got along with her stepmother and thus spent much of her youth in care of a grandmother. Lively and intelligent, she received an excellent education. By 1839, she was living with her sister's family at Springfield, the new Illinois state capital. There Mary met a number of rising politicians, including STEPHEN A. DOUGLAS [11]. Her leading suitor, however, was a tall, gaunt young lawyer named Abraham Lincoln. Following a stormy two-year courtship, during which Lincoln once broke off their engagement, the couple married in late 1842.

Outwardly the match seemed an odd one, as the moody, gangling Lincoln towered over the vivacious, refined Mary. During their twenty-three years of marriage, Lincoln's frequent absences and inattentiveness sometimes infuriated his temperamental wife. Yet despite their arguments (Mary once whacked her absentminded husband on the nose with a piece of firewood after he thrice failed to respond to her request that he put another log on the fire), they remained deeply in love. Though reared in an aristocratic style, Mary faithfully raised their children and handled the domestic chores of their crowded household. Scoffing at an unfavorable comparison between her husband and Douglas, Mary responded: "Mr. Lincoln may not be as handsome a figure . . . but the people are perhaps not aware that his heart is as large as his arms are long." In return, Lincoln worked long hours to raise the family's standard of living and patiently endured his wife's occasional outbursts.

Both Lincolns shared a keen interest in politics. A Whig like her husband (and like him eventually a Republican), Mary's awareness of and involvement in politics was for the time unusual, as was the decision that the entire family accompany Lincoln to Washington during his 1846–1848 stint as Illinois congressman. She always encouraged her husband to seek higher office and even tried to explain his position on slavery to friends in Kentucky.

Exhilarated by the 1860 presidential victory, Mary understood the symbolic value of an elegant executive mansion and active social schedule. Convinced that her appearance could help overcome the criticism sometimes occasioned by her husband's plebeian background, she outfitted herself at stylish East Coast shops. Glittering soirees and receptions helped to shore up the president's flagging morale during the military disappointments of the early war years. Shocked by the dilapidated condition of the White House and armed with a twenty-thousand-dollar furnishing allowance from Congress, Mrs. Lincoln transformed the crumbling thirty-one-room edifice into a public showplace. Shipments of new carpets, curtains, furniture, and wallpaper started arriving even as the Civil War began.

All acknowledged that Mary Lincoln stamped her personality on the Washington scene. Critics, however, questioned whether it was appropriate to purchase a one-hundred-ninety-piece French Limoges china service while thousands of Americans were dying. More serious, she wildly overspent her generous allowance. Her desperate efforts to keep her debt a secret by selling old furniture, and even manure from the White House stables, failed; the president was furious with Mary's incompetent handling of her budget, and would have been even more so had he learned about the personal debt she had accumulated while buying her own clothing and jewelry.

Mary's emotional health was fragile. After the death of her third son,

The box (right) at Ford's Theater in which Mary Todd Lincoln and her husband sat on the night of the assassination.

Willie, in February 1862, she sank into a deep depression (Edward, the Lincoln's second son, had died in 1850). Mrs. Lincoln wore mourning clothes for nearly a year. She hosted several White House seances in an effort to speak with the departed. Although she resumed an abbreviated schedule of public appearances in 1863, her health steadily deteriorated. Irritable, nervous, and depressed, she proved less and less effective in supporting her husband as he battled his own demons.

By asserting her control over official entertainments, directing a spectacular refurbishing of the executive mansion, urging her husband to abolish slavery, and appearing at receptions, hospitals, and army camps, Mary Todd Lincoln merits inclusion among the one hundred most influential persons of the Civil War. Her unconventional behavior and determination to expand the role of the president's wife, however, sparked great controversy. She was grief-stricken by her husband's assassination, and her increasingly erratic actions led her eldest and only surviving son, Robert, (her fourth son, Tad, had died in 1871) to attempt to declare her incompetent in 1875. Fearing a return to a mental institution, where she had been held for nearly four months during her competency trial, Mary fled to the French resort city of Pau. Poor health forced her to return to the United States, where she died from a stroke in 1882.

54

Franklin Pierce

(1804–1869)

Longtime Democratic Party loyalist Franklin Pierce defeated his Whig rival, WINFIELD SCOTT [37], in the 1852 presidential contest, carrying twenty-seven of the thirty-one states. Not until Woodrow Wilson's 1912 election would a candidate again accumulate such a preponderance of electoral votes from both North and South. The Democrats also secured comfortable majorities in both houses of Congress. Many hoped the triumph, coming on the heels of the Compromise of 1850, foreshadowed a healing of the nation's divisions. Unfortunately, Pierce, though handsome and affable, had neither the wisdom nor strength of character needed for the difficult task.

Born in 1804 at Hillsborough, New Hampshire, Franklin Pierce graduated from Bowdoin College in 1824 and became a lawyer. His father had twice been elected governor, and Franklin served four years in the state legislature and two terms in Congress. In 1837 he secured a seat in the Senate, but resigned five years later to return to his law practice. Pierce was appointed a brigadier general in the Mexican War. His active service, however, was limited by illness and a painful groin injury suffered as result of a riding accident.

A traditional Jacksonian Democrat, the "Young Hickory of the Granite

Hills" believed in limiting the federal government's influence over domestic affairs. He opposed most social reform movements, while supporting territorial expansion. His friends in the Democratic Party brilliantly managed Pierce's dark horse campaign in the 1852 party convention. He secured the nomination over several better-known rivals, including STEPHEN A. DOUGLAS [11] and JAMES BUCHANAN [26], on the forty-ninth ballot. Though opponents made light of his Mexican War experiences (Pierce was "the hero of many a well-fought *bottle*," they charged), the united Democratic Party helped him to an easy triumph in the general election.

On the eve of his inauguration, Pierce and his wife saw their only surviving son killed in a railroad accident. The distraught first lady devoted most of the next four years writing letters to their three dead sons, and the accident was a tragic foreboding of the bleak times to come. Once in office, Pierce appointed confirmed expansionists to several key diplomatic posts. Seeking to exploit the burgeoning "Young America" brand of nationalistic growth, the Pierce administration made clear its desire to acquire Cuba, encouraged American adventurers abroad, and secured from Mexico a potential route for a transcontinental railroad by purchasing the southern strip of what is now Arizona and New Mexico. Rather than uniting the nation behind this spread-eagle nationalistic fervor, however, the president's efforts reinforced growing Northern fears that expansion seemed only destined to win new areas for slavery.

A Democratic loyalist, Pierce sought above all else party unity. He seemed unable or unwilling to understand the growing Northern opposition to the expansion of slavery into new areas. The pliable Pierce supported Stephen Douglas's ill-fated Kansas-Nebraska Act, which repealed the Missouri Compromise and opened the newly created territories of Kansas and Nebraska to slavery. Northern voters reacted furiously. In the off-year congressional election of 1854, Democrats held 63 of their 67 slave-state seats, but they retained only 25 of the 91 seats they formerly held in the free states.

Hard on the heels of this political disaster, a foreign policy debacle further embarrassed the Pierce administration. In the Ostend Manifesto, three American ministers in Europe threatened Spain with force if it did not sell Cuba to the United States. This ill-timed action seemed but another blatant attempt to secure new lands for slavery; it further discredited Pierce in the eyes of many in the North. Meanwhile, angry extremists among both abolitionists and slave owners poured into Kansas; the situation deteriorated into virtual civil war as the Pierce administration lay prostrate.

Pierce tried unsuccessfully to win renomination, but the Democratic Party rejected him in favor of James Buchanan. Returning to New Hampshire, Pierce reentered public life sporadically in support of last-ditch efforts to avert the Civil War and in opposition to the administration of ABRAHAM LINCOLN [1]. He died in 1869. Among the worst of our presidents, Franklin Pierce left the nation far more divided than he had found it, and thus helped cause the Civil War.

55

Mary Chesnut

(1823–1886)

Mary Boykin Miller Chesnut, wife of a plantation owner and prominent politician, offers in her personal journals the best insider's account of Confederate society. Seven manuscript volumes of her wartime diaries, covering February–December 1861 and nearly four months of 1865, still survive. In the early 1880s Chesnut attempted to create a major work for publication, completing over twenty-five hundred manuscript pages before her death. In 1905, the Appleton Company published a heavily edited volume of her work as *A Diary From Dixie*. A second, even more altered edition, was published in 1947. Only with the 1981 publication of *Mary Chesnut's Civil War*, edited by noted historian C. Vann Woodward, did general readers get the full flavor of Chesnut's own writing.

Mary Boykin Miller was born in 1823 in Statesburg, South Carolina. Her father, Stephen Decatur Miller, owned several hundred slaves and, as governor and U.S. senator, had been a leading advocate of South Carolina's attempt to nullify a federal tariff during the Jackson administration. At seventeen, Mary Miller married James Chesnut Jr., who had recently inherited one of the most valuable estates in South Carolina. The two made their home south of Camden at Mulberry Plantation, and by the late 1840s had accumulated over five hundred slaves.

Unlike Mary's father, James Chesnut was a political moderate. He served twelve years in the state legislature before becoming a United States senator in 1858. Mary and he moved to Washington, where they became part of the nation's social elite. Upon the election of ABRAHAM LINCOLN [1] as president they returned to South Carolina to help support secession. James Chesnut was elected to the first Confederate Congress and acted as aide to P. G. T. BEAUREGARD [35] during the Fort Sumter, South Carolina, siege and First Bull Run, Virginia, campaign. Though Chesnut lost his congressional seat that fall, he served on the South Carolina Executive Council until fall 1862, when he joined the staff of President JEFFERSON DAVIS [5]. He and Mary moved to Richmond, returning to South Carolina two years later when Chesnut became a brigadier general of reserves.

Well educated and childless, Mary Chesnut began keeping a wartime

North view of Mulberry, Chesnut Plantation, South Carolina

diary in February 1861. With an eye to history, she recorded the comings and goings of the Confederacy's leading luminaries as well as slaves and plain folk. A close friend of Davis and his wife, Varina, Chesnut defended the Confederate president and blasted those who failed to meet her standards of patriotism. Featuring contemporary gossip, rumors, quarrels, romances, literary and historical references, and personal experience and insights, her diaries remain the most illuminating account of Confederate life behind the lines during the Civil War.

Countless historians have used Chesnut's account as a source for their studies of life within the Confederacy. Witty and talented, she chafed at the limits placed on women during the nineteenth century. Her husband's concept of honor, which prevented him from openly seeking the offices and appointments she believed he deserved, often left her frustrated. "Why was I born so frightfully ambitious?" she wondered in her original entry for August 16, 1861, when James remained in the Confederate Senate rather than taking the more glamorous step of joining the army. "Oh that I were a man!" she exclaimed that October. Always opinionated, Mary hated slavery and equated the plight of slaves to that of women: "There is no slave, after all, like a wife," she proclaimed in the 1880s version of her manuscript.

After the war, the Chesnuts returned home to ruined plantations and legal entanglements. James remained in politics and Mary ran the household, setting up a small dairy business to provide needed cash. Her husband died after a stroke in 1885; a heart attack killed Mary the following year. Her diaries offer an unrivaled glimpse of day-to-day life among the Southern aristocracy, and help us understand the war's impact upon the Confederacy.

56

Edmund Kirby Smith

(1824–1893)

Edmund Kirby Smith commanded the Confederacy's Trans-Mississippi Department from early 1863 through the end of the Civil War. On being transferred to this post, which encompassed all Confederate territories west of the Mississippi River, he reportedly asked: "Am I thus to be sent into exile?" Although far from the larger campaigns in Virginia, Tennessee, Mississippi, and Georgia, his responsibilities were huge and difficulties great. Hampered by shortages of men and material, Kirby Smith did a credible job organizing the area into a virtually autonomous region often called "Kirby-Smithdom."

The son of Joseph Lee Smith and Frances Marvin Kirby, Edmund Smith was born in St. Augustine, Florida, in 1824. Groomed for a military career, he entered West Point in 1841 and overcame extreme nearsightedness to graduate twenty-fifth in a class of forty-one four years later. Smith fought in the Mexican War, winning brevet promotions after Cerro Gordo and Contreras. He adopted the name Kirby Smith in tribute to a brother, known as "Kirby" to his family, who died during the Mexican War. Kirby Smith then taught mathematics at West Point and commanded the military escort for the Mexican Boundary Commission, also acting as the expedition's botanist.

In 1855 he was promoted to captain and transferred to the newly created Second Cavalry Regiment. Stationed in Texas and New Mexico, he excelled as a cavalryman. Wounded fighting Indians in New Mexico in 1859, he was advanced to major the following year.

Kirby Smith resigned his commission after his native Florida's secession from the Union. His military experience proved invaluable. After serving as chief of staff to JOSEPH E. JOHNSTON [12], Kirby Smith commanded a brigade that arrived just in time to help win the First Battle of Bull Run, Virginia, and suffered a serious wound in the process. While recuperating at nearby Lynchburg, Virginia, he met and married Cassie Selden, with whom he would have eleven children.

In early 1862 Kirby Smith assumed command of the Department of East Tennessee, Kentucky, North Georgia, and Western North Carolina. That fall, in conjunction with BRAXTON BRAGG [30], he marched into Kentucky, won the Battle of Richmond there, and temporarily cleared the Cumberland Gap of Federal troops. Occupying Lexington, Kentucky, and even threatening Cincinnati, Kirby Smith had to fall back into Tennessee as Bragg retreated following the inconclusive Battle of Perryville, Kentucky. Like many fellow Confederates, he sharply criticized Bragg's management.

Despite the failure of the Kentucky offensive, Kirby Smith emerged with his own reputation intact. Another promotion left him second in seniority among all Confederate lieutenant generals, behind only JAMES LONGSTREET [19]. In 1863 President JEFFERSON DAVIS [5] sent Kirby Smith west to take charge of the Trans-Mississippi Department. The move proved a good one. Kirby Smith was a hard worker and good organizer but was dismayed by the lack of resources at his disposal. His admiration for Davis became an especially valuable asset after the fall of Vicksburg, Mississippi, severed direct communications with Richmond. In February 1864 he was promoted to the rank of full general. From his headquarters, located variously at Alexandria and Shreveport, Louisiana, and Marshall, Texas, Kirby Smith strove to fend off Union offensives as well as set up the rudiments of government and cooperate, as best he could, with other Confederate officials. Under his direction, the Trans-Mississippi Department established a postal system, levied taxes, and conscripted men for military duty.

With the surrender of the major Confederate armies by Lee and Johnston, Kirby Smith initially vowed to continue the struggle until President Davis made his way west. Finally convinced the cause was hopeless, Kirby Smith signed surrender terms at Galveston, Texas, on June 2, 1865. He then went to Mexico and later Cuba in hopes of establishing a colony of Confederate exiles, but in November 1865 returned to the United States. After brief forays into the insurance and telegraph businesses, he set up a military school in Kentucky before becoming president of the University of Nashville in 1870. He resigned five years later to teach mathematics at the University of Sewanee, where he remained for eighteen years. Edmund Kirby Smith died at Sewanee in 1893, the last surviving full general of either army.

57

Irvin McDowell

(1818–1885)

Irvin McDowell had the misfortune of being appointed to command the Union army assembled south of the Potomac River in the opening stages of the Civil War. As a career military officer, he recognized that his troops were not ready for a major battle. Under pressure from President ABRAHAM LINCOLN [1] and other government officials, however, McDowell was forced into action prematurely. The resulting defeat at the First Battle of Bull Run, Virginia, shattered his public reputation; more important for the Union war effort, the disastrous beginning set a somber tone for future Federal activities in the east.

Born at Columbus, Ohio, in 1818, McDowell graduated twenty-third in his 1838 class of forty-five cadets from the U.S. Military Academy. Following a tour of duty along the Canadian border, he returned to West Point from 1841 to 1845 as adjutant and tactical instructor. McDowell served as aide-de-camp to Gen. John Ellis Wool during the war against Mexico, winning a brevet promotion for his actions in the Battle of Buena Vista. He remained on staff duty after the war, serving in various departmental headquarters and War Department bureaus until 1858, when he was detailed to Europe as a military observer.

At the outbreak of war between North and South, McDowell held the rank of major and was serving on the staff of Lt. Gen. WINFIELD SCOTT [37]. Boasting twenty years' military experience, McDowell enjoyed the confidence of his nation's highest-ranking military officer. His lengthy service in Washington had also endeared him to several congressmen and cabinet officers. Appointed brigadier general, he assumed command of the Department of Northeastern Virginia and with it the largest Union field command. He worked energetically to transform this mob into an army; pushed by Lincoln and others, McDowell drew up an ambitious plan to outflank a Confederate force assembling at Centreville, Virginia.

Thirty-seven thousand men strong, McDowell's forces enjoyed a decided advantage over the twenty thousand Confederates, commanded by P. G. T. BEAUREGARD [35], in his front. But to preserve this numerical superiority, another Union force, led by the aged general Robert Patterson, had to prevent thirteen thousand additional Confederates under JOSEPH E. JOHNSTON [12] from linking up with Beauregard. Patterson failed, and most of Johnston's troops arrived in time to reinforce Beauregard.

With limited military intelligence available, McDowell nonetheless attacked on July 21. His plan called for a feint against the Confederate center, followed by what he hoped would be a crushing blow against the enemy left flank and rear. The plan was a good one, depriving Beauregard of the defensive advantage of Bull Run Creek and the field fortifications he had constructed in his army's front. Initially, McDowell's assault went well, but his green troops quickly tired and lost their unit integrity. The enemy rallied around the stand of Virginians under STONEWALL JACKSON [20], and a subsequent Southern counterattack drove the Union forces from the field in disarray.

McDowell was held responsible for the defeat. Relegated to a corps command, he did poorly in the Second Battle of Bull Run, Virginia, where he was falsely accused of drunkenness, incompetence, and treason. Cleared of these charges, McDowell was in 1864 assigned to command the Department of the Pacific, where he devoted most of his attentions to dealing with the Mormons in Utah and coordinating campaigns against the Indians. Following the war, he served effectively as commander of the Departments of the East, the South, and the Division of the Pacific. He retired from the army in 1882 and died three years later.

The hospitable McDowell was a teetotaller who compensated by consuming massive amounts of food. His inability to remember faces and names made it difficult for him to inspire personal loyalty among even those who respected his military professionalism. His lack of combat command experience prior to the Civil War also proved a serious defect. Given the situation, he nonetheless did about as well as could reasonably be expected at First Bull Run. After the war, many Union generals, including Grant, believed McDowell had been unfairly blamed for the defeat.

58

Benjamin Butler

(1818–1893)

Alawyer by profession, Benjamin F. Butler was the Union's most conspicuous political general. By appointing Butler, a prominent Democrat, to
important military positions, President ABRAHAM LINCOLN [1] helped unite a
divided Northern society. Naming men with little military training or experience was dangerous, a conclusion established by Butler's poor wartime
record.

Born in New Hampshire in 1818, Butler moved with his widowed
mother to Massachusetts at an early age, where he became a schoolteacher
and a prominent criminal lawyer. Entering politics as a Jacksonian Democrat,
he was elected to the Massachusetts state house in 1852. Butler also gained
a brigadier generalship in the state militia, largely by virtue of his political
stature. As a delegate to the 1860 Democratic National Convention, he ini-

tially supported the nomination of JEFFERSON DAVIS [5] for president. Later, Butler backed JOHN C. BRECKINRIDGE [60], the candidate of the party's southern wing.

When war erupted, however, Butler sided with the Union. In April, his troops seized control of and repaired railroad lines connecting Washington and Annapolis; the following month, he occupied Baltimore and declared that he would brook no secessionist opposition. For his services in securing Union control over Maryland, a slave state which had not seceded, Lincoln rewarded Butler with an appointment as major general of volunteers. But Butler's order declaring escaped slaves who had come to his camps as "contraband of war" caused concern, and his reputation was damaged by the unsuccessful skirmish at Big Bethel, Virginia, in June 1861. He did better that August by occupying Confederate fortifications off the Hatteras Inlet, North Carolina.

In April 1862, DAVID G. FARRAGUT [13] ran his fleet past the forts guarding New Orleans, thus opening the South's largest city to Federal occupation. Commanding the fifteen thousand troops which followed the navy, Butler entered the Crescent City on May 1. As the city's military governor, he proved competent if controversial. With his troops greatly outnumbered by the city's secessionist population, Butler hoped to overawe the masses by making examples of a few. A man who tore down the flag over the U.S. Mint was hanged; after a woman jettisoned the contents of a chamber pot off her balcony onto Farragut's head, Butler threatened to treat women who insulted his troops as prostitutes. Such actions made Butler one of the most hated men in the South; known as the "Beast" by some New Orleanians, others derisively referred to him as "Spoons" for allegedly stealing silver tableware from a private home. More substantive were charges that he and his brother profited from the sales of confiscated property. Tired of the controversies, Lincoln replaced him in December 1862 with NATHANIEL P. BANKS [59].

Butler nonetheless remained a powerful political figure. Both Lincoln and his chief rival for the upcoming Republican presidential nomination, SALMON P. CHASE [21], reportedly promised him a vice-presidential slot in return for his support. Privately angling for top billing from a major political party, Butler instead accepted Lincoln's offer of command of the Department of Virginia and North Carolina in late 1863. Early the following year Butler's Army of the James, consisting of nearly forty thousand men, attempted to move up the James River to isolate Richmond from the south. But he moved too slowly, allowing the Confederates to seal up his army between the James and Appomattox rivers, in the words of U. S. GRANT [2], "as if it had been in a bottle strongly corked."

Dispatched with 3,500 troops to quell anticipated election day riots in New York City in November 1864, Butler once again handled the task of dealing with troublesome civilians with aplomb. He repeated his oft-demonstrated inability to lead troops in combat situations later that year in an unsuccessful attempt to capture Fort Fisher, North Carolina. After his reelec-

tion Lincoln no longer had to bow to political concerns, and Butler, whom
Lincoln once characterized as being "as full of poison gas as a dead dog," was
removed from military command. After the war, Butler returned to politics.
He was elected to Congress and served as governor of Massachusetts, having
presented himself at various times as a Democrat, Republican, and Green-
backer. In 1884 he ran unsuccessfully as the Antimonopoly and Greenback
Party candidate for president. He died in 1893.

Butler's flirtation with so many different political parties suggests that
ambition and the quest for the presidency drove his decisions. His suspicious
appearance—balding head, seedy mustache, and cocked left eye—did nothing to allay the fears of anxious contemporaries. Yet despite all his faults, this
political general represented an important part of the multifaceted Union
coalition which won the Civil War.

*Union officers faced a crowd of hostile citizens when they landed to demand the
surrender of New Orleans.*

59

Nathaniel P. Banks

(1816–1894)

Nathaniel Prentiss Banks was one of the most controversial figures of the Civil War. He owed his Civil War appointments to his political connections. After compiling a mediocre record leading Union troops in Virginia in 1862, he was transferred to command the military Department of the Gulf, which encompassed much of occupied Louisiana. In this position he sought to subdue Texas, but despite enjoying superiority in numbers and resources, Banks proved unable to capture significant chunks of it. He also received sharp criticism from abolitionists for failing to act more swiftly to abolish the old plantation economy of southern Louisiana.

In 1853, Banks served as president of the Massachusetts constitutional convention and was elected to Congress. Opposed to the expansion of slavery, he won reelection, this time on the ticket of the American Party (Know-Nothing). After forging a coalition with the newly established Republican Party, in early 1856 Banks was elected house speaker on the one hundred thirty-third ballot. The following year Banks, now a Republican, defeated a three-term incumbent for the Massachusetts governorship.

Upon the outbreak of the Civil War, Banks accepted an offer from President ABRAHAM LINCOLN [1] to become a major general of volunteers. Although Banks had no military experience, he helped transfer reliable Massachusetts volunteers to quell secessionist threats in the state of Maryland, and received command of the Department of the Shenandoah, in Virginia. There, in the spring of 1862, he tangled with Confederate troops led by STONEWALL JACKSON [20]. Despite enjoying numerical superiority, Banks was baffled by Jackson's marches up and down the Shenandoah Valley. Banks somewhat redeemed himself later that summer during the Second Bull Run campaign, when he nearly won a sharp fight at Cedar Mountain, Virginia, against his old nemesis, Jackson.

In December 1862 Banks replaced BENJAMIN BUTLER [58] in command of the Department of the Gulf, with headquarters at New Orleans, Louisiana. The following spring, he pushed up the Mississippi River to Port Hudson, which surrendered only after the fall of Vicksburg. Under pressure to mount at least a token threat to Maximilian's French-sponsored coup in Mexico, Banks spent the remainder of the year probing the Texas Gulf coast. After one Federal invasion force was thwarted at Sabine Pass, Texas, Banks, hoping to interdict the cotton trade into Mexico, captured Brownsville, Texas.

Banks had long hoped to strike against Mobile, Alabama, the Confederacy's last major Gulf port. Although ULYSSES S. GRANT [2] agreed with Banks, HENRY HALLECK [27] instead insisted upon a move up the Red River into cotton-rich western Louisiana and eastern Texas. Banks, however, bungled the job again. Boasting thirty thousand men and aided by a strong river flotilla, he enjoyed a nearly two-to-one numerical superiority over Confederate forces led by RICHARD TAYLOR [78]. Taylor dealt Banks a major setback at the Battle of Mansfield, Louisiana. Union troops fended off another Confederate attack the next day at Pleasant Hill, Louisiana, but the absence of expected reinforcements from Arkansas and the falling waters of the Red River, which threatened to strand the Union gunboats, unnerved Banks, who retreated back to southern Louisiana.

As commander of an occupied territory Banks also had enormous social, economic, and political responsibilities. To restore a semblance of prosperity to southern Louisiana, he forced most of the region's former slaves back to their old plantations under a contract labor system. Criticized by those who feared that this too closely resembled slavery, Banks had at least ensured the formal demise of the "peculiar institution" and supervised labor conditions reasonably well. As military governor, he also engineered the election of a moderate civilian government in Louisiana suitable to President Lincoln.

It is for these acts, rather than for his military failures, that Banks merits his ranking among the most influential persons of the Civil War. After the Confederacy collapsed, Banks returned to politics and served four terms as a Republican member of Congress. He bolted the party in 1872, regaining his seat two years later as a Democrat. Banks then returned to the Republican fold, sandwiching congressional victories in 1876 and 1888 around his tenure as United States marshal for Massachusetts. He died in 1894.

60

John C. Breckinridge

(1821–1875)

A handsome, elegant figure who at age thirty-five was elected vice president of the United States, John C. Breckinridge was also the unsuccessful Southern Democratic candidate for president in 1860. Though he had earlier favored abolition, Breckinridge was by then asserting that the federal government had to protect slavery in the territories. A former Unionist and one of the South's most respected mid-nineteenth century figures, Breckinrige, by his demands of 1860, demonstrated the gaping division between even moderate Northern and Southern leaders on the eve of the Civil War. Defeated by ABRAHAM LINCOLN [1], Breckinridge eventually cast his lot with the Confederacy. Rising to the rank of major general, late in the war he became the last and most competent Confederate secretary of war.

The grandson of Thomas Jefferson's attorney general, John Cabell Breckinridge was born near Lexington, Kentucky, in 1821. He graduated from Centre College in 1839 and was admitted to the state bar at age twenty. Breckinridge ventured west to Iowa for two years before opening his legal practice in Lexington. During the war with Mexico, he was commissioned a major in the Kentucky volunteers, but saw no action. He entered politics in 1849 as a Democrat, winning a term in the state legislature and two terms in Congress. Impressed by his oratorical skills and personal charm, the Democratic National Convention selected him as the vice-presidential running mate of JAMES BUCHANAN [26] in 1856. Breckinridge, however, rarely influenced the new administration's policies, and the president did not invite him to a private meeting for three and a half years.

In December 1859 the Kentucky legislature selected Breckinridge for the United States Senate, the term to begin when he completed his tenure as vice president. Alarmed by the Republican Party's growing political power and the raid of JOHN BROWN [14] on Harpers Ferry, Breckinridge now began preaching the need to ensure the protection of slavery in the territories. In the summer of 1860 Southern Democrats nominated him for the presidency. Still, he hoped to preserve the Union, and supported a deal in which he and two rival candidates—STEPHEN A. DOUGLAS [11] (representing most Northern Democrats) and John Bell (nominee of the new Constitutional Union Party)—would withdraw in hopes that their supporters might unite behind a single candidate and defeat the Republican, ABRAHAM LINCOLN [1]. The deal was never consummated, and even if it had been, reuniting the old Democratic coalition would have been difficult. Knowing his defeat was certain, Breckinridge nonetheless resolved to carry on. He received nearly nine hundred thousand votes and carried eleven southern and border states.

After the election, Breckinridge still hoped to prevent secession. He served in the Senate, defending Southern interests, until Union troops began entering Kentucky. In October 1861 he resigned from the Senate; in the next month he helped organize a provisional state government and joined the Confederate army.

Despite his lack of military training, Breckinridge proved a capable commander. He fought at Shiloh, Stones River, Chickamauga, and Missionary Ridge. Like virtually every other general officer in the Confederate Army of Tennessee, he detested BRAXTON BRAGG [30], who in turn charged that Breckinridge had been drunk at Missionary Ridge. Breckinridge then assumed command of troops in southwestern Virginia. He defeated Union troops led by Franz Sigel in the Battle of New Market, Virginia, in May 1864, then fought at Cold Harbor, Virginia, and with JUBAL EARLY [81] in the Shenandoah Valley. On February 4, 1865, President JEFFERSON DAVIS [5] named Breckinridge his secretary of war. Unlike his predecessors, Breckinridge asserted himself: He played a major role in convincing Davis not to resort to guerrilla tactics in the war's final days.

Breckinridge fled the country after the fall of the Confederacy. After spending time in Cuba, Europe, and Canada, he returned to the United States upon the Christmas 1868 proclamation of a general amnesty by President ANDREW JOHNSON [6]. Breckinridge opposed the Ku Klux Klan and supported reconciliation with the North. He died in 1875. Like that of his fellow Kentuckian, JOHN CRITTENDEN [88], Breckinridge's family was cruelly divided by the Civil War: While he and his three sons fought for the Confederacy, two of his cousins remained loyal to the Union. One of those cousins had two sons who served with the Union and two who joined the Confederate Army.

61

Thaddeus Stevens

(1792–1868)

United States congressman and political leader Thaddeus Stevens was once depicted as an evil, vindictive man responsible for humiliating the South during Reconstruction. His reputation among historians, however, has steadily risen during the last two decades. An uncompromising defender of racial equality, the irascible Stevens is now seen in a more favorable light as an advocate of civil rights and economic reform.

Thaddeus Stevens was born in Danville, Vermont, in 1792. While Thaddeus was still a youth, his father disappeared, leaving his mother to care for her four small boys. Sickly, born with a clubfoot, and coming from humble beginnings, Stevens always professed special sensitivities toward outsiders and the oppressed. Despite his family's struggles, Stevens attended Dartmouth College and graduated in 1814. After practicing law for ten years at Gettysburg, Pennsylvania, he acquired part-ownership of an iron manufacturing company. Stevens was elected to the Pennsylvania legislature in 1833 as an Anti-Mason. Serving until 1841, he advocated free public education and defended the protective tariff as a necessary means of shielding not only his own industry but also the jobs of his employees.

Elected to Congress as a Whig from 1849 to 1853 and a Republican from 1858 to 1868, Stevens denounced slavery, slaveowners, and anyone who advocated compromise on the question with invective rarely heard on the House floor. Slavery was "a curse, a shame, and a crime"; any legislation which allowed the expansion of slavery into the territories or which attempted to conciliate Southern interests stank of "the coward breath of servility and meanness." He was acknowledged the most radical member of the Republican Party. The delay of ABRAHAM LINCOLN [1] in ending slavery and his caution in confiscating rebel property were, in Stevens's view, unacceptable, and the congressman made clear his disgust with such temporizing.

An advocate of black suffrage, Stevens also denounced the restoration policies of Presidents Lincoln and JOHNSON [6] as too lenient toward the South. He contended that former Confederates, by raising arms against their country, were traitors who had forfeited all their constitutional rights. The South should be treated as a "conquered province." Stevens further recognized that unless substantive changes occurred in the South, readmission of the former Confederate states would weaken or eliminate altogether the Republican majority in Congress. He thus took a leading role in the passage of military reconstruction, the Fourteenth and Fifteenth amendments, the impeachment of Johnson, and the extension of the Freedmen's Bureau. Stevens also hoped Congress would carve up old plantations among former slaves, but such a move proved too radical for his colleagues.

Stevens was honest, courageous, intensely partisan, a master of parliamentary tactics, and an effective Republican Party floor leader. As chairman of the House Ways and Means Committee during the Civil War, he shepherded through several key economic measures, including the income tax, the use of paper currency, and the widespread sale of government bonds to help finance the war. His view of Reconstruction also reflected his determination to protect the underprivileged and unrepresented. Better than most, Stevens understood that unless freedmen were assured equal access to land and jobs, whites would continue to dominate Southern life.

Stevens never married and lived for years with a black housekeeper. Reviled by white Southerners, he refused either to confirm or deny rumors that the relationship was less than proper. Stevens was buried in a small, integrated cemetery in Lancaster, Pennsylvania, a highly unusual move for the time and a lasting testimony to his belief in the "Equality of Man before his Creator."

62

John Pope

(1822–1892)

Dismissed by some Civil War enthusiasts as the hapless loser of the Second Battle of Bull Run, Virginia, John Pope had a major impact on the war in the west. As one of the chief architects of the war's campaigns against the Northern Plains Indians, Pope's views gradually shifted from advocating extermination of the tribes to a more reasoned policy, which acknowledged that corruption had made fair dealings with the Indians virtually impossible. Dashing and handsome, he also held several important commands during Reconstruction and the post–Civil War conflicts against the Indians.

Born in Louisville, Kentucky, in 1822, Pope lived most of his youth in Illinois, where his father, Nathaniel, became a prominent political figure. John graduated from the U. S. Military Academy in 1842, ranked in the top third of his class. He saw duty in Florida and served with Zachary Taylor's army in the Mexican War, where he won one brevet promotion. Pope then played a leading role in surveying the Red River Valley of the North and the arid Southwest.

Pope served as one of four military representatives who accompanied President-elect ABRAHAM LINCOLN [1] from his Springfield, Illinois, home to his inauguration. Pope secured an appointment as brigadier general of volunteers in May 1861 and was ordered to Missouri, where he helped to organize Unionist elements against pro-Southern guerrillas. In early 1862 he took command of the Army of the Mississippi. In this role Pope again did well, pushing down the Mississippi River and forcing the Confederates to abandon New Madrid, Missouri, and strong positions on Island No. 10, which guarded an S-bend on the river. Boosted by appointments to major general of volunteers and brigadier general of regulars, as well as by favorable reporting from journalists who accompanied his campaign, Pope's star indeed shone bright.

At the end of the unsuccessful Peninsula campaign in Virginia of GEORGE MCCLELLAN [7], Lincoln transferred Pope east to command the newly formed Army of Virginia. The bombastic Pope promptly alienated the men of his new command by comparing them unfavorably to troops in the west. He was outgeneraled by ROBERT E. LEE [4] at the Second Battle of Bull Run, Virginia. Seeking a scapegoat for the debacle, Pope brought charges against Gen. Fitz-John Porter for disobedience, disloyalty, and misconduct against the enemy. Porter was found guilty and cashiered, but spent the next twenty years clearing his name. The factions created by the Porter-Pope feud would divide the army for a generation.

Whatever the validity of Pope's charges against Porter, Second Bull Run had been an unmitigated Federal disaster. Lincoln exiled Pope to the Department of the Northwest, then embroiled in the Sioux War of 1862. From this new command, headquartered in St. Paul, Minnesota, Pope initially spoke of "exterminating" hostile Sioux. Pressed by more serious emergencies against the Confederates, Union officials never gave Pope the manpower or supplies he desired, and his offensives of 1863, 1864, and 1865, though expanding the growing white influence in Minnesota, the Dakotas, and Montana, never provided the crushing blows he envisioned.

Given command of the sprawling Division of the Missouri in early 1865, Pope came to understand better the complexities of Indian-white relations. Frustrated by the nefarious influence of self-interested politicians and the corruption-riddled Indian Bureau, he proposed the transfer of Indian affairs from the Interior to the War Department. The army, Pope reasoned, would provide the security and honest dealing needed to reform Indian relations. Though gaining the support of numerous military officials, Pope's proposals were never fully implemented.

Following Appomattox, Pope headed several key commands, including the Third Military District (Georgia, Alabama, and Florida), the Department of the Lakes, the Department of the Missouri, and the Division of the Pacific. Late in his career he developed into an effective military administrator. Against Robert E. Lee's tactical genius, however, Pope had been no match.

63

Oliver O. Howard

(1830–1909)

Union general and commissioner of the Bureau of Refugees, Freedmen, and Abandoned Lands, commonly referred to as the Freedmen's Bureau, Oliver Otis Howard left a mixed Civil War legacy. As a military officer, Howard, though brave in battle, was only a mediocre general. He was, however, one of few high-ranking Northern officers who truly sympathized with the concerns of blacks during and after the Civil War. As such, Howard was a logical choice to head the Freedmen's Bureau, which Congress established in March 1865 to supervise the federal government's assistance programs for former slaves.

Howard was born at Leeds, Maine, in 1830. After his father's death in 1839, he was raised by an uncle. He graduated from Bowdoin College in 1850 and entered the U.S. Military Academy, from which he graduated four years later, fourth in his class. For the remainder of the decade he held various regular army posts, in the meantime marrying and fathering two children. Accepting a position with the Maine volunteers at the onset of the Civil

War, Howard lost his right arm as a result of a wound suffered at the Battle of Fair Oaks, Virginia; he would receive the Medal of Honor for his heroism in 1893. Howard returned to active duty two months later, in time to participate in the Second Battle of Bull Run, Virginia. Later that year, he fought in the battles of Antietam, Maryland, and Fredericksburg, Virginia.

Howard's personal courage, combined with the support he received from Maine politicians, led to his rapid promotion. By March 1863 he commanded the XI Corps, Army of the Potomac. During the Battle of Chancellorsville, Virginia, his corps held the army's left flank. Howard ignored indications that an attack was imminent, thus allowing the Confederates under STONEWALL JACKSON [20] to catch XI Corps completely by surprise. Although Howard gamely attempted to rally his command, he bears much of the responsibility for the shattering Union defeat there. He failed to restore his flagging reputation in the Battle of Gettysburg, Pennsylvania, when his corps retreated during the first day's fighting.

In September 1863 Howard was transferred to the western theater. His West Point pedigree, intelligence, and devotion to the Union cause gained the attention of WILLIAM T. SHERMAN [3], who named him to lead a corps in the Army of the Tennessee. A grateful Howard proved extremely loyal to Sherman, a characteristic that the latter believed outweighed his subordinate's mediocre combat record. Indeed, after the death of James B. McPherson, Sherman selected Howard to command the Army of the Tennessee, which he led during the final stages of the Atlanta campaign and throughout the March to the Sea.

Near the war's conclusion, President ANDREW JOHNSON [6] appointed Howard to head the newly created Freedmen's Bureau. A pious teetotaller who genuinely cared for blacks, Howard nonetheless faced major obstacles in his new post. The president, for example, prevented him from fully redistributing abandoned Southern lands among the former slaves. With less than a thousand field agents, many of whom did not share their commissioner's zeal, the bureau found it difficult to effectively provide educational opportunities, resolution of contract disputes, or courts for its charges. Although he personally was exonerated, Howard's administration was plagued by charges of corruption. Much discredited, the power of the Freedmen's Bureau was gradually reduced until its abolition in 1872.

Howard, meanwhile, continued to press for social reform. He was instrumental in the establishment of a college for black people in Washington, D.C., which was named Howard University in his honor. After serving as that institution's first president, Howard resumed his active military duties, acting as a peace agent in talks with the Apache Indians for the Grant administration. In 1877, while commanding the Department of the Columbia, Howard participated, again without distinction, in the campaign against Chief Joseph and the Nez Percés. Resigning in 1894, he continued to write (he authored nine books and numerous magazine articles), to lecture, and to support the Republican Party until his death in 1909.

Stephen Mallory

(1811–1873)

Confederate Secretary of the Navy Stephen Mallory is recognized as one of the ablest cabinet members of President JEFFERSON DAVIS [5]. Mallory designed two strategies for breaking the Union naval blockade that threatened supply lines vital to Southern success. First, he directed the construction and purchase of commerce raiders that might destroy enough Northern merchant vessels to draw off Federal warships otherwise assigned to blockade duty, thus rendering the blockade ineffective. The second stratagem was more visionary. Rather than complementing his merchant raiders with traditional wooden ships, Mallory hoped that powerful ironclad vessels might counter the enemy's superior numbers and break the blockade. Unfortunately for Mallory, the Confederacy devoted neither the technological resources nor the money necessary to secure enough reliable ironclads to defeat the North. Although Confederate seamen such as RAPHAEL SEMMES [93] destroyed large

163

The Virginia *and the* Monitor *(foreground) exchange gunfire off Hampton Roads, Virginia, March 9, 1862, in the first battle between ironclad warships.*

numbers of Union merchant ships, the North stubbornly maintained its blockade.

Stephen Russell Mallory was born at Trinidad, British West Indies, in 1811. After his father's death just two years later, Stephen's mother opened a boardinghouse in Key West, Florida. Despite having less than four years' formal education, Mallory became a lawyer and held several government positions in the Key West area. Married to the daughter of a wealthy Pensacola family, he was elected to the United States Senate as a moderate Democrat in 1851. Appointed chair of the Senate Committee on Naval Affairs, he worked tirelessly to improve the U.S. Navy. In addition to helping force the navy to retire overage and ineffective officers, Mallory also pressed for development of an iron-encased floating battery, but failed to secure sufficient funding to complete the craft.

Mallory urged conciliation following the 1860 election of ABRAHAM LINCOLN [1], but he had long been a champion of Southern interests, and, when it became clear that Florida would secede, he resigned his Senate seat. With the formation of the Provisional Government of the Confederate States of America, President Jefferson Davis selected Mallory as secretary of the navy. The choice seemed natural: The two were personal friends; Davis needed a Floridian in his cabinet; and Mallory had as much naval expertise as any other prominent Southern politician.

Mallory faced an enormously difficult task. During the early weeks of the war, the Confederate Navy consisted of just twelve small ships and about three hundred officers. Further, naval funding would remain limited, as would cooperation with the War Department. Undaunted, Mallory enthusiastically began trying to purchase and build a navy. With mixed success, his agents combed the naval yards of Europe. Most notable was the acquisition of sleek commerce raiders from Britain, especially the *Alabama*, captained by Raphael Semmes. As the war turned against the Confederacy, however, ambitious efforts to buy additional vessels abroad usually came to naught.

Mallory was also an innovator. Despite the inadequacy of the South's industrial plants, especially following the loss of Nashville, New Orleans, Memphis, and Norfolk in the first year of the conflict, the Confederacy managed to commission twenty-two ironclads during the war, a testimony to the ingenuity and hard work of Navy Department officials. Mallory also explored other experimental weapons and tactics, including naval mines (called torpedoes during the Civil War), submarines, torpedo boats, and secret amphibious raids, although such efforts usually had little immediate benefit. Given the South's enormous disadvantages, however, such schemes were probably necessary if the Confederacy hoped to meet the Federal fleets on anything approaching even terms.

After the evacuation of Petersburg, Virginia, by ROBERT E. LEE [4] Mallory fled Richmond with the rest of the Davis administration. Concluding that defeat was certain, he opposed efforts to turn to guerrilla warfare in the conflict's latter days. He was imprisoned at Fort Lafayette, New York, for nearly ten months. Afterward, he resumed his law practice and opposed the military's role in Reconstruction, and the institution of black male suffrage. He died in 1873.

Known for his penchant for fine wines and mint juleps, Mallory was a hard-working, conscientious administrator whose innovations and ingenuity helped the Confederate navy fight the U.S. Navy on something approaching equal terms. Perhaps his biggest failure lay in his inability to persuade his government to devote sufficient attention to naval affairs or coastal defense. Widely criticized during his lifetime, Mallory has generally received better marks from historians than from his own contemporaries.

65

John C. Pemberton

(1814–1881)

Though a Pennsylvanian by birth, John C. Pemberton joined the Confederate cause with the secession of his adopted state, Virginia. He is important chiefly for having surrendered Vicksburg, Mississippi, the greatest Confederate stronghold on the Mississippi River, to ULYSSES S. GRANT [2] in July 1863. This loss divided the Confederacy into two parts. It ranks along with the Battle of Gettysburg as the worst Confederate defeat of the war.

The second of thirteen children, John C. Pemberton was born in Philadelphia in 1814. He graduated from West Point in 1837, twenty-seventh in a class of fifty. His classmates included BRAXTON BRAGG [30] (ranked fifth), JUBAL EARLY [81] (eighteenth), and JOSEPH HOOKER [36] (twenty-ninth), all of whom also became prominent Civil War generals. He served in the Seminole and Mexican Wars, and during the latter conflict suffered two wounds and won two brevet promotions. In 1846, Pemberton married the daughter of a wealthy Southern shipowner while stationed at Fort Monroe, Virginia. They had five children. Although the rest of his family pleaded for him to remain loyal to the Union upon the South's secession, the combination of his Southern wife and his own states' rights philosophy led him to cast his lot with Virginia.

Initially accepting a lieutenant colonelcy from Virginia, in November 1861 Pemberton was appointed brigadier general in the Confederate army. Transferred to Charleston, South Carolina, he rose to major general and department commander. There Pemberton earned the enmity of South Carolinians by recommending that Fort Sumter—site of the opening shots of the war—be abandoned as of no military value to Charleston's defense. President JEFFERSON DAVIS [5], however, respected his abilities, and in October 1862 Pemberton assumed command of the Army of Mississippi. In the process, Davis also arranged Pemberton's promotion to lieutenant general.

Pemberton's chief task was the defense of Vicksburg, the key to maintaining communications between Richmond and Texas, Arkansas, and western Louisiana. A skilled military engineer, he set about improving the city's already formidable defenses. In mid-December, he dispatched EARL VAN DORN [92] and a strong cavalry force against the supply depot of ULYSSES S. GRANT [2] at Holly Springs, Mississippi. By severing the Union supply line, Van Dorn's raid checked the overland drive against Vicksburg for several months. Union assaults that month against well-defended Chickasaw Bluffs, Mississippi, north of the city, also came to naught.

In spring 1863, Grant vainly tried to bypass Vicksburg by digging a canal through the swamps west of the river. Despite repeated failures, Grant remained undaunted even as Pemberton concluded that the danger had passed. As a Union cavalry raid through central Mississippi diverted attention, Grant cut loose from his supply lines and marched part of his army overland west of the Mississippi River. Several Union gunboats and transports ran past the citadel's guns about midnight on the evening of April 16–17, then ferried Grant's column across the Mississippi River at Bruinsburg, Mississippi, some forty miles below Vicksburg.

Had Pemberton struck quickly, while the Union forces were still divided, he might have defeated his opponent in detail, but Grant had fooled his enemies. By the time Pemberton and JOSEPH E. JOHNSTON [12], now commanding a separate Confederate force at Jackson, Mississippi, realized their danger, it was too late. Additional Union troops from north of Vicksburg joined Grant, who was now positioned squarely between the divided Confederates. Grant defeated Pemberton's command at Champion's Hill and the Big Black River, Mississippi, and by May 18 had surrounded Vicksburg and its thirty thousand defenders. On July 3, after a six-week siege, Pemberton asked for terms. The beleaguered Confederates, with less than half their men now available for duty, surrendered the next day.

Paroled in accord with the terms of capitulation, Pemberton was excoriated by the Southern press, which now attacked his Northern ancestry and accused him of treason. The Pennsylvania native waited for eight months for another assignment. Finding no command at his rank of lieutenant general, he resigned his commission, accepted a lieutenant colonelcy, and dutifully served out the remainder of the war in an artillery regiment. He died in Philadelphia in 1881.

66

Herman Haupt

(1817–1905)

Herman Haupt ranks as perhaps the least recognized hero of the American Civil War. More than anyone else, Herman Haupt designed, organized, and implemented the Union's successful system of military railroad transportation. This enabled the North to have two million men in arms and to bring to bear its great industrial might. In developing the Union rail system, Haupt performed a signal service to his country.

Born in Philadelphia in 1817, Haupt secured an appointment to the U.S. Military Academy at the tender age of fourteen through the influence of a distant family relative who was serving in Congress. He graduated thirty-first out of a class of fifty-six cadets in 1835. Commissioned a brevet second lieutenant in the Third Artillery Regiment, Haupt resigned after one month with his unit. He then worked as a draftsman and engineer on several rail-road projects, also teaching for a time in Gettysburg, Pennsylvania.

In 1849, Haupt accepted a post as the Pennsylvania Railroad's first transportation engineer. Two years later he published his *General Theory of Bridge Construction,* which became a standard engineering text. After a brief stint as chief engineer of a Mississippi railroad firm, he rejoined the Pennsylvania line in a similar post. Haupt oversaw completion of the main line from Philadelphia to Pittsburgh, amassed a small fortune, and resigned from the company in 1856 to take charge of a massive attempt to construct a four-and-a-half-mile long railroad tunnel through the Hoosac Mountains of Massachusetts. He devoted the next six years to the project, battling a hostile press, inadequate working capital, and fluctuating state politics. In 1862 the state finally assumed his contract, but Haupt never fully regained his personal fortune.

As Union generals became increasingly aware of the railroad's importance to modern military activities, Haupt accepted an appointment as colonel on the staff of Gen. IRVIN MCDOWELL [57]. Haupt named himself "Chief of Construction and Transportation, U.S. Military Railroads" and threw his energies into developing a system of building, repairing, and operating these vital arteries. Initially, he personally oversaw the construction of several major projects and used his well-honed talent at solving transportation bottlenecks to ensure the timely arrival of reinforcements and supplies to needed areas. Especially important were his efforts to move troops to the Second Battle of Bull Run, Virginia. The ever-quotable ABRAHAM LINCOLN [1] marveled about one of Haupt's miracles, a four-hundred-foot-long trestle bridge built eighty feet high by unskilled labor in less than two weeks: "That man, Haupt, has built a bridge . . . over which loaded trains are running every hour, and upon my word, gentlemen, there is nothing in it but beanpoles and cornstalks."

After solving the immediate crises in rail transport, Haupt devoted more time to anticipating the needs of generals in the field. He developed prefabricated truss bridges and devised better methods for reshaping bent rails to allow quicker reconstruction of lines destroyed by retreating Confederates. His transportation corps performed extraordinary feats; two days after the Battle of Gettysburg, for example, the rail lines were open again, allowing vital supplies to flow into the stricken Pennsylvania college town. Haupt also recognized the advantages to be gained by destroying the enemy's rail system and designed mobile devices for such purposes.

Haupt, who had refused to accept a federal salary, quit the military on September 14, 1863, rather than lose the freedom of action that had been essential to his success. After the war he worked for several railroad companies and tinkered with various schemes, ranging from improved pneumatic drills to condensing milk. But due to lingering financial problems stemming from the Hoosac travails, Haupt worked until his death in 1905.

Railroads made it possible to supply and move huge Civil War armies.

Largely through Haupt's efforts, the Union developed efficient methods of building, repairing, and operating systems which met the demands of complex strategical operations. Even after he left military service, Haupt's legacy continued to be felt through the efforts of those who had developed their expertise under his guidance. His skillful handling of the railroads was unmatched by anyone in the Confederacy.

In developing the Union rail system, Haupt made it easier for troops to be supplied

67

Charles Francis Adams

(1807–1886)

Grandson of John Adams and son of John Quincy Adams, Charles Francis Adams never reached the political heights attained by his forebears. Nonetheless he continued the family's exemplary record of national service. After two terms in Congress, he was United States minister to England from 1861 to 1868. While in London, Adams helped prevent a breakdown in relations between Great Britain, whose position as the world's greatest naval power dictated that of the rest of Europe, and the United States. His careful approach ensured that England not only refused to recognize Confederate independence, but also limited its sales of war materials to the South.

Born in Boston in 1807, Charles Francis Adams spent most of his youth in Russia, France, and England, where his father held various diplomatic posts. After returning to America, the younger Adams graduated from Harvard College in 1825. He then studied law and handled his father's business interests. An abolitionist, he was the Free-Soil Party's vice-presidential candidate in 1848. In the early 1850s, Adams edited and published ten volumes of his grandfather's works. Elected to Congress for the first of two terms in 1858, he urged conciliation and moderation during the secession crisis.

Strongly backed by incoming Secretary of State WILLIAM SEWARD [8], Adams was named minister to England in March 1861. A brief meeting with President LINCOLN [1], however, left the new appointee unimpressed. "You are not my choice. You are Seward's man," Lincoln reportedly informed Adams. Discomforted by the brusque send-off, Adams inherited a difficult situation upon his arrival in England. His chief, Seward, had an unfortunate penchant for making inflammatory statements. Had Adams shared with the British the exact details of many of Seward's dispatches, relations between the United States and England would have been seriously imperiled. Fortunately, Adams grasped the delicate nature of U.S.-British relations and managed to convey Seward's meaning without unnecessarily angering the British.

Britain had adopted a neutral position, conferring belligerent status upon the Confederacy but stopping short of granting outright recognition. This stance reflected the mixed British attitudes toward the war. A division of the United States would reduce a rival's commercial power and the threat to British Canada. English textile mills were heavily dependent upon Southern cotton; shortages due to a war would thus hurt the British economy. On the other hand, a lengthy disruption of American political stability would hurt trade, and Northern wheat (and eventually corn) rivaled Southern cotton in importance. Finally, opposition to slavery ran deep in many segments of British society, especially the working class.

Minister Adams played an especially important role in two major diplomatic crises. One occurred in late 1861, when two Confederate diplomats were crossing the Atlantic aboard the British-flagged *Trent*. A U.S. warship stopped the *Trent* and seized the two Southerners as "contraband of war." The affair led to threats from both sides, but an outright breach in relations was averted when the Confederate diplomats were released.

The second major controversy related to the construction of Confederate warships in Britain. Early on, Southern agents contracted for the purchase of two cruisers, eventually named the *Florida* and the *Alabama*. Adams protested their release to the Confederacy, but by the time he had convinced British officials of their military intent, both had sailed. Together, they sank or captured well over a hundred Northern merchant vessels. Attacks by these and other Confederate ships increased insurance rates and ravaged the American merchant marine fleet. As the tide of war turned in favor of the North, however, and Lincoln announced the Emancipation Proclamation, Adams found the British much easier to convince. At Adams's behest in April 1863, the British government seized several ships, most notably two ironclad rams then under construction for Confederate use. Adams returned to the United States in 1868. After completing publication of twelve volumes of his father's diaries, his memory began to fail, and he died in Boston in 1886.

Throughout the Civil War, Adams's steadiness had impressed British officials. Though Lincoln and Seward had set American policy, Adams had implemented it in a professional, tactful manner, thus making an important contribution to the North's victory.

68

Wade Hampton

(1818–1902)

One of the wealthiest men in the antebellum South, Wade Hampton developed into a superb wartime cavalryman. More significant, however, were Hampton's actions during and after Reconstruction. As governor of South Carolina from 1877 to 1881 and U.S. senator from 1881 to 1891, he supported a return to conservative rule in the South. Unlike many of his fellow Democrats, however, Hampton refused to engage in race-baiting tactics or propaganda. His failure to maintain control of the South Carolina Democratic Party perhaps symbolized the decline of the traditional patriarchal power elite in favor of more overtly racist politicians who urged the complete disfranchisement and segregation of blacks.

Born into one of South Carolina's most prominent families in 1818, Wade Hampton graduated from South Carolina College in 1836. After studying law, he returned to his family's Millwood plantation home. Hampton's holdings expanded into Mississippi and Louisiana, and he eventually owned

173

some three thousand slaves. A powerfully built man, Hampton proved an excellent manager and businessman. He married in 1838; after his first wife's death in 1855, he remarried three years later. He fathered three sons and three daughters in these unions. Regarding public service as something of an obligation, Hampton sat in the state house and senate for a series of terms during the 1850s. During that time he opposed reopening the African slave trade as well as immediate disunion. Secession, he believed, was a legal right, but the time for so dramatic a step was not yet at hand.

Hampton nonetheless believed his loyalty was to South Carolina rather than the Union. An imposing and muscular six feet tall, he volunteered as a private soldier upon the outbreak of war. Eager to capitalize on Hampton's reputation, the governor instructed him to raise and command a military unit, which was formed in short order. Hampton was slightly wounded at the First Battle of Bull Run, Virginia, then accepted a promotion to brigadier general, and received another wound during the Battle of Seven Pines, Virginia.

Hampton was then transferred to the cavalry under J. E. B. STUART [33], where he distinguished himself as an able leader of mounted troops. After repeated skirmishes his men were heavily engaged at Brandy Station, Virginia, where one of his brothers was killed. Hampton himself fell wounded in hand-to-hand combat the following month at Gettysburg, later admitting that the battle had been "useless." Promotion to major general and division command followed Gettysburg. After Stuart's death, in August 1864 Hampton took command of the cavalry of the Army of Northern Virginia. He won the battle of Trevilian Station, Virginia, then, in early 1865, was transferred to his native South Carolina. There Hampton vainly attempted to harass the advance of WILLIAM T. SHERMAN [3] into his native state.

Hampton took a more active interest in politics after the Civil War. Defeated in his bid for governor in 1865, he supported HORACE GREELEY [31] and the Liberal Republicans in 1872. He claimed victory in his state's controversial gubernatorial race of 1876. Only with Rutherford B. Hayes's accession to the presidency, however, did Hampton actually take office. He promised fair treatment for blacks and, unlike many of his fellow Democrats, supported limited black suffrage. Hampton opposed the Populists, however, and found himself increasingly isolated by the reactionary turn of South Carolina politics even while serving two terms in the U.S. Senate. When the South Carolina legislature selected his archrival, Ben Tillman, to take Hampton's Senate seat, he accepted President Grover Cleveland's offer to become U.S. commissioner of railroads two years later. Hampton died in 1902, his excellence as a Civil War cavalry leader overshadowed in later life by his loss of political power following Reconstruction.

69

Walt Whitman

(1819–1892)

In his 1837 "American Scholar" address to Harvard's Phi Beta Kappa chapter, Ralph Waldo Emerson challenged his fellow scholars to define and produce the type of literature appropriate to American democracy. "Our day of dependence, our long apprenticeship to the learning of other lands, draws to a close," Emerson explained. Walt Whitman, more than any other single figure—at his best unconventional, unrestrained, sensual, and emotional— helped to create a uniquely American poetic heritage. On a practical level he acted as a "wound-dresser" to hospitalized Civil War soldiers. Profoundly influenced by the suffering of his fellow countrymen, Whitman captured their agony better than any other contemporary writer of fiction.

Born in Huntington, New York, in 1819, Walt Whitman spent most of his youth in Brooklyn, where he attended public schools until age eleven. He then took up clerking, was apprenticed to a printer, and taught school. During the 1840s and 1850s, Whitman wrote for and edited various periodicals in New York, New Orleans, and Brooklyn. He loved mingling with America's city folk as he dabbled in oratory and phrenology in addition to his writing. Through his essays and short fictional pieces, he exulted in the freedoms allowed by America's democracy.

In 1855 Whitman published his first major work, *Leaves of Grass*, which originally included twelve poems and a long preface. Heavily influenced by his reading of William Shakespeare, Thomas Carlyle, Johann Wolfgang von Goethe, and especially Emerson, the original edition of *Leaves of Grass* included many of Whitman's most famous pieces, such as "Song of Myself" and "I Sing the Body Electric." He added new entries, many of which described the nation broken by war, to later editions, so that by the time of his death, the work included 350 poems.

Whitman was an active participant in the Civil War, and the war in turn profoundly shaped his poetry. To him, the war represented a challenge to the Union and democracy, the keys to his entire being. At forty-two years of age he was too old for active military duty. But one of his brothers, George, would serve four years, fight in twenty-one battles, and spend almost five months in Confederate prisons. Upon learning that George had been wounded at Fredericksburg, Virginia, Whitman rushed to the improvised field hospital where his brother was recuperating. Struck by the suffering, intimacy, and heroism found at these chaotic Civil War hospitals, Whitman remained in the Washington area, raising money, food, tobacco, and clothing to distribute to the sick and wounded. He calculated that he made over six hundred hospital visits, during which he claimed to have ministered to nearly one hundred thousand men.

Whitman recognized the greatness of President ABRAHAM LINCOLN [1]. For several years, Whitman had been working on poems commemorating the common soldier's sufferings. His collection of wartime poetry, *Drum-Taps*, was scheduled to go to press when word arrived that Lincoln had been assassinated. Whitman decided the book would be incomplete without a long poem devoted to the murdered president. Thus he produced the finest single poem about the war, "When Lilacs Last in the Dooryard Bloom'd," which appeared with the appended work, *Drum-Taps and Sequel*, published in October 1865. The opening stanza of "Lilacs" reflects the author's sensuality and passion:

> When lilacs last in the dooryard bloom'd,
> And the great star early droop'd in the western sky in the night,
> I mourn'd, and yet shall mourn with ever-returning spring.
>
> Ever returning spring, trinity sure to me you bring,
> Lilac blooming perennial and drooping star in the west,
> And thought of him I love.

Harewood hospital in which Walt Whitman gave comfort to the wounded

Whitman continued to write after the war ended, but only his *Democratic Vistas* (1871), a collection of philosophical and political essays, approached the quality of his earlier masterpieces. Still confident in America's destiny, he nonetheless acknowledged the nation's continuing growing pains. *Specimen Days* (1882) is a collection of notes, which Whitman jotted down, that contains his wartime observations (previously published in 1875 as *Memoranda During the War*). These poignant notes comprise Whitman's hospital experiences and his observations of war-time Washington and are among his most powerful and touching writings.

Rakish in appearance, with trademark felt hat and flowing beard, Whitman loved to be photographed. In 1873, he settled in Camden, New Jersey, where he lived the remainder of his life. Having suffered a series of strokes, he finally succumbed in 1892 to pulmonary emphysema. His poetry, itself shaped by the Civil War, had expressed the hopes, dreams, and sorrows of those who had experienced the conflict.

70

Napoleon III

(1808–1873)

Charles Louis Napoleon Bonaparte, the nephew of Napoleon Bonaparte, was president and emperor of France from 1848 until 1870, when he was captured during the Franco-Prussian War. A man of visionary goals and ambitions for himself and for France, Napoleon III had neither the personality nor the talent to fully implement his grandiose plans. Keenly interested in foreign expansion and glory, he hoped to use the American Civil War as an opportunity to set up a French-sponsored government in Mexico under an Austrian archduke, Ferdinand Maximilian. The move infuriated the United States, but with a much larger crisis closer to home, Federal officials at first did little to block the French aggression. Sympathetic with Southern interests, Napoleon III nonetheless refused to side openly with the Confederacy in the absence of British cooperation. His failure to intervene rendered the South's cause all the more difficult.

Louis Napoleon Bonaparte was the third son of Louis Bonaparte, who was a brother of Napoleon I and for several years King of Holland. His childhood was marked by his parents' separation and the French empire's collapse. Louis Napoleon determined from a rather early age that he must

178

restore his family's dynasty. Following a brief dalliance with Italian nationalists, he soon claimed to be his uncle's true successor and heir to the French crown. In 1836, he proposed that the garrison at Strasbourg march upon Paris and seize the government. Louis Napoleon was instead arrested and exiled. After six months in the United States, he returned to France and in 1840 made another unsuccessful effort to gain the throne. He was arrested and spent the next six years in prison before escaping to London.

Up to this point most international observers had viewed Louis Napoleon as something of a foppish buffoon. His calls for a return to the legendary days of his uncle, however, had hit a popular chord among the people of France. In 1848, in the wake of a successful revolt against the regime of Louis Philippe, he returned and was elected president of the Second Republic by a landslide vote. Mixing his genuine sympathy for the masses and promises of social and economic reform with claims that he would protect the people against the authoritarianism of the French Assembly, he dissolved the latter body, crushed a republican countercoup, and in 1852 proclaimed himself Napoleon III, Emperor of the French.

Under his rule, France achieved remarkable economic growth. Baron Haussmann, Napoleon's prefect of the Seine, oversaw the dramatic transformation of Paris into a modern city complete with efficient sewer and water systems, grand avenues, and beautiful public parks. In his foreign policy, Napoleon was extremely aggressive, expanding France's colonial domain in Indochina, Lebanon, West Africa, and several Pacific islands, and entering the Crimean War against Russia. In 1861, France joined Spain and Great Britain in the Convention of London, in which they declared that they would jointly occupy Veracruz in order to collect payment for Mexico's overdue foreign debts. The English and Spanish quickly withdrew, but some thirty thousand French troops moved inland and established Maximilian's regime.

Napoleon III's international adventurism, first in Italy and then in Mexico, made many enemies. Unwilling to risk a confrontation with the Union without British support, he rejected a Confederate offer in July 1862 of a huge cotton shipment and an alliance against Mexican resistance to French power in return for diplomatic recognition and naval assistance. His refusal to offer direct aid deprived the Confederacy of a potentially powerful ally. At the end of the Civil War, the U.S. government sent fifty thousand troops to south Texas, a clear signal of American displeasure with continued French support for Maximilian. Beset by rising domestic pressures, growing Prussian strength, and increasing Mexican opposition, Napoleon III was forced to abandon Maximilian, who was executed by the Mexicans in 1867.

In the 1869 elections, humiliated by the Mexican adventure, Napoleon's government lost 45 percent of the vote to the opposition. His fall came during the Franco-Prussian War. Shocked by early military setbacks along the border and weakened by chronic health problems, he gamely took the field with his armies. Captured in 1870 by the Prussians at Sedan, Napoleon III went into exile. He died at Chislehurst, England, in 1873.

71

Alexander Hamilton Stephens

(1812–1883)

Alexander Stephens was the vice president of the Confederacy, and his most significant act was his authorship of much of the Confederate constitution, a work based on that of the United States. He was born in 1812 at Crawfordville, Georgia. His mother died a month after his birth; his father remarried but died when Alexander was only fourteen. But Alexander Hamilton Webster, headmaster of a local academy, took a keen interest in the precocious young man and secured enough sponsors to loan his protégé the funds to enter college. Out of respect for his benefactor, Stephens adopted Hamilton as his middle name. He graduated from Franklin College (now the University of Georgia), used his small inheritance to repay the loan, and briefly taught school before becoming a lawyer.

After several terms in the state legislature, Stephens won election to Congress in 1843. A Whig, he was fiercely independent in his voting pattern and was a vocal critic of the Mexican War. Tiny in stature, with a boyish face, and constantly battling poor health, he challenged several rivals to duels and was once nearly stabbed to death during a fight. Although a champion of states' rights, Stephens nonetheless supported the Compromise of 1850 and helped to convince the Georgia state convention to reject secession that year.

He then backed the controversial Kansas-Nebraska Act and, with the decline of the Whig Party, in 1854 became a Democrat. He retired from office in 1858, returning to his now flourishing plantation, Liberty Hill, where he grew cotton. He owned thirty-two slaves.

Stephens opposed political extremists on both sides. He knew ABRAHAM LINCOLN [1] from his days in Congress; fearful that the Republicans would destroy slavery and supportive of secession in theory, he still did not believe conditions in 1860–61 mandated such a radical move. Elected to the Georgia secession convention, Stephens voted against leaving the Union. Out of either state loyalty or a desire to protect his stake in Southern society, however, he accepted his election to the Provisional Congress of the Confederate States. That body—perhaps in deference to Stephens's political prominence, to Georgia's influence, or in hopes of attracting former Unionists—elected him the new nation's vice president.

Stephens was a terrible choice. A better critic than achiever, his poor health and independent-mindedness rendered him uncooperative and ineffective. His relations with President JEFFERSON DAVIS [5] quickly deteriorated, leaving the vice president to spend most of the war sulking at home, loudly criticizing the administration for its intrusions into individual liberties, particularly its enactment of conscription. States' rights and liberty for white men must be maintained, he argued, even if it meant losing the war. Having long opposed Davis's policies, in February 1865 Stephens was one of three Confederate representatives to the Hampton Roads peace conference, but the meetings with Lincoln to work out an early end to the war never stood much chance of success.

With the Confederacy's collapse, federal troops arrested Stephens at his home in May 1865. Authorities detained him at Fort Warren (Boston) until October. In a remarkable gesture of defiance, Georgia legislators named him to the U.S. Senate in January 1866. Outraged Northerners refused to allow the former Confederate vice president a seat so quickly after the war and began to impose harsher terms of Reconstruction. True to his nature, Stephens rejected any hint of compromise with the North. An accidental fall had left him unable to walk without assistance, but his district elected him to his old House seat in 1873. Georgia having by then complied with congressional demands, Stephens took his seat, holding it until 1882. Elected governor of Georgia that year, he died in early 1883.

It would seem that Stephens, as vice president of the Confederacy, deserves a higher rank among Civil War figures, but he had little influence on either the secession movement or the affairs of the Confederacy, save to make Jefferson Davis's life miserable. Stephens's uncompromising concepts of honor and liberty made it impossible for him to work effectively for the Confederate cause. Too, his pallid, shrunken body reflected his continuing bouts with neuralgia, rheumatism, poor digestion, and migraine headaches, and he remained bedridden for extended periods throughout his life. By personality and physical health, he was ill-suited for such an important post.

72

Edmund Ruffin

(1794–1865)

The greatest antebellum advocate of Southern agricultural reform, Edmund Ruffin is now most famous for his untiring promotion of secession. He became an ardent defender of slavery and during the 1850s was a visible champion of secession. Through his travels, appearances at Southern commercial conventions, published editorials, and voluminous private correspondence, Ruffin constantly expounded his belief that the South must seek independence. His absolute refusal to compromise, however, limited his political effectiveness, thus making him less significant than other Southern firebrands, ROBERT RHETT [16 (tie)] and WILLIAM YANCEY [16 (tie)].

Born to a prominent Tidewater, Virginia, family in 1794, Edmund Ruffin entered William and Mary College at age sixteen, but was suspended for failing to keep up with his academic assignments. He served during the War of 1812 before marrying and inheriting his father's estate. Troubled by the region's declining productivity, Ruffin experimented with the application of marl, a calcareous substance that helps neutralize the acidity of sterile soils. Combining marl with fertilizers, crop rotation, and better drainage and plowing, he dramatically improved his agricultural yields.

Ruffin published the results of his experiments in farming journals and eventually in a book, *An Essay on Calcareous Manures* (1832). He also edited his own journal, the *Farmer's Register,* from 1833 to 1842. Commissioned to study agricultural practices in South Carolina, Ruffin served four terms as president of the Virginia State Agricultural Society. In 1843 he acquired lands in Hanover County which he transformed into a successful plantation, "Marlbourne," which he operated until retiring from active farming in 1855.

Ruffin also maintained an interest in politics. He served three years in the Virginia state senate but found the compromises often necessary to effect political change distasteful. Though in 1831 he had defended a black wrongfully accused of being part of Nat Turner's slave rebellion, Ruffin's defenses of slavery and denunciations of abolitionists grew increasingly radical. By the 1850s he emerged as an irreconcilable secessionist. Through pamphlets, serials, and a novel, *Anticipations of the Future* (1861), Ruffin sought to influence fellow Southerners in print. His wide travels throughout the South also afforded him ample opportunity to express his extreme views.

In 1860, Ruffin welcomed the election of ABRAHAM LINCOLN [1] on the theory that the Republican's victory would lead South Carolina to secede. He eagerly made his way to the Palmetto State to watch the proceedings and was given the pen used to sign South Carolina's Ordinance of Secession. Dismayed by the failure of Virginia and the upper South to immediately follow this lead, Ruffin urged an attack upon Federal positions at Fort Sumter. "The shedding of blood," he argued, "will serve to change many voters in the hesitating states, from the submissive or procrastinating ranks, to the zealous for immediate secession." On hand to watch the bombardment of Federal positions there, Ruffin was allowed to fire several of the cannon himself. Some accounts even have the sixty-six-year-old fire-eater firing the first shot of the war.

With the belated secession of his native Virginia, Ruffin hurried home in time to lob a few ceremonial artillery rounds at retreating Federal troops at First Bull Run, Virginia. The fortunes of war turned against him, however. The fighting left his holdings around Richmond destroyed, forcing Ruffin to move to a smaller farm at Redmoor, Virginia. Embittered and despondent due to his personal losses, the fall of Richmond, and the surrender of ROBERT E. LEE [4] at Appomattox, he spent two months planning his suicide. On June 17, 1865, he concluded the last entry of his diary:

> And now with my latest writing and utterance, and with what will be near my latest breath, I here repeat and would willingly proclaim my unmitigated hatred to Yankee rule—to all political, social, and business connections with Yankees, and the perfidious, malignant, and vile Yankee race.

Edmund Ruffin then sat back in his chair, placed the muzzle of his gun in his mouth, and, with a forked stick, pulled the trigger and ended his own life.

73

Clement Vallandigham

(1820–1871)

Clement Vallandigham was the chief spokesman for the "Copperheads," Northern Democrats who opposed the Civil War. Arrested and exiled to Canada in 1863 for his denunciations of the war, he ran as the Democratic Party's candidate for the Ohio governorship while out of the country. Vallandigham also was "Supreme Grand Commander" of the Sons of Liberty, a pro-Confederate group whose actual role in antiwar conspiracies remains somewhat cloudy. In June 1864, he defied his exile and returned to the United States, where he helped to draft the Democratic Party's peace platform in that year's presidential contest.

Clement Laird Vallandigham was born at New Lisbon, Ohio, in 1820. He attended Jefferson College, Pennsylvania, but left the school after a philosophical dispute with its president. Vallandigham then passed the Ohio bar, gaining a reputation as an eloquent defender of states' rights and individual liberties. In 1845 he was elected to the legislature and the following year, at the age of twenty-six, he became speaker. A fiery orator, Vallandigham was enamored of the South and a sharp critic of abolitionists. He narrowly won a seat in the U.S. Congress in 1858 and served as secretary of the National Democratic Committee two years later.

With the outbreak of the Civil War, Vallandigham opposed all military appropriations designed to help fight the conflict. Defeated in 1862 largely as a result of Republican gerrymandering of his old district, Vallandigham, in his farewell speech to Congress, denounced the suspension of the right of habeas corpus, which he charged had "made this country one of the worst despotisms on earth for the past twenty months." Rather than continue the futile conflict on behalf of blacks, Vallandigham argued, Northwestern whites should seek peace with the Confederacy. In spring 1863 the new military commander of the Department of the Ohio, AMBROSE BURNSIDE [52], issued an order threatening those who committed "expressed or implied" treason with trial by a military court. On May 1, Vallandigham, in an address at Mount Vernon, deliberately baited Burnside by criticizing this "wicked, cruel, and unnecessary war," which was being fought "for the purpose of crushing out liberty and erecting a despotism . . . for the freedom of the blacks and the enslavement of the whites."

Four nights later, soldiers routed Vallandigham out of his house and placed him under arrest. A military commission quickly found Vallandigham guilty and sentenced him to imprisonment for the duration of the war. Horrified that Burnside's order might transform Vallandigham into a martyr, LINCOLN [1] commuted the sentence to banishment from the country. On May 25 Vallandigham was escorted to Confederate lines south of Murfreesboro, Tennessee. He met with several Southern officials before sailing with a blockade-runner to Windsor, Canada, even as he mounted a campaign-in-exile as the Democratic Party's nominee for the governorship of Ohio. Buoyed by victories at Gettysburg and Vicksburg, however, the Republicans buried Vallandigham, who received less than forty percent of the vote. Ohio soldiers had voted ninety-four percent Republican.

Still defiant, Vallandigham returned to the United States and continued to speak out against the war. Not wanting to create a martyr, Lincoln refused to order his arrest. Vallandigham drafted large sections of the 1864 Democratic Party platform, which called for an immediate end to hostilities. Although the Democratic candidate, GEORGE MCCLELLAN [7], tried to distance himself from the peace platform, this radical statement undoubtedly hurt the party's chances in many quarters.

Vallandigham was handsome, sincere in his beliefs, and utterly uncompromising. He launched several unsuccessful efforts to regain his political influence after the war, but retained his law practice. In 1871, while demonstrating how the victim of one of his accused murder clients had been shot, Vallandigham accidentally killed himself. The considerable support for Vallandigham reflected the opposition to black rights and deeply held sympathies for the Southern way of life among many Northern voters.

74

Harriet Tubman

(c. 1821–1913)

The vaunted "underground railroad" of the antebellum period was hardly the well-organized operation of popular lore. Rather than a series of "conductors" leading massive numbers of slaves along various "stations" to their freedom, its success depended largely on the courage, resourcefulness, and luck of the relatively small numbers of fugitives themselves, most of whom had undergone the most arduous segments of their journeys before ever contacting any Northern sympathizers. Though general histories usually overstate the numbers of participants, the network of food, money, safe houses, transportation, and guidance, however small and informal, was seen by many Southerners as a significant threat to their culture, which was built upon slavery.

The railroad analogy is misleading, but if ever there was a "conductor," it was Harriet Tubman, who escaped from slavery to become a leading abolitionist. Named Araminta at her birth on Maryland's Eastern Shore about 1821, she called herself Harriet after her mother. Either an owner or over-seer gave her a severe head blow as a child, leading to recurrent narcoleptic seizures. Harriet preferred the relative autonomy of field work to domestic labor, where she would be under closer supervision. In 1844 she married a free black, John Tubman. Fearing that she would be sold into the Deep South after her owner's death in 1849, Harriet escaped to Pennsylvania. Her autobiography, written by a friend and published in 1869, describes her arrival in the Keystone State: "When I found I had crossed that line, I looked at my hands to see if I was the same person. There was such a glory over everything; the sun came like gold through the trees, and over the fields, and I felt like I was in Heaven."

But personal freedom was not enough. After working as a domestic ser-vant in Philadelphia, Tubman raised enough money to return South, only to find her husband living with another woman. Still defiant, she spirited her sister and two children into freedom, the first of at least fifteen trips she made into Maryland, during which Harriet guided from two to three hundred persons out of bondage. Wearing a multitude of disguises, often brandishing a pistol to deter any of her charges from changing their minds, and carrying liberal amounts of paregoric to quiet restless babies, Tubman was the most effective and daring of those who led fugitives from slavery. Triumphantly, she rescued her parents in 1857. Fearful Maryland slaveowners offered a bounty of $40,000 for her capture.

In the North, Tubman gained the alliance of several key abolitionists. Even so, fearing the Fugitive Slave Law, which rewarded federal commis-sioners with ten dollars for every black returned to slavery, she relocated to Ontario, Canada, until 1858. Taking more direct action than most of her fellow abolitionists during the Civil War, Tubman acted as a spy, scout, and nurse for Union forces operating from the Sea Islands of South Carolina. She even assisted in several daring raids against Confederate railroads, bridges, and plantations.

Tubman remarried in 1869 to a Civil War veteran, Nelson Davis, who died in 1888. In New York, she helped to establish a home for aged ex-slaves and, after a thirty-year struggle, won a small monthly government pension for being a war widow. Tubman died of pneumonia in 1913 at her home in Auburn, New York, truly a Moses to those she had delivered from slavery.

75

John Schofield

(1831–1906)

A Civil War general who went on to become secretary of war and commanding general of the United States army, John McAllister Schofield held several important wartime commands. Responsible for military affairs in Missouri during a critical period of the war, he did much to keep that bitterly divided state under Union control. As head of the Army of the Ohio, he also performed capably during the campaign against Atlanta under WILLIAM T. SHERMAN [3]. Later, Schofield defeated Confederate forces under JOHN BELL HOOD [38] in the Battle of Franklin, Tennessee. During Reconstruction, Schofield, a political moderate, headed military affairs in Virginia. He proved a compromise choice as secretary of war (1868–1869), thus helping to avert a constitutional crisis during the troubled latter days of the administration of President ANDREW JOHNSON [6].

The son of a Baptist preacher, Schofield was born in southwestern New York State in 1831. He moved with his parents to Freeport, Illinois, where he attended local schools and helped out with the family farm. Rejecting the ministry, Schofield briefly tried surveying and schoolteaching before receiving an appointment to the U.S. Military Academy in 1849. Despite narrowly averting dismissal for having allowed some younger cadets in his charge to be hazed by fellow upperclassmen, he graduated seventh in his class of fifty-two in 1853. Among his classmates were PHILIP H. SHERIDAN [18] and John Bell Hood.

After graduation, Schofield served in garrison duty in South Carolina and Florida before returning to West Point as an instructor in the Department of Natural and Experimental Philosophy. There he married the department chairman's daughter, Harriet Bartlett. Dissatisfied with the slow pace of promotion in the antebellum army, Schofield took a one-year leave of absence in 1860 to teach at Washington University in St. Louis.

With the outbreak of the war, Schofield worked to keep Missouri under Federal control. The most populous state west of the Mississippi River, Missouri ranked third nationally in the production of corn, sixth in livestock, and first in lead. Schofield assisted Nathanial Lyon in seizing the St. Louis arsenal and enrolling volunteers. By November 1861, Schofield, now a brigadier general in command of the state militia, felt comfortable enough to funnel increasing numbers of troops out of Missouri to other fronts.

In July 1862, Schofield took command of the District of Missouri. Holding various positions, he remained a central figure in the military administration of Missouri and Kansas for the next eighteen months. Confederate guerrillas and raiders proved his chief military threat; politically, the state's tenuous Unionist government was divided among those who sought an immediate end to slavery and a harsher policy against Southern sympathizers and those who advocated a more conservative stance. Schofield's attempts to chart a moderate course, however, pleased few in Missouri or Kansas. On several occasions, delegations to Washington sought his removal; generally, however, President LINCOLN [1] supported Schofield, as did ULYSSES S. GRANT [2] and HENRY HALLECK [27], who appreciated Schofield's determination to provide reinforcements for campaigns against Vicksburg.

Schofield's Missouri ordeal ended in January 1864, when he took command of troops at Nashville and eventually led the Army of the Ohio. He then participated in Sherman's campaign against Atlanta. Following the fall of Atlanta, Schofield helped to prevent John Bell Hood's Confederates from retaking Tennessee. At Franklin, Hood attacked Schofield in a desperate attempt to prevent his old West Point comrade from linking up with a larger Union command located at Nashville. In his largest independent action of the war, Schofield fended off Hood's attacks with heavy losses to the Confederates. Transferred east, Schofield later captured Wilmington and Goldsboro, North Carolina.

After the war, Schofield performed a variety of unusual services. He was the government's choice to command a mixed force of Union and Confederate veterans and Mexican volunteers should it be necessary to use force against Maximilian's regime in Mexico, and was dispatched to France in an effort to further pressure NAPOLEON III [70] to withdraw his support for Maximilian. Schofield then oversaw military reconstruction in Virginia before becoming secretary of war in the latter days of the Johnson administration. Returning to active duty after Grant's election, Schofield spent 1872 and 1873 in Hawaii investigating the defensibility of Pearl Harbor should the United States acquire the islands. From 1876 to 1880 he was superintendent of West Point.

On Sheridan's death in 1888, Schofield became commanding general of the army. Unlike most others who held this post, he saw his position largely as military adviser to the secretary of war and president; in taking this view, he avoided needless controversy. As commanding general Schofield worked effectively to reduce desertion and to foster a greater sense of professionalism among the officer corps. He retired from active duty in 1895 and died eleven years later.

Some of the worst fighting of the Battle of Franklin raged around the Carter house.

76

William S. Rosecrans

(1819–1898)

Until his disastrous defeat at the Battle of Chickamauga, Georgia, William S. Rosecrans had been one of the Union's most successful generals. After assuming command of the Army of the Cumberland, he had, through skillful maneuvering, forced the Confederates to abandon strategic Chattanooga, Tennessee, the northern gateway to Georgia and Alabama, but Rosecrans's mistakes during and after the ensuing Battle of Chickamauga irreparably damaged his military reputation.

Born in Ohio in 1819, Rosecrans secured an appointment to the United States Military Academy, from which he graduated fifth in his class in 1842. This high ranking allowed him to receive his commission as second lieutenant in the much sought-after Corps of Engineers. Subsequent military assignments included a four-year stint as instructor at West Point. He resigned his commission in 1854 to enter private business.

Rosecrans volunteered for duty at the beginning of the Civil War. As a Democrat, a Catholic, and an experienced officer, he seemed an especially valuable commodity to the LINCOLN [1] administration, and received a Regular Army appointment as brigadier general on May 16, 1861. He did well in the early campaigns of GEORGE McCLELLAN [7] in western Virginia. After several months' command of the Departments of the Ohio and Western Virginia, Rosecrans was transferred west, where he gained command of the Union Army of the Mississippi. He angered his superior, ULYSSES S. GRANT [2], by failing to close a trap laid for a small Confederate army at Iuka, Mississippi, but successfully defended Corinth, Mississippi, against enemy attack.

On October 30, 1862, President Lincoln named Rosecrans, now a major general, to succeed DON CARLOS BUELL [95] in command of the Army of the Cumberland. Dubbed "Old Rosy" by his men, Rosecrans proved an intelligent if somewhat excitable and overcautious commander whose profane outbursts belied his devout Catholicism. Brave in combat, he took Murfreesboro, Tennessee, and fought off determined Confederate assaults in the bloody Battle of Stones River, Tennessee. For this effort, Lincoln, besieged by antiwar Democrats and desperately needing a victory, wrote gratefully to the major general, "God bless you, and all with you."

Nevertheless, Rosecrans had suffered thirty-one percent casualties at Stones River. These debilitating losses, combined with continuing difficulties in securing the huge stockpiles of supplies, horses, and mules he believed necessary to launch an offensive, delayed Rosecrans for five months. Finally, under persistent pressure from Washington officials, on June 24 he pushed south from Murfreesboro. Following a brilliant campaign during which only six of his men were killed, Rosecrans occupied Chattanooga six weeks later.

Triumph then turned into disaster. Just south of Chattanooga, the Confederate Army of Tennessee under BRAXTON BRAGG [30] counterattacked Rosecrans in the Battle of Chickamauga. The Federals fended off repeated Southern attacks on September 19. As the assaults continued the following day, Rosecrans mistakenly ordered one of his divisions to shift its position, thus creating a gap in the Union front. By chance, JAMES LONGSTREET [19], freshly arrived from Virginia to reinforce Bragg, had selected just this point for a renewed attack. As the Union line collapsed, Rosecrans panicked, with only the stubborn defense of troops led by GEORGE THOMAS [29] saving the army from complete collapse as the bluecoats fell back to Chattanooga.

Ousted in favor of Thomas as commander of the Army of the Cumberland, Rosecrans served for nearly a year as head of the Department of the Missouri. Convinced that he needed more troops to maintain Union control there, his constant requests for reinforcements led to his removal on December 9, 1864. Rosecrans never received another command, finally resigning from the army three years later. A Democrat, he went into private business and was later elected to two congressional terms from California. Rosecrans died near Los Angeles in 1898.

Rosecrans despised Grant, whom he held responsible for many of his own errors. As chairman of the House Military Affairs Committee, he was one of very few who opposed the appointment of a nearly impoverished Ulysses S. Grant to full general on the retired list. During the Civil War, Rosecrans's successes in the Battle of Corinth and in capturing Chattanooga were clearly overshadowed by his defeat at Chickamauga and by his tendency toward overcaution.

77

James Henry Carleton

(1814–1873)

Most Civil War books concentrate on the battles between the Confederate and Union armies and the accompanying social, economic, and cultural developments which changed the country forever. Unfortunately, the impact of the war in the far West is often overlooked in the process. Typical is the relative obscurity of James Henry Carleton, who helped guarantee that the New Mexico Territory remained in the Union and also oversaw the defeat of the Navajo Indians during the Civil War.

Born in Maine in 1814, James Henry Carleton was commissioned in that state's militia during the boundary disputes with British Canada (1838–1839). Securing a second lieutenancy in the regular army, he served with the First Dragoon Regiment and won a brevet promotion at the Battle of Buena Vista during the Mexican War. Carleton compiled an impressive record during the next decade, conducting a successful expedition against the Jicarilla Apaches in 1854, serving as a military observer in the Crimean War, and leading a government investigation of the infamous Mountain

Meadows Massacre in Utah.

When the Civil War began, Carleton's regulars helped to overawe potential Confederate sympathizers in southern California. He then organized an expedition to reinforce Union troops in New Mexico, under threat by a Confederate force led by Henry Hopkins Sibley. Having collected about twenty-three hundred men, Carleton's "California Column" arrived just as Sibley's command began disintegrating in the wake of the Battle of Glorieta. Carleton restored Federal authority in Tucson, then pushed into western Texas and completed the rout of Sibley's army.

Appointed a brigadier general (and eventually major general) of volunteers, Carleton assumed command of the military Department of New Mexico in September 1862, a position he held for the remainder of the Civil War. His main enemies now became the Indians—chiefly Mescalero and Chiricahua Apaches, Navajos, Comanches, Kiowas, and Kiowa-Apaches—who had for centuries challenged Spanish, Mexican, and American intrusions into the Southwest. With the recent withdrawal of many Federal garrisons to face the Confederate threat during the Civil War, Indian raids often increased, thus sparking intense retaliation by federal and state governments now accustomed to raising and equipping large numbers of troops. Carleton's resulting campaigns were marked by his determination to crush those tribes deemed hostile. After they had been whipped into submission, the tribes would be moved to reservations a safe distance from white settlements, where they would be taught farming and American-style civilization.

A stern disciplinarian whose autocratic methods resulted in establishing a virtual dictatorship over New Mexico, Carleton was a ruthlessly effective Indian fighter. In his old friend Christopher "Kit" Carson, the famous frontiersman, Carleton found the ideal tool to implement his designs. The Mescalero Apaches were the first to feel Carleton's hard hand of war. By mid-1863, most of the once fearsome Mescalero Apaches had been relocated to newly established Fort Sumner, in a region known as the Bosque Redondo.

Carleton next turned his attention to the Navajo, numbering about twelve thousand. If they wanted peace, they would have to surrender and relocate to the Bosque Redondo alongside the Mescaleros. All who did not would be treated as hostile. Throughout the latter half of 1863, the Navajos eluded the Union columns, but Carleton had just begun. On December 31 he urged his field commanders to press home their campaigns. "*Now,* while the snow is deep," Carleton insisted, "is the time to make an impression on the tribe." In early January, Carson struck a large Navajo encampment at Canyon de Chelly, destroying huge quantities of winter food supplies. Exhausted and impoverished by the relentless chases, thousands of Navajo surrendered and made the long trek to Bosque Redondo. Navajo military resistance had been permanently ended.

Carleton's subsequent campaigns against the Kiowas, Comanches, and Chiricahuas were less decisive, and probably increased the determination of

Fort Marcy, Santa Fe, headquarters of the Territory of New Mexico

these groups to continue their armed opposition to white expansion. After the Civil War, he left New Mexico to resume his career with the regular army. He died of pneumonia in 1873.

Most contemporaries found Carleton to be a thoroughly unlikable individual, but by helping to defeat the Confederate invasion of New Mexico and launching campaigns which eventually crushed the Navajo, Carleton ranks among the most significant persons of the Civil War. Recognition of this importance, however, should not be confused with the assumption that his policies settled the Indian controversy after the war. They did not. The Bosque Redondo experiment proved a disaster; after years of spirit-numbing poverty, the Navajos returned to their homeland in 1868, where the government established a new reservation.

78

Richard Taylor

(1826–1879)

The late Douglas Southall Freeman, one of the greatest Civil War historians, believed that Richard Taylor was the one "Confederate general who possessed literary art that approached first rank." A gentleman planter and Southern aristocrat, Taylor is most famous for his Civil War military exploits. Untrained as a soldier, he nonetheless developed into one of the Confederacy's ablest generals. After serving under STONEWALL JACKSON [20] in the Virginia campaigns of 1861 and 1862, Taylor was transferred to his home state of Louisiana, where he effectively harassed numerically superior Union forces until the war's close. He then entered Democratic Party politics as a bitter critic of Reconstruction and defender of Southern virtue. His opinionated and stridently anti-Federal memoirs, *Destruction and Reconstruction: Personal Experiences of the Late War*, profoundly influenced postwar Southern debates about the conduct of the Civil War and Reconstruction.

The son of future president Zachary Taylor and brother-in-law of future Confederate president JEFFERSON DAVIS [5], Richard Taylor was born in Kentucky in 1826. The family moved frequently due to the father's military assignments, but young Dick spent most of his time away from his parents attending school. Cultured, dashing, and independent in spirit, he graduated from Yale in 1845 but did not settle down until 1848, when his father assigned him managerial duties over one of his plantations. Soon Richard convinced his father to purchase another plantation, called Fashion, in St. Charles Parish, Louisiana.

On Zachary Taylor's death in 1850, Richard Taylor inherited one hundred forty-seven slaves and the Fashion estate, which also brought with it a mortgage of $100,000, payable in four years. The area's rich sugar cane production usually generated considerable income, but his extravagant lifestyle and a disastrous freeze in the fall of 1856 drove him ever deeper into debt. Still, Taylor became one of the region's most influential men. His politics reflected the discomfort many moderate Southerners had with the nation's political parties. Initially a Whig, he briefly joined the American (Know-Nothing) Party during the mid-1850s. Fear of the newly formed Republicans finally led Taylor to become a Democrat. He was no radical, however, and in the disputed 1860 Democratic National Convention at Charleston, he urged Southern fire-eaters not to walk out of the meeting.

At the outset of the war Taylor traveled to Pensacola, Florida, where he acted as civilian aide-de-camp on the staff of BRAXTON BRAGG [30]. Elected colonel of a Louisiana regiment, Taylor and his men arrived in Virginia too late for the First Battle of Bull Run. He served as brigade commander in Stonewall Jackson's Shenandoah Valley, Virginia, campaign in spring 1862, although severe rheumatoid arthritis hampered him throughout the Seven Days Battles, Virginia. Nevertheless, his talent for battle had earned the attention of Jackson, who helped Taylor become the fourth non-West Pointer appointed major general in the Confederate Army.

In August 1862, Taylor received command of the District of Western Louisiana. He was a natural choice for this command, but a lack of resources and manpower plagued his efforts to retake New Orleans or cut the supply lines of ULYSSES S. GRANT [2] west of the Mississippi during the Vicksburg, Mississippi, campaign. In 1864, Taylor initially retreated before the forces of NATHANIEL P. BANKS [59] during the Red River campaign. On April 8, however, Taylor turned and struck the Federals at the Battle of Mansfield, Louisiana. With his own nine thousand men outnumbered by the twelve thousand Union troops who participated in the battle, Taylor nonetheless drove the enemy back in disarray, capturing twenty cannon and some two hundred wagons. Although another Confederate attack the next day at Pleasant Hill, Louisiana, failed, Banks abandoned his offensive.

Taylor earned his promotion to lieutenant general, but sullied his reputation in an attack against EDMUND KIRBY SMITH [56], his superior officer and commander of the Trans-Mississippi Department. Smith, claimed Taylor, had deliberately withheld reinforcements that might have allowed him to annihilate Banks's entire command. The ugly feud which resulted tarnished the records of both men. Taylor served out the rest of the war commanding the once-proud Army of Tennessee, which had never recovered from its losses under JOHN BELL HOOD [38] at the Battle of Nashville.

Taylor died in 1879, a week after publication of his *Destruction and Reconstruction.* Forcefully written, its descriptions of the war's campaigns and pro-Southern denunciations of congressional Reconstruction swayed subsequent debates about the course and results of the Civil War.

Rebels and Yankees exchange gunfire during the Seven Days Battles, Virginia, 1862.

Albert Sidney Johnston

(1803–1862)

Although he was believed by some contemporaries to be America's ablest military officer at the outset of the Civil War, Albert Sidney Johnston's short wartime record is fraught with controversy. A longtime friend of Confederate President JEFFERSON DAVIS [5], Johnston assumed command of Department No. 2, the western theater of operations, in September 1861. Beset by shortages of men, equipment, and supplies, he launched a surprise attack against the Federals under ULYSSES S. GRANT [2] at Shiloh, Tennessee, but fell mortally wounded during the first day's fighting.

Born in Kentucky in 1803, Johnston attended Transylvania (Kentucky) University for two years before entering the U.S. Military Academy. He graduated in 1826, eighth in his class of forty-one. Johnston resigned his commission after eight years' military service. His wife's death in 1836 convinced him to go west, where he fought in the Texas Revolution and served for two

199

years as secretary of war for the Republic of Texas. Elected colonel of a Texas regiment during the Mexican War, he distinguished himself in the Battle of Monterrey and in 1849 accepted a commission as a major in the U.S. Army.

Standing just over six feet tall and weighing nearly two hundred pounds, Johnston seemed every inch the professional soldier. In 1855, Secretary of War Davis, who had been Johnston's junior at both Transylvania and West Point and had fought beside him in Mexico, appointed his fellow Kentuckian colonel of the newly created Second Cavalry Regiment. Johnston commanded the "Mormon expedition," which occupied Utah in 1857. He handled this difficult task well enough to receive a brevet promotion to brigadier general and, in 1860, appointment to command the Department of the Pacific. Opposed to secession, he nonetheless rejected an offer of high command in the United States Army and threw in his lot with Texas, his adopted state.

Confident in his old friend's abilities, Davis, as provisional president of the Confederacy, consolidated the west under Johnston's unified command, but with fewer than forty thousand poorly armed men scattered from Kentucky to Arkansas, Johnston inherited a crisis. His aggressive bluffs in Kentucky unnerved WILLIAM T. SHERMAN [3] and DON CARLOS BUELL [95]; in central Tennessee, however, incompetent subordinates lost strategic Forts Henry and Donelson in February 1862. The heartland of the Confederacy now lay exposed to the Federal threat. Belatedly recognizing the danger, Davis dispatched P. G. T. BEAUREGARD [35] to act as Johnston's second-in-command and arranged for thousands of reinforcements. At Beauregard's behest just over forty thousand Confederates, including Johnston's Kentucky command, formed at Corinth, Mississippi. Seventeen miles away lay Ulysses S. Grant and a slightly smaller Union force at Pittsburg Landing, Tennessee. Thirty thousand additional Federal troops were en route. A decisive attack, the Confederates hoped, might destroy Grant before the reinforcements arrived.

Johnston erred in leaving the details of the march from Corinth to Pittsburg Landing to Beauregard, whose complex plans proved far beyond the abilities of the green army. The ensuing traffic snarl delayed the attack, originally planned for April 4, for two days. Beauregard and the newly arrived BRAXTON BRAGG [30] both advised against continuing; Johnston, still popular with his troops though now denounced by most of the Southern press, determined to strike. The initial assault at Shiloh Church just southwest of Pittsburg Landing went well. Atop his horse, Johnston seemed to be everywhere, encouraging and cajoling his men as they drove back the surprised Federals, but just after two o'clock that afternoon, a bullet severed a major artery in his right leg above the knee. Unaware of the wound's seriousness, Johnston bled to death before medical attention arrived. Command passed to Beauregard, who called off the attacks later that day. Grant, reeling from the sudden onslaught, steadied his forces as Federal reinforcements arrived that evening. The following day Grant counterattacked, winning back the lost ground and forcing Beauregard back to Corinth.

Union boats at Pittsburg Landing. Grant's headquarters was located in the Tigress *(center)*

Historians have disagreed about the impact of Johnston's premature death upon the Confederate cause. His supporters emphasize his delay of the Union army in Kentucky, his inspirational combat leadership, and his successful concentration of his forces in the face of the numerically superior enemy. Some believe that had Johnston not been killed, the Confederates would have won the Battle of Shiloh. Critics, however, maintain that Beauregard, not Johnston, was the guiding force behind the collection of Confederate troops at Corinth and note that Johnston recklessly exposed himself to enemy fire. Whatever the case, by leaving to Beauregard authority over planning the march and battle dispositions at Shiloh, Johnston made a fatal error in judgment that cost the Confederacy dearly.

80

Henry Bellows

(1814–1882)

Henry Bellows, the nineteenth century's leading Unitarian reformer, owes his rank in this volume to his role as founder and president of the U.S. Sanitary Commission. Set up to assist sick and wounded Union soldiers and their families in the absence of other Federal support groups, the Sanitary Commission raised some seven million dollars in cash along with fifteen million dollars in donated supplies. The massive organization comprised some seven thousand local aid societies and maintained branch offices in ten cities in addition to its Washington headquarters. Although some impatient reformers criticized Bellows's pragmatic style, which favored gentle suasion rather than open confrontation in his efforts to improve conditions, it is difficult to envision a more aggressive personality leading such a diverse coalition of business, medical, and civic interests.

Born in Boston in 1814, Henry Whitney Bellows graduated from Harvard College at age eighteen. He taught school in New York and acted as private tutor to a wealthy Louisiana family before graduating from Harvard Divinity School in 1837. Following a brief ministry in Mobile, Alabama, he took leadership of a church which was eventually known as All Souls. An effective, inspirational speaker, Bellows energized the church and took part in numerous charitable activities. He delivered his most notable theological address, "The Suspense of Faith," in 1859, in which he hoped that a universal church might counteract what he saw as the moral decay of contemporary Protestantism.

The U.S. Sanitary Commission grew out of the New York Aid Society into a national crusade. The army initially opposed the idea, as did President LINCOLN [1], who referred to such an auxiliary as a "fifth wheel to the coach." Despite these objections, the president signed the order that created the new group on June 13, 1861. Bellows's organizational skills immediately came to the fore. To fill the gaps left by existing military hospital services, the Sanitary Commission did everything from helping to care for sick or wounded soldiers to assisting dependents and veterans in securing their pension claims. Thousands of volunteers, many of them women, supplemented the work of over five hundred paid agents. Giant sanitary fairs, which featured parades, auctions of donated merchandise, and raffles, not only rallied public support for the war but also raised over four million dollars for the Sanitary Commission and allied agencies.

Most controversial were the Sanitary Commission's efforts to change the army's medical bureau. Commission personnel advised soldiers to take steps to improve camp health by proper placement of latrines, improving cooking, and securing better water supplies. The interference irked many army doctors, but complaints about such issues paled in comparison to the furious opposition to the thousands of women volunteers within the commission. "Sensation preachers, village doctors, and strong-minded women" must be prohibited from military hospitals, argued some army bureaucrats, but the Sanitary Commission became a national political force. A law passed in April 1862 suspended the medical branch's strict seniority system, thus allowing progressive young surgeons to gain higher rank. Lincoln also took the commission's advice and appointed William H. Hammond, a thirty-three-year-old firebrand, surgeon general. Hammond's cooperation with Bellows and the Sanitary Commission undoubtedly saved thousands of lives and comforted countless others.

After the war, Bellows embarked upon a second crusade—this time to organize the country's Unitarian churches into a "National Conference." The initiative first stunned his followers, accustomed to the individualism stressed by their traditional doctrine. Bellows, however, argued that churches needed to play a central role in religious life. Only through a concerted, organized effort, he argued, could the churches deal with society's problems. Many Unitarians rejected this as heresy, but Bellows gradually expanded the numbers who joined his National Conference. A moderate who was willing to compromise on minor points of doctrine in order to achieve his larger goal, he thought it essential to provide religious liberals with at least a minimal institutional framework. He remarried in 1874, five years after the death of his first wife. Bellows died in New York in 1882.

81

Jubal Early

(1816–1894)

Scrappy, aggressive, and cantankerous, Jubal Early ranks among the best officers in the Army of Northern Virginia under ROBERT E. LEE [4]. "Old Jube" was in the thick of the fighting at First Bull Run, the Seven Days, Second Bull Run, Antietam, Fredericksburg, Chancellorsville, Gettysburg, and the Wilderness. From June to November 1864, Early commanded the Army of the Valley, given the task of saving the Shenandoah Valley, Virginia, and diverting Union troops from the Army of the Potomac. His men marched over 1,600 miles and at one time threatened Washington itself before being driven out of the Valley by PHILIP SHERIDAN [18]. After the war, Early defended Lee's reputation against any hint of criticism and became a leading figure in developing the ideology of the "Lost Cause," which attributed the Confederacy's defeat to overwhelming Union numerical and industrial superiority rather than to any Southern failures.

Jubal Anderson Early was born in Franklin County, Virginia, in 1816, the third of ten children in a family of prosperous Virginia farmers. He was sent to the U.S. Military Academy in large part to help him forget his grief over his recently deceased mother. There Early's excellent academic scores were somewhat offset by numerous demerits for misbehavior; still, he graduated eighteenth in a class of fifty in 1837. Commissioned in the artillery, he served briefly in the Second Seminole War before resigning in 1838. Early became a lawyer, entered politics as a Whig, and was appointed the commonwealth's attorney. He volunteered during the war against Mexico but saw no combat.

As a delegate to the Virginia secession convention, Early spoke out against leaving the Union, but upon Virginia's secession, Early, like Lee, volunteered to defend his state. Commissioned a colonel, he won a promotion to brigadier general after First Bull Run, Virginia. Wounded in the early stages of the Peninsular Campaign, Virginia, Early led a skillful counterattack at the Battle of Antietam, Maryland. At Fredericksburg, Virginia, his counterstroke restored a sagging Confederate line and secured him a promotion to major general. Another excellent performance at Chancellorsville, Virginia, reinforced his growing reputation as combat commander. There he held Confederate positions against Union forces led by John Sedgwick while Lee concentrated the bulk of the army against JOSEPH HOOKER [36]. Early tenaciously held his line long enough for Lee to defeat Hooker and then turn on Sedgwick, defeating both piecemeal.

Early's record to that date rivaled that of any division commander in Lee's army. At Gettysburg, Pennsylvania, however, Early's failure to push more aggressively against Union positions atop Culp's Hill sparked a good deal of criticism. He also seemed uncharacteristically hesitant at the Battle of the Wilderness, Virginia. Promoted to lieutenant general and given command of the Second Corps after Richard Ewell's retirement in late May 1864, Early was ordered to the Shenandoah Valley the following month. With a command never totaling more than fourteen thousand five hundred men, he outmaneuvered several enemy forces and briefly threatened Washington. In retaliation for Union destruction of his beloved Shenandoah, in late July he ordered that Chambersburg, Pennsylvania, be burned. So far, he had succeeded brilliantly, diverting thousands of troops who might otherwise have reinforced Grant, but Early's overconfidence would get the best of him. Now faced by the dangerous Philip Sheridan, he suffered stinging defeats at Winchester, Fisher's Hill, and Cedar Creek and was forced to abandon the Shenandoah Valley.

Following Appomattox, Early fled the country for Mexico and then to Canada. He resumed his Virginia law practice in 1869 and eight years later became director of the Louisiana State Lottery. A frequent lecturer, he wore only gray, refused to apologize for his role in the war, and helped to organize the Southern Historical Society. Early contributed numerous articles and essays during his lifetime, although his *Autobiographical Sketch and Narrative of the War Between the States* was published posthumously. He fought bitterly with his old comrade in arms, JAMES LONGSTREET [19], over the latter's criticism of Lee's handling of the Battle of Gettysburg. In joining this feud, Early greatly influenced subsequent histories of the conflict.

Reputedly the most profane man in the Army of the Northern Virginia, Early was one of very few who dared to swear in Lee's presence. He sported a long gray beard and usually wore a slouch hat adorned by a black ostrich plume. Few subordinates appreciated Early's biting sarcasm, but his superiors recognized his considerable military talents. An unreconstructed rebel to the end, he died in 1894, still a bachelor.

The battle of Gettysburg, Pennsylvania, July 1–3, 1863

82

William Gilmore Simms

(1806–1870)

The South's preeminent man of letters of the mid-nineteenth century, William Gilmore Simms did much to foster the development of a distinct Southern culture. Incredibly prolific, Simms published over eighty books of poetry, fiction, history, and biography. These works, which ranged in subject matter from the aristocratic Tidewater to the southwestern frontier, illustrated his section's rich diversity. As editor of numerous journals, he further guided the direction of antebellum Southern literature. Simms's fervent support for slavery and secession permeated his fiction, lectures, and voluminous private correspondence. Through these, Simms became an influential voice for the Southern aristocracy.

William Gilmore Simms was born in Charleston, South Carolina, in 1806. After the death of his mother in 1808, his father left him in the care of Jane Gates, his maternal grandmother. Though his formal education was erratic, the young Simms developed a passion for books and literature. A workaholic, by age twenty-one he had helped to found and edit a literary magazine, written two volumes of poetry, and been admitted to the South Carolina bar. During the mid-1830s he gained national recognition as a novelist. Criticized for working too hastily, Simms's work is sometimes flawed by internal inconsistencies, redundancy, and careless grammatical errors, but at its best, his writing captures the vitality and character of the antebellum South.

Immensely ambitious, Simms believed he could create a distinctly American literature by focusing on American historical themes and by dealing with the South—the region he knew best and which, in his view, best represented the ideals of the Founding Fathers. In essence, Simms hoped to write the Great American Novel by writing the Great Southern Novel. In so doing, he hoped to preserve a world that combined the beauty of Appalachia, the culture of Western Europe, and the rugged individualism of the mystical frontier. Though he admitted that he never actually fulfilled his literary promise, his torrent of published writings yielded a considerable income. His father-in-law contributed to his growing wealth by generously providing him with a four-thousand-acre South Carolina estate, the Woodlands, which included seventy slaves.

Simms vigorously defended traditional Southern institutions. He was a powerful public speaker and served a term in the South Carolina legislature from 1844 to 1846. More significant was his voluminous correspondence with prominent Southern politicians and intellectuals. Simms felt threatened by the North's growing industrial and economic power, which he believed endangered Southern order and influence. To counter this peril, he advocated expansion into Texas, the Southwest, and the Caribbean and became increasingly vocal in his defense of slavery. In 1856, as the sectional crisis deepened, he embarked on an ill-fated though courageous lecture tour of the North. His defense of the South won few friends there, and the criticism he received helped to confirm his belief in the desirability of Southern independence.

Simms strongly supported the secession movement of 1860–61. The election of ABRAHAM LINCOLN [1], wrote Simms, meant that "Black Republicanism . . . would run riot over the land. . . . If the South submits, the Black Republicans are confirmed in their power, their predictions, their supremacy." As was his habit, Simms threw himself into the Confederate cause, writing lengthy letters full of military and political advice. Financially ruined by the destruction of Woodlands by the army of WILLIAM T. SHERMAN [3], Simms churned out fiction, poetry, and history in order to support his family after the war until his death in 1870. Though often ignored by modern literary critics, he profoundly influenced mid-nineteenth century Southern thought and culture. He outlived both of his wives, but Simms was survived by only six of his fifteen children.

83

Justin Smith Morrill

(1810–1898)

A New Englander and member of Congress from 1855 to 1898, Justin Smith Morrill sponsored two of the most important pieces of legislation to come out of the war. The Morrill Tariff, passed in early 1861, was a decidedly protectionist measure that alienated Southerners who still held some loyalty to the United States. The Morrill Land-Grant College Act, enacted the following year, gave federal land to the states in order to support agricultural and mechanical colleges. Proceeds from sale or lease of these lands were used to offset costs at the sixty-nine land-grant institutions eventually established under the program, thus making higher education possible for many who would otherwise have been unable to afford tuition.

The eldest son of a prosperous farmer and blacksmith, Justin Smith Morrill was born in 1810 at Strafford, Vermont. He left school at age fifteen to go to work as a clerk in a local store. After a short stint at Portland, Maine, he returned to Strafford and by 1834 had become a business partner with his old employer, a local judge. Morrill succeeded splendidly, making enough money to retire to his farm in 1848. Three years later he married Ruth Barnell Swan; one of their two sons lived to maturity. Formerly a Whig, Morrill quickly converted to Republicanism upon the former party's demise. Pro-temperance, antislavery, and proud of his working-class Vermont roots, he was an ardent protectionist who opposed the tariff reductions of 1857.

Morrill also took an interest in educational reform, concluding that federal aid to state agricultural colleges would encourage more scientific farming and make it possible for more young men to attend school. In December 1857 he introduced a measure which would grant the states federal land, the revenue from which would support universities. Initially, western congressmen opposed giving the land, for most of it, though located in the west, would be given to the eastern states. Morrill's measure passed both houses in February 1859, but President JAMES BUCHANAN [26] vetoed the bill, contending that it was an unconstitutional expansion of the federal government.

The South's secession in the months following the election and inauguration of ABRAHAM LINCOLN [1] made possible the implementation of Republican Party principles, which included Morrill's reforms. His wartime tariff reflected his distrust of Great Britain, his desire to increase revenue in order to avoid inflationary monetary policies, and his determination to protect American manufacturing and labor. In December 1861, Morrill reintroduced his land-grant bill. Supported by Senator BENJAMIN WADE [49], the measure was now linked to a Homestead Act, which westerners generally favored. Attracting broad popular support, in June 1862 the Morrill Land-Grant College Act passed both houses by a comfortable margin. President Lincoln quickly signed it into law.

The land-grant act, which owed its passage to the wartime withdrawal of Southern opponents from Congress, would be Morrill's most lasting legislative triumph. It provided every participating state with thirty thousand acres (ten thousand more than in his earlier 1857 proposal) of federal land per member of congress. Eventually, the program diverted over thirteen million acres of land to support higher education. In 1890, a second act began providing annual subsidies to each land-grant college.

In 1867 Morrill took a seat in the Senate, which he held for the rest of his life. He served on the Joint Committee on Reconstruction and voted to convict President ANDREW JOHNSON [6]. As a member of the Building and Grounds Committee Morrill influenced the conception and design of several of the capital's most enduring public structures, including the Washington Monument and the Library of Congress. Chair of the Senate Finance Committee on several occasions, he remained a strong protectionist and opposed adoption of paper money or the silver standard. Morrill also opposed the eight-hour work day and woman suffrage. The venerable politician died in 1898, his forty-three consecutive years in Congress establishing what was then a record for longevity.

Morrill was generally conservative on social issues. The absence from Congress of the Confederate states during the Civil War had made possible passage of his protective tariff and his more lasting land-grant college act, which greatly expanded the federal government's involvement in education.

Sterling Price

(1809–1867)

Antebellum politician and Confederate general in the west, Sterling Price enjoyed only mixed success as a military commander. Victorious in the war's early months at Wilson's Creek and Lexington, he went on to lose the battles of Pea Ridge, Iuka, Pilot Knob, and Westport. Price focused his efforts largely on redeeming Missouri from Federal occupation. Brave in battle and popular with his own men, the handsome, fatherly Price nonetheless quarreled with every one of his superiors, whether military or civilian. President JEFFERSON DAVIS [5] labeled him "the vainest man I ever met."

Sterling Price was born to a family of wealthy Virginia slaveholders in 1809. After attending Hampton-Sidney College, he moved with his parents in 1830 to Missouri. There he established a tobacco farm, acquired several dozen slaves, and married. Five of his children lived to maturity. He served several terms in the state legislature until he won a congressional seat in 1844. Price resigned to fight in the Mexican War, eventually becoming a brigadier general. During the march from Missouri to New Mexico and the invasion of Chihuahua, he displayed the traits which would characterize his military career. His troops adored him for his bravery, defiance of orders that he dismount his cavalrymen, and lax discipline. His superiors, however, found him independent to the point of insubordination.

On his return to Missouri, Price steadily expanded his plantation until he became one of the state's biggest landholders. A Democrat and an Episcopalian, he was elected governor in 1853. Like most Missourians, Price feared disunion and the war it might bring. Elected president of the state's secession convention, he supported that group's resolution that "there is no adequate cause for the withdrawal of Missouri from the Union," while at the same time warning the federal government not to intervene in the state's internal affairs. Efforts to maintain peace in Missouri collapsed on June 11, however, during a meeting that Price attended at the Planters' House Hotel in St. Louis.

Convinced that his loyalties lay with the Confederacy, Price began mobilizing troops. In August, he defeated Union forces led by Nathaniel Lyon at Wilson's Creek, Missouri. In September he captured Lexington, Missouri, its three thousand strong Federal garrison and a large stock of weapons. He found Missourians less willing to rally to the Confederate colors than he expected, however, and was forced back into northwestern Arkansas. Commanding the newly organized Army of the West as a recently appointed major general, he was wounded in the defeat at Pea Ridge, Arkansas, and transferred east of the Mississippi River to help reinforce Southern armies facing offensives under ULYSSES S. GRANT [2] into southern Tennessee and Mississippi. Furious at having been ordered to abandon his plan against Missouri, Price twice went to Richmond and publicly denounced President Davis.

Price was transferred back to Arkansas in spring 1863. That July, he participated in the unsuccessful Confederate assault on Helena, Arkansas. Called "Old Pap" by his men, he took temporary command of the District of Arkansas shortly thereafter. Forced to evacuate Little Rock that September by superior Union forces, Price always longed for a return to Missouri, where he still hoped his appearance would trigger an outpouring of support for the Confederacy. He got his chance in August 1864. Leading three divisions, Price planned to move swiftly into southeastern Missouri and seize St. Louis, recruit troops, gather supplies, and impress upon the population the righteousness of the Southern cause. Heavy losses in a foolish attack against entrenched Union forces at Pilot Knob, Missouri, however, forced Price to abandon efforts against St. Louis in favor of a western sweep toward Kansas. He barely escaped annihilation at Westport, Missouri, dashing whatever small hope remained that Missouri could be recaptured.

After the war Price tried to establish a Confederate colony at Carlota, Mexico. Named after the wife of Emperor Maximilian, the settlement once numbered some two hundred and fifty ex-Confederates, but the emperor's sagging fortunes forced its abandonment by the summer of 1866. Impoverished and broken in health and spirits, Price returned to Missouri, where he died the following year of cholera. His failure to win over his beloved Missouri is suggestive of the Confederacy's limited appeal there as well as in the other border states of Kentucky, Maryland, and Delaware.

85

Frank Leslie

(1821–1880)

The most eminent journalistic entrepreneur of the mid-nineteenth century, Frank Leslie founded, managed, and published several major periodicals. *Frank Leslie's Illustrated Weekly* was America's first successful illustrated news weekly, its artists portraying contemporary events in vivid sketches with accompanying news accounts designed for a broad readership. "Never shoot over the heads of the people," he advised his staff. Although eventually outpaced in circulation numbers by *Harper's Magazine, Leslie's* coverage of the Civil War provided an exceptionally good record of the war, with up to twelve correspondents and eighty artists compiling three thousand scenes of military events.

Frank Leslie was born Henry Carter at Ipswich, England, in 1821. His father, a prosperous manufacturer, sent him off as a teenager to London to learn the glove business, but the younger Carter soon began submitting drawings to the *Illustrated London News* under a pseudonym, Frank Leslie. After six years of drawing and of directing that paper's engraving department, he came to New York in 1848. Successful work on several projects allowed him to begin his own publication, *Frank Leslie's Lady's Gazette of Fashion and Fancy Needlework,* in 1854. Capitalizing on the public's craving for illustration and the fashionable hoopskirt dresses just coming into style, Carter's *Gazette* flourished. Profits from this venture allowed him to acquire the *New York Journal of Romance.*

In December 1855, Carter launched his most ambitious project, *Frank Leslie's Illustrated Newspaper.* A sixteen-page folio sold for ten cents per copy. The fledgling weekly broke new journalistic ground in the United States by combining vivid illustrations with lively stories about contemporary events. A miscellaneous collection of news, fine arts, sports, and serial fiction, *Leslie's* circulation often surpassed one hundred thousand. Stories ranged from coverage of the raid on Harpers Ferry by JOHN BROWN [14] to New York's "swill milk" racket, an exposé of the contemporary practice of feeding cows with refuse from distilleries, then selling the milk of the unhealthy animals to the general public.

In 1857, Carter formally changed his name to Frank Leslie, continuing to expand his empire of periodicals. Now competing against several publications which had adopted his style, especially *Harper's* and the *New York Illustrated News,* Leslie's newspaper maintained a neutral stance on the war, offering to buy sketches from both sides and datelining one dispatch from "Charleston, Republic of South Carolina." *Frank Leslie's Illustrated Weekly's* coverage of the war's early years was especially strong, but lack of capital, the retirement of his best field artist, and Leslie's insistence on launching five new publications during the war years eventually took its toll on quality. Circulation was also hurt by Leslie's attempt to maintain balanced war coverage.

FRANK LESLIE'S ILLUSTRATED NEWSPAPER.

Detail from one of Leslie's weeklies

Leslie led a tumultuous personal life. In 1860, he separated from his first wife, living for a time with Miriam Florence Squier and her husband, both of whom became editors in the Leslie publishing empire. Mrs. Squier and Leslie each secured difficult divorces in the early 1870s, then married in 1874. For a few years, the couple entertained in grand style and traveled the world, mixing with royalty and entertaining their readers with stories and pictures of the rich and famous. But despite boasting an aggregate circulation of half a million copies a week, the depression of the mid-1870s reduced profits, forcing Leslie's publishing company into partial receivership.

Despite his later problems, through his regular weekly and special pictorial history supplements Frank Leslie had helped the Northern public learn about and understand the American Civil War. His newspapers also preserve a superb record of America's greatest conflict. Leslie died in early January 1880; his talented wife changed her name to that of her husband, Frank Leslie, and seized the publishing opportunity afforded by the assassination of President James Garfield to restore circulation of the empire's flagship publication, the *Illustrated Weekly.* A better editor and business manager than her second husband, she restored her wealth and died in 1914, leaving most of her two-million-dollar estate to the cause of woman suffrage.

86

Little Crow

(1803?–1863)

Many readers forget that the American Civil War also featured fierce conflicts between Indians and non-Indians. Among the largest of these confrontations broke out in 1862, pitting the Dakota Indians against the Federal and Minnesota territorial governments. The fighting ultimately resulted in the ouster of the Dakotas from Minnesota.

Perhaps the most prominent of the Dakotas (a term meaning "allies," used by the Mdewakanton, Wahpekute, Sisseton, and Wahpeton tribes of the Eastern Sioux) was Little Crow, a Mdewakanton chief and shaman. Born about 1803, Little Crow, called Taoyateduta ("His Red Nation") by his own people, witnessed the severe decline of the fortunes of his tribe. As hereditary chief of a Mdewakanton village, he signed the Mendota Treaty of 1851, but vehemently protested the U.S. government's failure to prevent white intruders from encroaching upon Indian lands or to ensure that money promised to the tribes by the treaty actually wound up in the hands of Indians. Little Crow also signed an 1858 agreement which further reduced Indian lands and again saw most Indian allotments pocketed by white traders and negotiators. Egotistical and ambitious, he was disappointed when tribal elders elected a rival as head chief in spring 1862. Hoping to regain his former prestige, Little Crow attempted to associate himself more closely with white-allied factions, cutting his hair, taking up farming, and sporting a velvet-collared frock coat.

By August 1862, relations between the Dakotas, soldiers at Fort Ridgely, Minnesota, and Indian bureau officials had deteriorated badly as government agents refused to distribute expected food allotments and cash annuities. On August 17, a group of young Wahpetons murdered five whites. Little Crow at first resisted calls for general warfare, arguing that the Indians had no chance for victory. After being called a coward (and perhaps in hopes of securing the head chief's post), he reversed his earlier stance and organized a full-scale attack at and around the Redwood Agency. Little Crow's raiders killed up to four hundred whites the next day, August 18.

Fortunately for the whites, the Indians divided their forces, with Little Crow and one group focusing on Fort Ridgely while others concentrated on the settlement at New Ulm, Minnesota. Defeats in the attacks on both places

Contemporary rendering of the execution of thirty-eight Indians involved in the rebellion led by Little Crow.

demoralized Little Crow's followers; support from other Dakotas slowed to a trickle. Meanwhile, the Minnesotans assembled reinforcements for a counterattack. The Battle of Wood Lake, Minnesota, on September 23, 1862, proved another decisive setback for the war faction among the Dakotas. By the end of October, some two thousand Indians had been taken prisoner. A military commission sentenced over three hundred of them to be hanged; President ABRAHAM LINCOLN [1], recognizing the flimsy nature of much of the evidence, reduced that number to thirty-eight. On the day after Christmas, the nation's largest public execution was carried out at Mankato.

Meanwhile, Little Crow had escaped and headed west. With the onset of winter, the Minnesotans called off the pursuit, but reports continued to place Little Crow at the center of a large Indian alliance in the Dakota Territory. Major General JOHN POPE [62], recently arrived from the east, organized another offensive, which began in the summer of 1863. Little Crow slipped back into Minnesota to steal horses, but while picking berries he was killed by a settler, just weeks before Pope's columns bested the Sioux in several engagements in present-day North Dakota.

While Little Crow supported accommodation with the whites for most of his life, it seems characteristic of the tragedies of Indian-white relations that he came to be a leader of a major Indian war. His scalp remained on public display for years at the Minnesota State Historical Society before eventually being returned to his descendants for proper burial. Fighting against the Sioux continued after Little Crow's death, blending with more general conflicts that inflamed much of the Great Plains, thus diverting valuable resources from the North's larger effort against the Confederacy.

Dorothea Dix

(1802–1887)

Among the most effective of nineteenth-century American reformers, Dorothea Dix is best known as a champion of humane treatment for the mentally ill. Before the Civil War, she lobbied several state legislatures for the creation of publicly supported asylums. In an age when society discouraged women from assuming active public roles, Dix's persistence and thorough knowledge of the conditions of jails, almshouses, and penal institutions made her a formidable humanitarian force. During the Civil War, she became a powerful advocate for the widespread introduction of women nurses into military hospitals. As superintendent of women nurses, Dix helped not only to improve care for the sick and wounded but also to open a new professional career option for future generations of women.

    Dorothea Dix was born in 1802 at Hampden, Maine. Uncomfortable with life at her parents' home, at age ten she moved to Boston to be with her grandmother. "I never knew childhood," Dix later remembered; by age fourteen she was teaching school. She soon opened the Dix Mansion in Boston, a school for girls, which, in addition to the normal emphasis on moral development, boasted an unusual academic focus on the natural sciences. A Unitarian, Dix also wrote several books on morals and behavior, one of which, *Conversations on Common Things,* underwent at least sixty editions and remained in print through the Civil War. Chronic lung problems, however, forced her to give up her school by 1835. After a sojourn to England, she returned to Boston, nearly an invalid.

Dix's own suffering perhaps intensified her compassion for the mentally ill. Having rallied somewhat by 1841, Dix opened a Sunday School class at the East Cambridge House of Correction (Massachusetts). Shocked by the maltreatment of the mentally ill persons held there, she undertook a thorough two-year study of the state's provisions for mental care. Rather than creating separate asylums, government officials had simply placed the mentally ill in jails, almshouses, and private homes. Her blistering report described the inhumane living conditions and common reliance upon chains, ropes, and beatings to control the mentally ill. In 1843, Massachusetts began to enact some of her reforms.

Not satisfied with this state victory, Dix made the cause a national one. Battling poor health, an entrenched bureaucracy, the public's limited notions of government's social responsibilities, and criticisms of a woman's involvement in public policy matters, she took her case to Congress and state legislatures across the land. Dix seemed indefatigable. As of 1845, she claimed to have traveled ten thousand miles and visited eighteen state penitentiaries, three hundred county jails, and over five hundred almshouses and other institutions. Largely due to her efforts, during the late 1840s and early 1850s eleven legislatures promised to create state hospitals. In 1854, however, President Franklin Pierce vetoed a $12,000,000 package for creating a national asylum that she had backed.

Dix traveled to Europe during the mid-1850s, helping to secure the founding of mental hospitals in Scotland and Italy. In June 1861, she was appointed "Superintendent of Female Nurses," with exclusive power to select and assign women nurses to military hospitals. Many in the male-dominated world of medicine, however, resented a woman having such broad authority. Dix formed an uneasy coalition with officials from the U.S. Sanitary Commission. Despite enjoying the support of Secretary of War EDWIN STANTON [9], her authority was somewhat reduced by Surgeon General William Hammond. Dix retained her authority to select female nurses, but the male medical officer in charge of a military hospital assumed "control and direction" of her nurses.

Dix was tall, spare, and often authoritarian, but she was one of the most skilled political tacticians of the nineteenth-century reformers. Dix resumed her crusade for better mental hospital care following the Civil War. She died in 1887 at a home given to her by a hospital she had helped establish at Trenton, New Jersey.

John Crittenden

(1787–1863)

One of the last great antebellum political figures, John J. Crittenden proposed a last-ditch compromise intended to avert the Civil War. The failure of Crittenden's effort revealed with stark clarity just how fractious the nation's political debates had become. Earlier, the Missouri Compromise (1820–1821) and the Compromise of 1850, while providing no permanent solution to the slavery controversies, had at least prevented breakup of the Union. By 1861, however, the perceived distance between North and South had grown too large for half-measures to seal the breach.

Born in Woodford County, Kentucky in 1787, John Jordan Crittenden finished his law courses at William and Mary College in 1807. He established his legal practice in Logan County, Kentucky, then secured an appointment as attorney general for the Illinois Territory. During the War of 1812 he served as an aide-de-camp. In 1815, Crittenden was chosen speaker of the Kentucky house; two years later, the legislature appointed him to fill out a vacant seat in the U.S. Senate. In 1819, he returned to Kentucky and transferred his legal practice to Frankfort, where he became one of the region's most noted defense attorneys.

Crittenden's support for John Quincy Adams was rewarded in 1827 with an appointment as the U.S. district attorney for Kentucky. Adams subsequently nominated Crittenden to the Supreme Court, but the Senate, now dominated by Andrew Jackson's supporters, refused to allow his name to come up for confirmation. In 1835, the Kentucky legislature elected Crittenden, a Whig, to another Senate term. Opposing Jackson's war on the national bank, he worked tirelessly for William Henry Harrison's 1840 presidential campaign. Crittenden then accepted Harrison's offer to become attorney general, but with the accession of John Tyler to the presidency following Harrison's death, Crittenden resigned in protest against the new chief executive's failure to follow Whig doctrine.

Crittenden still retained his support among Kentucky Whigs, who in 1843 engineered his reelection to the Senate. Like his fellow Kentuckian Henry Clay, Crittenden was unsure of the merits of national expansion. After concluding that Clay would never win the presidency, Crittenden backed Zachary Taylor in 1848, winning Taylor's gratitude but losing Clay's friendship. Upon Taylor's death, Millard Fillmore named Crittenden his attorney-general.

In 1854, Crittenden returned to the Senate. The expansion of slavery into the West, he believed, was a moot point, because "no sensible man would carry his slaves there if he could." A Unionist, he opposed the Kansas-Nebraska Act for having reopened the question of slavery in the territories. With the Whig collapse, he supported the Know-Nothing Party before backing the Constitutional Union ticket in 1860. Crittenden still denounced extremists on both sides, but with the election of ABRAHAM LINCOLN [1] Crittenden desperately tried to stave off disunion with an eleventh-hour compromise. He proposed a series of constitutional amendments which would have reestablished the old 36°30′ line once used in the Missouri Compromise. Slavery would be prohibited above and protected below this line; these rules could not be overridden by future amendments and would apply to all territories "now held, or hereafter acquired." Lincoln, however, signaled his opposition, and without Republican support any compromise was doomed.

Having failed to deter the South's dash for independence, Crittenden now resolved to prevent his own beloved Kentucky from seceding. Elected to the House of Representatives in June 1861, he believed the war should be fought to preserve the supremacy of the Constitution, not to interfere with the established institutions (such as slavery) of individual states. As such, he opposed the confiscation of Confederate property, the enlistment of black troops, and the Emancipation Proclamation. He died in 1863, survived by his third wife.

John Crittenden's inability to craft a compromise which might have averted the war had revealed the depths of the nation's sectional tensions. It also split families. In border states like Kentucky, the Civil War often pitted brother against brother. Nowhere was this more evident than in the case of the Crittenden family. Two of his sons became major generals during the war: George for the Confederacy and Thomas for the Union. Both survived the conflict, with Thomas remaining in the United States Army until 1881.

Clara Barton

(1821–1912)

Clara Barton was the founder of the American Red Cross, and ranks among the best-known women of the nineteenth century. She possessed enormous personal courage, fortitude, and self-sacrifice. Her contributions to American history are indeed impressive; Barton's impact on the Civil War, however, is sometimes overrated. Through hard work and resourcefulness, she helped to get supplies and medical care to those who most needed them. Yet her fiercely independent methods, which later served her so well in convincing Congress to create the Red Cross, made her difficult to work with and reduced her wartime influence.

Clarissa Harlow Barton was born at Oxford, Massachusetts, in 1821. One of five children, she began teaching school at age fifteen, and continued to do so through the early 1850s. In 1854 she moved to Washington and accepted a position in the Patent Office, only to lose the job with a change in presidential administrations two years later. Disturbed by the inadequacies of existing medical support for military personnel, Barton, with the onset of the Civil War, threw herself into caring for the sick and wounded. She began raising money and supplies for Northern soldiers. With her characteristic tenacity, she convinced the surgeon-general in mid-1862 to give her virtual carte blanche in nursing and comforting troops in need.

With Washington as her base, Barton spent most of the war with Union armies and hospitals in the eastern theater of the war. Her efforts were particularly apparent following the battles of Antietam, Maryland, and Fredericksburg, Virginia. She maintained her independence, often feuding with other Union nurses like DOROTHEA DIX [87], and remaining free of any association with the officially sanctioned U.S. Sanitary Commission. With the end of the war Barton engaged largely in the gruesome duty of identifying bodies exhumed from unmarked graves.

Her health shattered by these labors, in 1869 Barton went to Europe to recuperate on the orders of her doctors. With the outbreak of the Franco-Prussian War (1870–71), she joined international relief efforts and came into contact with the International Red Cross, established in 1864 by the Geneva Convention. After poor health forced her into temporary retirement back in the United States, she resolved to establish a similar organization in her own country. Years of intense lobbying followed; in 1882 the Senate finally ratified the Geneva Convention and formed the American Red Cross.

For the next twenty-three years Barton served as the organization's president. Under her leadership, the American Red Cross played an especially important role in providing relief to those hit by the Johnstown, Pennsylvania, flood of 1889 and the survivors of a hurricane which battered the Sea Islands in 1893. She also arranged aid shipments to Russia and Armenia and performed with her usual distinction in Cuba during the Spanish-American War. In 1900, Barton spent six weeks in Galveston, Texas, following a hurricane that killed six thousand persons.

As with most of her work, Barton conducted these efforts virtually on her own. Her refusal to delegate authority, inability to work with others, and failure to consult with other Red Cross personnel led to an internal revolt against her continued leadership. Her resignation in 1904 allowed for a much-needed restructuring of the organization. Though bitter about having been forced to resign, Barton remained active in charitable organizations until her death just outside Washington in 1912.

She was buried at her childhood home of Oxford. Barton's legacy remains the Red Cross organization she brought to the United States. During the Civil War, she had done much to ease the suffering of sick and wounded troops, but her inability to work effectively with others somewhat reduced her significance and explains her ranking below stalwarts like Dix.

90

Mary Ann Bickerdyke

(1817–1901)

Although sometimes obscured by the shadow of CLARA BARTON [89], Mary Ann Ball Bickerdyke arguably did more than Barton during the Civil War to demonstrate the important contributions women could make to military medicine. Before 1860, military nurses were exclusively male, but women like Bickerdyke shattered this barrier. Known affectionately as "Mother" Bickerdyke by the soldiers she helped, she often offended male physicians, who resented her outspoken challenge to societal notions that women should remain in the domestic sphere.

The details of Bickerdyke's early life are somewhat hazy. Born in 1817 at Knox County, Ohio, Mary Ann Ball claimed to have attended Oberlin College, although that institution's records do not support this assertion. Marrying Robert Bickerdyke in 1847, she moved to Cincinnati, where some assert that she assisted fugitive slaves. The Bickerdykes later moved to Galesburg, Illinois. In 1859, following her husband's death, Bickerdyke opened a business as a "botanic physician." Using knowledge acquired either from her family or while working as a doctor's assistant, she treated her clients with herbal teas and compresses.

With the onset of the Civil War, Bickerdyke's Congregational Church sent her to Cairo, Illinois, to assist in the care of Union soldiers. Setting aside the period's fashionable hoops for a more practical gray calico dress, she entered her field of battle brusquely determined to provide patients with better food and cleaner facilities, an attitude that engendered the affection of those under her care but angered many male physicians. Bickerdyke also insisted that she be allowed to go to field hospitals near the front as Grant's army advanced south into Tennessee and Mississippi. It became her custom to scour the battlefields at night with a lantern to find wounded soldiers who might otherwise have been forgotten.

Bickerdyke returned north in late fall 1862. After a brief rest, she embarked upon a successful fundraising tour in Illinois and Wisconsin for the United States Sanitary Commission, during which time she continued to advocate the wider employment of women nurses at military hospitals. Having won the attention of GRANT [2], she returned to the front. During the Vicksburg, Mississippi, campaign Mother Bickerdyke adopted the command

Celebrating the eightieth birthday of the "Mother" of nursing

of SHERMAN [3] as her own, securing the use of military railroads for Sanitary Commission supplies over his objection. In an incident which is probably only slightly apocryphal, a complaint about Bickerdyke's no-nonsense approach is said to have come to Sherman, who responded that he could do nothing as she outranked him. Indeed, she bragged that she was the only woman Sherman would permit at his front-line camps as he moved against Atlanta.

When Sherman's troops left Atlanta on their March to the Sea, Bickerdyke briefly returned north, where she reviewed the progress made in reorganizing Sanitary Commission hospitals and resumed her fundraising tours. On her way to rejoin Sherman's command after it reached the coast, she was diverted by reports about the deplorable condition of Union prisoners of war newly liberated from the former Confederate prison camp at Andersonville, Georgia. Focusing on the survivors, Bickerdyke helped bathe, bandage, and feed the former prisoners. She rejoined Sherman's army in time to ride in the triumphant victory parade through Washington.

Bickerdyke resigned from the Sanitary Commission on March 21, 1866, the same day the last Illinois volunteer was mustered out of the army. She later ran a hotel in Salina, Kansas, and conducted several fund-raising tours for charitable organizations. In 1886, Congress granted her a long overdue pension of twenty-five dollars a month. On her eightieth birthday, Kansas honored her with a statewide celebration of Mother Bickerdyke Day. Probably because of her lack of education, she did not write her wartime reminiscences, the absence of which helps explain her relative anonymity today. This pioneer of nursing and "Mother" to thousands of lonely, frightened, bedridden Civil War soldiers, died in Kansas in 1901, survived by one of her three children.

91

Herman Melville

(1819–1891)

One of nineteenth-century America's greatest writers, Herman Melville dealt extensively with Civil War subjects. Although Melville's underestimated collection of Civil War poetry, *Battle-Pieces and Aspects of the War,* does not equal the brilliance of *Drum-Taps* by WALT WHITMAN [69], it provides an excellent literary exposition on political and military aspects of the war. Melville hoped his poetry would encourage the nation to find lessons from its war wounds and quickly reunite in order to fulfill what he believed to be its moral destiny.

Herman Melville was born in New York City in 1819. His father's death in 1832 convinced Herman to leave school to help support his family. He took on a variety of jobs before going to sea in 1839 as a cabin boy. After four years abroad, during which time he briefly lived with some South Seas islanders, he returned to New York. Writing quickly to support his wife and family, his early novels brought enough income to enable him to purchase a farm at Pittsfield, Massachusetts, where he wrote *Moby-Dick* (1851). Though highly acclaimed by twentieth-century critics, contemporaries generally rejected this soaring narrative of an apocalyptic quest for a white whale. Four subsequent novels and collections of short stories during the 1850s also sold rather poorly.

A Democrat who doubted the wisdom of immediate emancipation, Melville nonetheless opposed secession and supported the effort to restore the Union. His wife, Lizzie, worked for the Ladies' Soldiers' Relief Association and Melville avidly followed the course of the military campaigns through newspapers, letters, and the experiences of relatives who saw active duty. Companies raised in Pittsfield served in the western campaigns, thus providing him with further insights into the conflict. In 1863, he sold his farm and moved with his family back to New York City. Turning to poetry as the genre best suited to express the intensity of war, Melville journeyed south to see the Army of the Potomac's encampment at Culpeper, Virginia.

Melville decided to compose a series of poems about the nation's wrenching experiences. By his own admission, the fall of Richmond in April 1865 stimulated most of the actual writing. *Harper's New Monthly Magazine* began printing some of his verse in early 1866, and a longer collection, *Battle-Pieces,* was published later that year. The latter collection recounted Melville's belief that the nation had fallen from grace only to achieve a postwar rebirth. With little mention of slavery and several tributes to the conservative GEORGE MCCLELLAN [7], former commander of the Army of the Potomac and unsuccessful Democratic presidential candidate, its contents illustrate Melville's belief that a speedy restoration of the former Confederate states into the Union, along with generosity and forgiveness to defeated enemies, would allow the nation to achieve its true destiny. As he concluded in his poetic tribute to the congressional testimony of ROBERT E. LEE [4] in 1866:

> Brave though the Soldier, grave his plea—
> Catching the light in the future's skies,
> Instinct disowns each darkening prophecy,
> Faith in America never dies.
> Heaven shall the end ordained fulfill,
> We march with Providence cheery still.

Receiving only lukewarm reviews, *Battle-Pieces* sold fewer than five hundred copies in the first year and a half following its publication. The popular failures of this and other writing led Melville in 1866 to take a job as a customs inspector, which he held for nineteen years. Just before his death in 1891, Melville started work on what twentieth-century critics have acclaimed as another masterpiece, *Billy Budd, Sailor* (published posthumously).

Standing nearly six feet tall, the ruggedly independent Melville never achieved the celebrity accorded him by modern readers during his own lifetime. Only recently has the importance of his Civil War poetry been recognized. Overtly political, unconventional in form and structure, and admittedly somewhat uneven, it nonetheless represents a great poet's examination of this distinctly American conflict through specific historical scenes and images.

92

Earl Van Dorn

(1820–1863)

Earl Van Dorn commanded Confederate troops in the western and Trans-Mississippi theaters during the early years of the Civil War. In 1862, he lost the Battle of Pea Ridge, Arkansas, and later launched a futile assault against Federal positions at Corinth, Mississippi. He redeemed himself, however, as a cavalryman, leading a strike force which destroyed the supply base of Ulysses S. Grant [2] at Holly Springs, Mississippi, thus forcing the Federals to abandon early efforts to move south against Vicksburg, Mississippi. His mixed combat record was itself debatable, but Van Dorn's doubtful marital fidelity made him one of the most controversial Confederate officers of the entire war and led to his early death.

Born near Port Gibson, Mississippi, in 1820, Earl Van Dorn was a great-nephew of Andrew Jackson. Nearly dismissed from the U.S. Military Academy for his unruly conduct, Van Dorn managed to graduate in 1842, fifty-second out of his class of fifty-eight, a group which included fourteen future generals. An impetuous man of small physical stature, Van Dorn won two brevet promotions during the Mexican War, suffering a foot wound during the assault against Mexico City. He then served a short tour of duty in the Third Seminole War before being transferred to duty with military asylums for disabled veterans in New Orleans and Pascagoula, Mississippi.

In 1855, Van Dorn received a highly prized appointment as captain of the newly created Second Cavalry Regiment. Boasting sixteen future Civil War generals among its officers, (including ROBERT E. LEE [4], GEORGE THOMAS [29], EDMUND KIRBY SMITH [56], ALBERT SIDNEY JOHNSTON [79], and JOHN BELL HOOD [38]), the Second Cavalry easily ranked as the army's most prestigious unit. After several desultory campaigns against the Comanches in Texas, Van Dorn, leading four companies and about one hundred Indian auxiliaries, struck a deadly blow against Buffalo Hump's Comanche village at Rush Springs, Indian Territory (today Oklahoma), in 1858. Despite suffering a severe arrow wound through his left lung and stomach, Van Dorn recovered in time to win another victory against the Comanches the following year in the Battle of Crooked Creek, Kansas. He won a long-deserved promotion to major in 1860.

Recognized as one of the antebellum army's best small-unit leaders, Van Dorn resigned his U.S. commission in early 1861 to join the Confederacy. Named a major general that September, he held various posts in Texas, Louisiana, and then Virginia before being transferred back west in January 1862. Hoping to take the war into Missouri, in early March he struck a Federal force at Pea Ridge, Arkansas. Although enjoying a sixteen thousand to eleven thousand numerical superiority, Van Dorn dissipated this advantage by splitting his forces. Short on ammunition, his men were routed in a two-day battle. This defeat ended any chance of a sudden Confederate thrust into St. Louis and prevented Van Dorn from reinforcing Albert Sidney Johnston's army in time for the Battle of Shiloh, Tennessee.

Still, Van Dorn was a good friend of fellow Mississippian JEFFERSON DAVIS [5], and he was transferred back to his home state, where as commander of the District of Mississippi he helped shore up defenses at strategically important Vicksburg. His ill-conceived attack against Union troops at Corinth, however, led to a military investigation. Although he was cleared of official misconduct, he had in the process angered many by declaring martial law. With the appointment of JOHN C. PEMBERTON [65] to lieutenant general, Van Dorn was relegated to the command of Confederate cavalry in the region. In this position, he once again demonstrated his skills as a mounted warrior, as evidenced by his raid against Holly Springs, but his defeats at Pea Ridge and Corinth had left the Confederacy vulnerable in the West.

Van Dorn was a handsome, convivial man and married Caroline Godbold in 1843. He was also long reputed to have engaged in a series of extramarital affairs. On May 8, 1863, Dr. George B. Peters entered Van Dorn's headquarters at Spring Hill, Tennessee, and shot and killed the general. Tried before a Confederate court, Dr. Peters was acquitted on grounds that he had merely taken revenge on Van Dorn for having had an affair with his wife. The doctor then divorced his wife, but the two later remarried. Caroline Godbold Van Dorn apparently never recovered from the shock of her husband's murder and lived out the rest of her life at her parents' home.

93

Raphael Semmes

(1809–1877)

Raphael Semmes was the best-known Confederate naval officer of the Civil War. As captain of the C.S.S. *Sumter* and later the C.S.S. *Alabama* he destroyed or captured over eighty U.S. registered merchant ships, more than any other naval officer in history. Although most of his actions came against unarmed merchant vessels, he also sank the U.S.S. *Hatteras,* an ironclad side-wheeler, off the coast of Galveston, Texas, while commanding the *Alabama*. Semmes's activities threatened the North's overseas trade and raised insurance rates to prohibitive levels.

Born in Charles County, Maryland, in 1809, Raphael Semmes was orphaned at age nine. He then lived with relatives in Georgetown and in 1826, through the influence of a wealthy uncle, secured an appointment as midshipman in the U.S. Navy. Promotion in the antebellum navy was slow, and it took eleven years before he became a lieutenant. In the process, he passed the bar exam and saw much of the world. Shortly after securing his promotion, Semmes married and was assigned to Pensacola, Florida. He settled his family in nearby Alabama and purchased three slaves to help his wife with domestic chores, further cementing his Southern ties.

During the war against Mexico, Semmes nearly found his naval career ruined when the ship he commanded sank during a storm. Exonerated by investigators, he went on to participate in the blockade of the Mexican coast and the amphibious assault against Vera Cruz. During an extended postwar leave in the early 1850s, Semmes practiced law in Mobile and compiled his memoirs of his wartime experiences, *Service Afloat and Ashore During the War With Mexico.* Recalled to duty in 1855, he conducted surveys along the Gulf and Atlantic coasts as well as performing various duties associated with lighthouses. He resigned his U.S. commission in February 1861, shortly after his adopted state of Alabama left the Union.

Semmes was soon appointed a commander in the Confederate navy. Traveling to New Orleans, he oversaw conversion of a condemned ship into a commerce raider, the *Sumter,* then eluded Northern blockaders and headed out to sea in June 1861. Although hampered by his ship's small size and slow speed, within the next six months Semmes sank or captured eighteen vessels. Trapped at Gibraltar by three Union warships, Semmes abandoned the *Sumter* and escaped to London, accompanied by his able first lieutenant John McIntosh Kell. On his way back to the Confederacy, Semmes received news of his promotion to captain and his assignment to command a new vessel, especially designed as a merchant raider. Built at Liverpool, it sailed from England, then rendezvoused with its captain, crew, and arms in international waters just off the Azores. In August, 1862, Semmes commissioned the ship, now called the *Alabama,* into the Confederate navy.

Over the next twenty-two months, Semmes sailed over 75,000 miles and burned sixty-four ships. Typically, *Alabama* would hail its intended prey for boarding; if the vessel attempted to flee, Semmes ordered a shot fired across its bow. A boarding party then searched the ship, bonding its cargo if it proved to be neutral property. If U.S.-owned, its passengers, crew, and any useful supplies were taken aboard the *Alabama* and the ship destroyed. Avoiding enemy warships whenever possible, Semmes plied Atlantic and Caribbean trade routes before refurbishing his ship near Capetown, South Africa. Heading east, *Alabama* cruised the Indian Ocean to the China Sea, then retraced its course back to Cherbourg, France.

Believing his health shattered by his extended patrols, Semmes planned on retiring from active naval service, but the appearance of the U.S.S. *Kearsage* threatened to trap *Alabama* in Cherbourg. On June 19, 1864, before cheering crowds, *Alabama* sailed out for its final voyage. After exchanging gunfire for over an hour, Semmes and crew abandoned ship. "We fought her until she could no longer swim," he later remembered, "and then gave her to the waves." Picked up by an English yacht that had been monitoring the action, Semmes eventually made his way back to Mobile, where he arrived in December.

The officers of the Confederate commerce raider Sumter. *Semmes is seated (center) and behind him is his executive officer, John Kell.*

Semmes then went to Richmond, accepted promotion to rear admiral, and assumed command of the James River Squadron. The fleet was scuttled with the fall of Richmond. Semmes served in the artillery until the Confederacy's final collapse. Arrested in late 1865 for allegedly having fled the scene of the *Alabama-Kearsage* engagement after showing a white flag, Semmes was freed after four months' imprisonment. He later served as a lawyer, a professor at what became Louisiana State University, and an editor. His *Memoirs of Service Afloat During the War Between the States* was published in 1869. He died in 1877 from food poisoning.

94

Hannibal Hamlin

(1809–1891)

John Nance Garner, vice president during Franklin D. Roosevelt's administration from 1933 to 1941, is said to have remarked to a young Lyndon B.
Johnson: "I'll tell you, Lyndon, the vice presidency isn't worth a pitcher full
of warm spit." Hannibal Hamlin, the first vice president of ABRAHAM LIN-
COLN [1], surely would have echoed this complaint. Hamlin thoroughly
enjoyed his seat in the Senate, which he held both before and after the Civil
War, but disliked the chiefly ceremonial job of vice-president, often decrying
his lack of power or influence. Still, he performed his public duties reasonably well, especially when compared to his Confederate counterpart, ALEXAN-
DER STEPHENS [71].

Hamlin was born in 1809 at Paris Hall, Maine. His father's death forced
him to return to the family farm and give up his plans to attend college. Still,
he managed to gain admittance to the bar. From 1836 until 1861, Hamlin
served at various times as governor and member of the Maine legislature and
in both houses of Congress. Firmly opposed to the expansion of slavery, he
helped draft the controversial Wilmot Proviso. By proposing that slavery be
excluded from any territory acquired as a result of the Mexican War, the
Wilmot Proviso set off a firestorm of controversy in Congress. After opposing

the Kansas-Nebraska Act, which repealed the Missouri Compromise and opened the Kansas and Nebraska territories to slavery, Hamlin switched to the Republican Party in June 1856.

In 1860, the Republicans nominated Hamlin to be Abraham Lincoln's running mate. A compromise choice, Hamlin boasted a consistent antislavery record, provided geographic balance to the ticket, and as a friend of WILLIAM SEWARD [8] helped consolidate the New Yorker's powerful faction within the Republican ranks. He accepted the post out of loyalty to party and country. The president did allow his running mate to select a fellow New Englander for the cabinet; Hamlin's choice, GIDEON WELLES [23], proved an excellent secretary of the navy but often quarreled with the vice president. Hamlin admitted that he had little influence over Lincoln even as he sought to prod the president toward emancipation and a harsher war policy. Still, in contrast to many other contemporaries, Hamlin never doubted Lincoln's good intentions.

Since his own selection had been a political one, it is perhaps fitting that Hamlin was ousted from the ticket in 1864 for political reasons. Concerned about his own candidacy, Lincoln did not stop others from lobbying for a replacement who offered greater political benefits. The reasons were obvious. Representing a small state in a safely Republican region, respected by, but not a favorite of, those within the party who wanted to challenge Lincoln: Hamlin was expendable. Thus the Union–Republican Party coalition convention rejected Hamlin in favor of a War Democrat, Tennessean ANDREW JOHNSON [6].

Though disliking the job, Hamlin nonetheless found the rejection personally humiliating. Still, he maintained a brave public front. With little to do in Washington as lame-duck vice president, he spent much of the summer of 1864 serving as corporal and company cook with his militia unit of the Maine Coast Guard in Kittery. Defeated in his bid to regain a spot in the Senate in 1865, he accepted a position as collector of the Port of Boston. In 1869, Hamlin returned to the Senate, where he would remain until 1881, happily handing out political favors and serving for four years as chair of the Foreign Relations Committee. Following a brief stint as U.S. minister to Spain, Hamlin died in 1891 in Bangor, Maine.

Sadly, Hamlin, who had always respected Lincoln, learned just before the president's death of the latter's willingness to accept an alternate running mate. The former vice president is reported to have replied wistfully: "I am sorry you told me that."

95

Don Carlos Buell

(1818–1898)

Commanding the Union Army of the Ohio early in the war, Don Carlos Buell never achieved the success that his prewar career had suggested. Like his friend GEORGE MCCLELLAN [7], Buell was an able administrator and firm disciplinarian who knew how to turn raw recruits into soldiers. Buell also shared with McClellan a sympathy for the Southern cause and a military caution which led their critics to suspect them of treason. Unlike McClellan, however, Buell never exuded the charisma and personal magnetism that would make his troops willing to die for him.

Born of Welsh ancestry in Ohio in 1818, Buell was raised by an uncle after his father's death. He graduated from West Point in 1841, ranked thirty-second in a class of fifty-two. Appointed a second lieutenant, Buell fought in the Seminole War and the war against Mexico, receiving brevet promotions for his gallantry in the battles of Monterrey and Churubusco. He survived a severe wound he suffered in the latter contest. After the war, Buell worked as a staff officer in the adjutant general's departments and had by 1861 risen to the rank of lieutenant colonel.

Appointed brigadier general in May 1861, Buell helped organize and train the Union Army of the Potomac. In November, McClellan selected Buell to replace WILLIAM T. SHERMAN [3] as commander of the Department of the Ohio. Leading the newly formed Army of the Ohio, Buell occupied

Bowling Green, Kentucky, and, after the fall of Forts Henry and Donelson, Tennessee, occupied Nashville in late February 1862. As did his old friend McClellan, Buell hated abolitionists and hoped that generous policies toward the occupied South would lead to a speedy reconciliation of the divided nation. Conciliatory orders governing Nashville, he believed, might entice neutral Tennesseans to the Union cause.

As Federal troops poured into central Tennessee, Buell received orders to move his thirty-five thousand troops south to join the army of ULYSSES S. GRANT [2] at Pittsburg Landing, Tennessee. Neither he nor Grant saw the need to hurry, so Buell, now a major general, marched at a leisurely pace. Only on the afternoon of April 6 did Buell's lead division reach Grant—just in time to reinforce sagging Union fortunes on the first day of the Battle of Shiloh, Tennessee. That night, much of the remainder of the Army of the Ohio arrived, spearheading Grant's successful counterattacks that turned defeat into victory.

After the fall of Corinth, Mississippi, HENRY HALLECK [27] dispatched Buell to move east against Chattanooga, Tennessee. Now a major general of volunteers, Buell found the going slow. Continually harassed as he repaired the Memphis and Charleston Railroad, he refused to punish civilians suspected of harboring guerrillas. Buell moved only ninety miles in three weeks. On July 8 Halleck warned him bluntly: "The President telegraphs that your progress is not satisfactory and that you should move more rapidly." Subsequent attacks by Confederate raiders NATHAN BEDFORD FORREST [44] and John Hunt Morgan further delayed the Army of the Ohio's advance. In August, when BRAXTON BRAGG [30] and EDMUND KIRBY SMITH [56] invaded Kentucky, Buell broke off his campaign to give chase. Continually prodded by Halleck, he finally struck one wing of the Confederate forces at Perryville, Kentucky, on October 8. In the ensuing fight, which Pulitzer Prize–winning historian James McPherson has labeled "a battle that set a new record for confusion among top brass on both sides," Buell's 37,000 men defeated a Confederate force of 16,000, but failed to achieve the crushing victory their superior numbers had made imminent.

Following the Battle of Perryville, Buell resumed his cautious pace, blaming his sluggishness on the lack of supplies. Out of patience at last, LINCOLN [1] replaced Buell with WILLIAM S. ROSECRANS [76] in late October. Though a military commission which investigated Buell's actions made no recommendations, he never returned to active command. He resigned his regular army commission on June 1, 1864, a week after he was mustered out of volunteer service. Buell later became president of a mining company and a pension agent. He died in 1898.

Buell's overly deliberate style was his downfall. Well trained and experienced, he demonstrated some abilities as a strategist, having recognized, along with Grant, that the Cumberland and Tennessee rivers held the best approaches to Nashville. But as an independent commander, Buell's caution and mediocre performance at both Shiloh and Perryville surely helped lengthen the war.

96

Eng.d by Geo E Perine NY

Gail Borden

(1801–1874)

While many readers are probably at least vaguely familiar with the name Borden, few know the details of the fascinating man who made the name famous or his contributions to the Civil War. Surveyor, inventor, and philanthropist, Gail Borden Jr. patented a process for condensing milk shortly before the war. Soldiers used his condensed milk and thus stimulated demand for Borden's product, allowing him to open new plants in New York and Illinois in addition to his original Connecticut facility. He went on to invent processes for condensing coffee, fruit juices, and extract of beef.

Born in 1801 in Norwich, New York, Gail Borden Jr. received less than two years' formal education, but learned the rudiments of surveying from his father. As a boy, he moved with his parents to Kentucky and later to the Indian Territory. In his early twenties, Borden went to Mississippi in hopes that the weather might relieve a persistent cough. There he taught school and worked as a surveyor. In 1829 he joined his parents in Texas, where he also surveyed, farmed, and raised stock. He played an active role in the Texas independence movement, serving on several committees of correspondence and publishing an important regional newspaper, the *Telegraph and Texas Register.* Borden was for a time tax collector and helped lay out the site of Houston. As a resident of Galveston during the late 1830s and 1840s, he invented a "locomotive bath house" for women to use in the Gulf of Mexico, acted as secretary for the real estate company that owned most of Galveston Island, and worked in the local temperance society. He also designed a terraqueous machine, a wagon-like vehicle meant to go on either land or water. In 1849 he combined dehydrated meat and flour to produce a meat biscuit. Seeking a worldwide market, he moved to New York, but his overly optimistic hopes of broader sales left him deeply in debt.

In 1853 Borden applied for a patent for condensing milk. Upon receiving approval three years later, he shifted his efforts away from meat biscuits. After two failures, with the financial assistance of Jeremiah Milbank he established a factory in Connecticut. Union soldiers found the product fairly palatable and easy to carry. Word spread to the general public, and booming Civil War sales allowed Borden to take an interest in four new factories in three states. Attracted anew by milder Southern climates, Borden began spending his winters in Texas once again after the Civil War. There he also established a meat-packing plant, a sawmill, and a copperware factory.

Borden was the father of seven children from three marriages (he outlived his first two wives). He was interested in education and humanitarian concerns and devoted much of his time to philanthropic issues in postwar Texas. Borden built a school for freedmen and another for white children; helped finance five churches; and supported numerous teachers, missionaries, ministers, and students.

Gail Borden Jr. died in 1874 in Borden, Texas, and was buried in New York. His condensed milk had helped sustain Union soldiers in the field; simultaneously, their demand for his product stimulated a whole new industry that would greatly facilitate the transport and storage of food products.

97

Philip Armour

(1832–1901)

Some of the richest men in nineteenth-century America began to accumulate their wealth during or shortly after the Civil War. Andrew Carnegie, Gustavus Swift, Leland Stanford, and C. P. Huntington fit this pattern, and as such might be seen as ranking among the war's one hundred most influential persons. Inasmuch as they tended to become wealthy either after the conflict or in a manner coincidental to the war, they are not included in the present volume. By contrast, Armour—grain dealer, meatpacker, and speculator—created a financial dynasty that had direct links to wartime activities. His inclusion in this book is intended to call attention to the enormous economic opportunities made possible by the outbreak of the war.

Philip Danforth Armour was born in 1832 in Madison County, New York. At the age of twenty, he joined thirty others in an overland trek to California, where he worked as a gold miner and in construction. After four years of hard physical labor, and with several thousand dollars in hand, Armour returned east. Dissatisfied with opportunities in New York, he soon relocated to Cincinnati, then to Milwaukee. There he became a partner in a wholesale grocery and commission firm.

In 1862 Armour married Malvina Belle Ogden of Cincinnati. He dissolved his original partnership the following year and with another investor formed a graindealing and meatpacking business. Armour became wealthy near the end of the war when pork prices soared. Convinced that the Confederacy's demise was imminent and that prices would soon plummet, Armour offered to deliver pork for future delivery at forty dollars a barrel. Assuming that prices would continue to rise, New York traders purchased huge amounts of pork futures from his partnership. Armour's hunch paid off. The Confederacy collapsed and pork prices fell to eighteen dollars per barrel. Thus he and his partner easily procured pork at the lower current price and resold it for forty dollars a barrel, netting a $2,000,000 profit.

Armour's financial empire continued to grow after the Civil War. He returned to the Midwest and joined forces with his brother Herman, who owned a Chicago grain commission business. In 1868 they added a pork-packing plant; by 1875 the firm of Armour and Company had emerged with Philip as its head. He established new industry standards by bringing in live hogs and supervising their slaughter at his processing plant; previously, hogs had typically been killed and dressed on small farms, then shipped to pork-packing centers during cold weather. He was always alert to cost-saving measures and pioneered new usages of waste products. When refrigeration became practical in the early 1880s, he bought his own refrigerated cars and established distribution points in eastern cities. Armour and Company also profited from the emerging canned meat and export industries.

In 1879, Philip and another brother, Andrew, established the Armour Brothers Bank in Kansas City, Missouri. Philip also continued to speculate in the futures market, making particularly lucrative investments in pork in 1879 and in wheat in both 1882 and 1897. By the end of the century his net worth was estimated at $50,000,000. Some fifteen hundred employees worked at his various plants.

Shortly after the Spanish-American War, Armour and other meatpackers were threatened by a potential public relations disaster when Commanding General of the Army NELSON A. MILES [98] claimed that Chicago meatpackers had shipped chemically "embalmed" beef to American soldiers. Although the allegations were not proven, Armour never recovered from this assault on his reputation. He relinquished active control of his businesses in 1899 and died two years later. Like many other tycoons of the Gilded Age, Armour gave generously to several philanthropic causes, but opposed collective bargaining and labor unions among his own workers. Of course, it was his ability to capitalize on the opportunities made possible by the Civil War that laid the foundation of Armour's financial empire, as was the case for many of his fellow late-nineteenth-century capitalists.

98

Nelson A. Miles

(1839–1925)

One of the North's "boy generals," Nelson Appleton Miles used the prominence he gained during the Civil War to vault himself onto the larger national stage. Though lacking in formal military training or education, Miles fought with the Army of the Potomac in virtually every major battle in the east, suffered four wounds, and rose from the rank of lieutenant to major general of volunteers. His splendid Civil War record illustrated the key role military amateurs could still play in deciding the conflict. Remaining in the army after the Civil War, he became his nation's most effective Indian fighter, helping to defeat such notables as Sitting Bull, Chief Joseph, and Geronimo. Appointed commanding general of the army in 1895, Miles led the invasion of Puerto Rico during the Spanish-American War.

 Born in 1839 in rural Westminster, Massachusetts, Nelson Miles set out in his late teens for the larger attractions of Boston. Following the First Battle

240

of Bull Run, Virginia, he borrowed enough money to organize and outfit a volunteer company. Clean-shaven and a strapping six feet tall, Miles accepted a lieutenant's commission in October 1861. His real breakthrough came during the Battle of Antietam, Maryland, where he helped spearhead the temporary breakthrough of the Confederate center, a site known forever after as Bloody Lane. With his senior officers either killed or wounded, Miles inherited command of his regiment on the spot. He urged that he be allowed to continue the advance, but his superiors, stunned by the heavy losses, ordered him to fall back, thus allowing the embattled Army of Northern Virginia under ROBERT E. LEE [4] the chance to recover.

Miles's bravery under fire sometimes approached foolhardiness, as was evidenced during the Battle of Fredericksburg, Virginia, when he tried to press home a futile bayonet attack against fortified Confederate positions atop the high ground. Only mildly chastened, he performed so heroically at Chancellorsville, Virginia, that he was later awarded the Medal of Honor. His brigade was again in the thick of the fighting at the Bloody Angle during the Battle of Spotsylvania, Virginia, and in the fruitless attack at Cold Harbor, Virginia. He ended the war a division commander.

Upon the capture of JEFFERSON DAVIS [5], Union officials assigned Miles the task of watching over the former Confederate president's imprisonment at Fortress Monroe, Virginia. It was a poor choice. Although a war hero, Miles was still only twenty-six years old and totally lacking in political experience. Concerned that Davis might escape, and inadequately supervised by his superiors, Miles naively ordered that "light anklets" be fastened around his prisoner's legs. In light of Davis's failing health, the shackling seemed an unnecessary humiliation. Newspaper accounts of this incident greatly embarrassed the Federal government and engendered considerable public sympathy for the former Confederate president.

In late 1866, Miles received a colonelcy in the much-reduced postwar regular army. After serving in North Carolina during Reconstruction, he was transferred west, where as commander of the Fifth Infantry Regiment he became a leading figure in the defeat of the Indians. He was a self-centered and ambitious man whose vanity earned him the enmity of virtually every superior. Miles's superb combat record, seniority, and relative youth, however, were enough to guarantee his continued advancement to higher command, culminating in his appointment as commanding general. Fascinated by technology but unable to comprehend the nation's emerging position as a world power, he remained to the end a hero of the Civil War rather than a leader who would move the U.S. Army into the twentieth century.

Following Miles's mandatory retirement from military service at age sixty-four, the post of commanding general was abolished in order to begin implementing gradual army reforms. Still vigorous despite his growing years, this boy general of the Civil War campaigned unsuccessfully for the presidency in 1904, played a leading role in filming a western movie with Buffalo Bill Cody, published three autobiographical accounts of his life, proposed that he lead an expeditionary force into Russia during the First World War, and testified in favor of Billy Mitchell and military aviation before Congress. In 1925 he died of a heart attack while with his grandchildren at the circus.

Miles's intrepid individual leadership was the stuff upon which Civil War battles depended. Officers personally accompanied their men into battle; all knew that the likelihood of injury or death was very high indeed. One anecdote especially captures the terrifying killing power of Civil War weaponry, absolutely essential to grasp if one hopes to understand the conflict. On their way back to Washington after Lee's surrender at Appomattox, the men of Miles's command marched back across their old battlefields. At Spotsylvania, Virginia, they dug up a tree, nearly two feet in diameter, which had been cut completely in half by *rifle fire*. Miles ordered the stump to be saved; it eventually came to be part of a Smithsonian Institution exhibit, a chilling reminder of the ferocity of the Civil War battlefield.

The battle of Chancellorsville, Virginia, May 3, 1863

99

Henry Wirz

(1823–1865)

The only Confederate official executed for war crimes after the Civil War, Henry Wirz was commandant of the notorious prison camp at Andersonville, Georgia. Found guilty after a quick trial during which he had little opportunity to defend himself, Wirz was hanged on November 10, 1865. His execution was clearly linked to the larger suspicion in the North of a Confederate conspiracy to treat Union prisoners of war inhumanely. Defenders of the Confederacy, on the other hand, saw Wirz's case as an example of unfair Northern retribution against a prostrate South.

Heinrich Hermann Wirz was born at Zurich, Switzerland, in 1823. Son of a tailor, Wirz was interested in medicine and would later falsely claim to be a physician. He married and fathered two children, but after a brief imprisonment ("it had to do with money," he later explained) and subsequent divorce, immigrated in 1849 to Massachusetts. Wirz remarried in Kentucky before moving again to Louisiana. With the outbreak of the Civil War, he enlisted in the Fourth Louisiana Infantry Regiment and advanced to sergeant. Wounded in his right wrist at the Battle of Seven Pines, Virginia, he joined the Confederate military prison system, headed by Gen. John H.

243

Crowded unsanitary conditions in the open caused many Union soldiers to succumb to disease at Andersonville prison camp.

Winder, and was soon promoted to captain. After a short stint at Richmond, in late 1862 Wirz commanded the prison at Tuscaloosa, Alabama, before being dispatched on a foreign service mission to Paris and Berlin.

Wirz returned in February 1864 and was assigned a month later to command the interior of recently established Andersonville Prison. Only partially completed before the first Federal prisoners arrived in February 1864, Andersonville consisted of a rude stockade surrounding over sixteen acres of land. Another ten acres would soon be added. Without adequate food, clean water, soap, shelter, or sanitation, living conditions in the camp quickly deteriorated. Barracks were practically nonexistent and typhoid fever and smallpox spread almost unabated. General Winder, who assumed overall command at Andersonville that June, was more concerned with security against escape and defense against a Union invasion force than the horrid conditions inside the camp. Thus Captain Wirz, whose authority was limited, perhaps bore more blame for the ensuing disaster than he probably deserved.

Even allowing for Winder's inadequacies, however, Wirz did little to ameliorate the situation at Andersonville, by far the largest of all Confederate prisons. Many contemporaries described him as a brutal, profane tyrant prone to outbursts of uncontrollable anger. By August 1864, over thirty thousand prisoners, mostly enlisted men, had been crammed into a site originally designed for ten thousand. Some prisoners were later transferred to other camps, and the Confederacy belatedly began to erect flimsy sheds for cover, but most of the latter facilities were quickly claimed by the "hospital." Nearly thirteen thousand bodies were buried in trenches, with diarrhea, dysentery, and scurvy claiming the most fatalities.

General Winder died in February 1865, leaving Wirz to assume all the blame for Andersonville's horrors. As the war wound down, most of his officers fled, but Wirz somewhat naively remained, paroling prisoners. Arrested in May 1865 by Union troops, he was tried before a military court three months later on charges of murder and mistreatment of prisoners. Sentenced to be hanged, his appeals for clemency went unanswered.

Assessing Wirz's role in the Andersonville disaster is difficult. He had little authority over many of the camp guards and, like the rest of the Confederacy, found supplies of any kind increasingly difficult to procure. The estimated mortality rate at Andersonville was twenty-nine percent (of the 45,000 men held there), slightly less than the thirty-four percent at Salisbury, North Carolina (which held 10,321 prisoners). The deadliest Northern prison was that at Elmira, New York, which claimed twenty-four percent of those incarcerated there. Some have sought to at least partially blame the horrors at Andersonville upon the breakdown of prisoner-of-war exchanges. Upon the Confederacy's refusal to exchange black military personnel, Federal officials broke off the practice in fall 1863. As the conflict continued, feeding and housing the POWs strained the South's remaining resources, so the Confederacy eventually backed down, and by the winter of 1864–65 thousands of prisoners were once again being exchanged. The temporary impasse had made Wirz's job more difficult, but did not excuse the large numbers of deaths under his watch that resulted from diseases spawned by simple malnutrition and exposure. Whether convenient scapegoat or the epitome of the cruel prison camp commandant, Wirz ranks among the one hundred most important figures of the Civil War.

John Chivington

(1821–1894)

Influential rather than likeable, John Milton Chivington made two major contributions to the Civil War. In 1862, his attack on an enemy supply train helped to turn back a Confederate invasion of New Mexico. Two years later, Chivington's unprovoked assault upon a peaceful Cheyenne Indian village at Sand Creek, Colorado, ignited the flames of a major Indian war. Indeed, the Sand Creek Massacre stands as one of the most horrific episodes in the history of the United States.

Born in 1821 near Lebanon, Ohio, Chivington was ordained a Methodist Episcopal minister. In 1860, he became presiding elder in his church's Rocky Mountain Conference at Denver. With the onset of the Civil War, Chivington, who strongly opposed slavery and was of large physique and ego, turned down an offer to become chaplain of the First Colorado Volunteer Cavalry Regiment, insisting instead upon a fighting commission. As major of the First Colorado, he led a raid on the Confederate supply train during the Battle of Glorieta Pass, New Mexico. The loss of its supplies forced the enemy to fall back in disarray all the way to Texas. Although a few fanatical Confederates would continue to dream of a western empire, Chivington's blow ended the most serious threat to Federal control of New Mexico.

Now acclaimed as the "Fighting Parson," Chivington advanced to colonel and assumed command of the military District of Colorado. From this new post, Indians, not Confederates, seemed the major enemy. He and the territorial governor, John Evans, hoped to expand white claims there by pushing the Indians to the upper Arkansas River. They also worried that the Federal government, more focused on affairs in the east than in far-off Colorado, would strip their department of troops. Enjoying virtual autonomy from his military superiors, believing that an Indian war was imminent, convinced that God was on his side, and aware that a successful campaign might further his own personal ambitions, Chivington determined to take matters into his own hands.

In spring and early summer 1864, Colorado volunteer cavalrymen combed the eastern part of the territory. Not surprisingly, Cheyenne, Kiowa, Comanche, Arapaho, and Sioux warriors struck back. Demands for action from angry Colorado citizens swelled even as a few Indian groups, including the followers of Black Kettle, sued for peace. Black Kettle repeatedly met with territorial and Federal officials, promising to lay down his arms and even to join the whites against other Indians. By the end of November Black Kettle's village numbered about 500 persons, mostly Southern Cheyennes. They were encamped along Sand Creek, forty miles from Fort Lyon, Colorado, comfortable in the promise that the government was soon to offer them needed rations.

Technically, however, Black Kettle's village was still considered hostile, as the army had not yet given its permission for the Indians to come in to Fort Lyon. Upon that technicality Chivington planned a surprise attack. On the night of November 28, he and over seven hundred men began a forced march from Fort Lyon. They arrived at the Indian encampment just after sunup the following day. Startled by the appearance of so many troops, Black Kettle raised an American flag and a white flag, assuring his followers that they would not be harmed.

John Chivington and his Colorado volunteers, however, thirsted for Indian blood. Only about thirty warriors formed anything resembling an organized defense; everywhere else there was wholesale slaughter. Men and women, the elderly and children—none were spared by Chivington's self-proclaimed avengers, who mutilated the bodies of many of the two hundred dead Indians who were left behind. Among those who escaped was Black Kettle, who died four years later during another army attack on his village, this time led by George Custer. Chivington's casualties numbered nine dead and thirty-eight wounded.

The Sand Creek massacre led to open warfare on the Southern Plains. Fittingly, the attack did not win Chivington the acclaim he had hoped. In 1865, three separate federal investigating bodies denounced his actions. Only by virtue of having been mustered out of military service did Chivington escape a court-martial. Moving to Nebraska, California, and Ohio before eventually resettling in Denver, he spent much of the rest of his life unsuccessfully defending his actions. He died of cancer in 1894. His success in destroying the Confederate supply train at Glorieta Pass was counterbalanced by the increased Indian warfare stemming from the slaughter at Sand Creek.

HONORABLE MENTIONS

Any attempt to compile a list of the 100 most influential persons of the American Civil War is sure to stimulate controversy. As friends, colleagues, and editors read this manuscript and discussed the subject with me, they offered frequent suggestions about people they believed should be included. I incorporated much of this advice, but rejected many characters whose contributions to the war's causes, course, and outcomes were more limited.

Still, 100 is an arbitrary number when dealing with a conflict as complex and important as this. As I pondered the final list, I concluded that another thirteen individuals deserved at least a brief description. Besides, readers should know why I decided not to include these persons in the main text. After all, the reasons why something is not included give the reader useful insights into the writer's biases. In the case of the Civil War, omissions from this list provide a convenient excuse to discuss, analyze, dissect, and argue about the greatest and most terrible conflict in American history. Should this for even a short time lead us to reflect thoughtfully and meaningfully upon our past, then a useful purpose will have indeed been served.

VARINA HOWELL DAVIS (1826–1906)

If this book had been about the 101 most influential persons of the American Civil War, Varina Howell Davis, the wife of JEFFERSON DAVIS [5], would have been number 101. Daughter of an aristocratic Mississippi family, Varina Howell married Davis in 1845. (Davis's first wife had died a decade earlier.) She proved a strong companion to her proud, talented husband, bearing him six children and managing their Brierfield plantation while he was away during the war against Mexico. On his election to the United States Senate in 1847 she accompanied him to Washington, where they maintained a residence for most of the next fourteen years. Their drawing room, featuring one of the city's more influential politicians and his vivacious wife, evolved into one of the capital's most prestigious social and political centers.

As first lady of the Confederacy, however, Varina Davis encountered much opposition. Her attempts to entertain only engendered criticism; elaborate galas were dubbed insensitive to the growing shortages on the home and battlefronts, while simpler affairs were challenged as diminishing the prestige of the presidential office. Fiercely supportive of her husband's policies, she challenged any who dared disagree and seemed to encourage the president's tendency toward overstubbornness. President Davis's health deteriorated badly during the war, leading Varina to devote increasing amounts of her time and energies to his care.

Feeling betrayed and humiliated by the Confederacy's collapse and her husband's subsequent imprisonment at Fortress Monroe, Virginia, Varina Davis worked tirelessly to preserve and protect his memory after the conflict. She acted as his personal secretary while he compiled his autobiography and wrote her own memoir, highly favorable to the deeds of her husband, after his death.

Without her care and support, Jefferson Davis's health would undoubtedly have been even worse than it was. Given his importance to the Southern cause, Varina Davis clearly merits close consideration for inclusion on any list of the Civil War's most influential persons.

JOSHUA L. CHAMBERLAIN (1828–1914)

Late-twentieth-century enthusiasts familiar with popular accounts of the Civil War will surely question the absence of Joshua Chamberlain from my list of 100. A native of Maine and professor at Bowdoin College before volunteering for the Union army, Chamberlain is a leading character in Michael Shaara's *The Killer Angels*, a Pulitzer Prize–winning historical novel about the Battle of Gettysburg, Pennsylvania. Chamberlain was also prominent in the made-for-television epic *Gettysburg* (based upon Shaara's book) and the award-winning Ken Burns documentary for the Public Broadcasting System, *The Civil War*.

Chamberlain is best remembered for his role commanding the Twentieth Maine Infantry Regiment during the second day of Gettysburg. Chamberlain's position, at the extreme left flank of the Union line along the lower slopes of Little Round Top, was indeed vital. Little Round Top overlooked the Union battle line; if the Confederates had either gained its peak or turned Chamberlain's flank, they might have rolled up the Union army and won a significant victory. Their failure to do so was in large part attributable to the heroic defense by Chamberlain and his men. Assaulted by enemy units twice the size of his own force, his men exhausted and nearly out of ammunition, he launched a desperate bayonet assault as twilight fell that drove back the enemy and securely anchored Little Round Top for the North.

Joshua Chamberlain was an excellent officer and a fine man. He deserved the Medal of Honor he subsequently received for his exploits at Gettysburg, his later election as governor of his home state, and the presidency of his alma mater, Bowdoin College. Yet serious students of the battle place Chamberlain's exploits, brave though they were, in more proper perspective. It was not Chamberlain, but Gouverneur K. Warren, who recognized the danger to the Union left at Little Round Top and ensured that Union troops were present there at all. And even if Chamberlain's position had been lost, in all likelihood the exhausted Confederates could not have properly exploited a breakthrough before darkness fell. The result would have been another of many defeats inflicted by the Army of Northern Virginia under ROBERT E. LEE [4] upon the Army of the Potomac, but hardly the end of the war. Finally, one might argue that Confederate mistakes—Lee's refusal to try to maneuver the Union forces out of strong defensive terrain; the absence of Southern cavalry until the battle's last stages; Richard Ewell's repeated failure to press home attacks; the delays by JAMES LONGSTREET [19] in carrying out Lee's orders—along with the steady Union generalship of GEORGE MEADE [22] and corps commander Winfield Scott Hancock were really the keys to the Union victory at Gettysburg.

ROBERT GOULD SHAW (1837–1863)

Robert Gould Shaw has also emerged as a well-known Civil War character. Like Chamberlain, the historical Shaw was indeed a fine person. A white man born to a prominent Boston family of abolitionists, Shaw commanded the Fifty-fourth Massachusetts (Colored) Regiment, the first African-American unit raised from the Northeast during the Civil War. Shaw, portrayed by actor Matthew Broderick in the superb film *Glory,* and his men spearheaded a doomed assault on Fort Wagner, South Carolina, one of several Confederate positions which protected the entrance to Charleston Harbor. Shaw, along with a good portion of his men, died in the attack, but in the process achieved the glory which is now associated with his name.

The son of wealthy philanthropists, Robert Gould Shaw attended but did not graduate from Harvard College. Shortly after the inauguration of LINCOLN [1], he volunteered for military service. He fought in the campaign against STONEWALL JACKSON [20] in the Shenandoah Valley, Virginia, in 1862 and then in the battles of Second Bull Run, Virginia, and Antietam, Maryland. In early 1863, Shaw accepted the colonelcy of the Fifty-fourth Massachusetts Regiment.

The assault on Fort Wagner came just after dusk on July 12, 1863. Union forces, including six regiments, briefly gained a foothold among the heavily defended Confederate positions before being driven back. Shaw died in the attack; both brigade commanders and four of the five other regimental commanders were also killed or wounded.

Deservedly, Shaw became a martyr among abolitionist groups in the North, but the near-suicidal attack he led failed. Charleston, the ultimate object of the Union operations of which Shaw's assault had been a part, would not fall into Union hands until February 1865. Thus his effect upon the war was relatively minor.

GEORGE ARMSTRONG CUSTER (1839–1876)

George Custer is another prominent Union general who some might expect to rank among the top 100 Civil War figures. Born in 1839, he graduated last in his West Point class of 1861, having racked up large numbers of demerits and floundered in many of his academic subjects. Only in riding and swordsmanship had Custer done well. Though a poor student, he developed into an excellent cavalry officer. Joining the Army of the Potomac shortly after the First Battle of Bull Run, Virginia, he fought in every major battle in the eastern theater after that except one. Custer's elan frequently gained the attention of his superiors, and he ended the war as a major general of volunteers. He seemed to enjoy a charmed life throughout the Civil War. Though he was habitually in the thick of the fighting and had nearly a dozen horses shot from under him, he suffered only one wound. His daring in the fighting at Brandy Station, Virginia, where the Union cavalry seemed a match for their Confederate counterparts for the first time, was especially important for the North.

Earning a lieutenant colonelcy in the much-diminished postwar army, Custer led the Seventh Cavalry to several important victories against the Southern Cheyenne and Sioux. His luck, however, ran out in June 1876 along the banks of the Little Bighorn River, Montana.

George Custer undeniably ranks among the most famous Indian fighters in American history. He was also an excellent mid-level Civil War officer. But because he held no major independent commands during this conflict, by no means does he merit inclusion among the Civil War 100.

GEORGE PICKETT (1825–1875)

Perhaps the most famous Confederate military figure missing from my "100" list, George Pickett spearheaded the unsuccessful assault against the Union center on the third day at Gettysburg, Pennsylvania. Born in Virginia, he moved as a teenager to Illinois, where he owed his appointment to the United States Military Academy largely to ABRAHAM LINCOLN [1], who knew and liked Pickett's uncle. Pickett graduated from West Point in 1846, ranked dead last in a class of fifty-nine. Though no schoolbook soldier, he won two brevet promotions during the Mexican War.

Pickett did well in the Seven Days Battles (Virginia), where he took a severe wound and earned a promotion to major general. After missing the first two days of fighting at Gettysburg, Pennsylvania, his division (which then numbered just under five thousand men) formed the nucleus of Lee's dramatic charge against Union positions along Cemetery Ridge. Shortly before two o'clock on the afternoon of July 3, 1863, Pickett's three brigades, along with eight others, moved from the protective cover of a tree line along Seminary Ridge across a mile of gently sloping open ground into the teeth of withering Northern fire. A few Confederates reached the Federal lines, but the attack disintegrated. "Great God, where, oh! where is my division?" wondered a tearful Pickett as he surveyed the carnage.

The next morning, only one in five of Pickett's men reported for duty. He remained a division commander for the rest of the war, forever associated with what came to be known as "Pickett's Charge" on that fateful day in Pennsylvania. In his memoirs Pickett later blamed LEE [4] for the disaster: "that old man [Lee] . . . had my division massacred at Gettysburg." Although he was an important division leader in the Army of Northern Virginia, the fact that Pickett never held a significant independent command convinces me that he does not merit ranking among the Civil War 100.

AMBROSE POWELL HILL (1825–1865)

The best Confederate division commander of the Civil War, A. P. Hill was born in Virginia and graduated from West Point in 1847, fifteenth in a class of thirty-eight. Though he believed slavery to be immoral, he supported states' rights and thus resigned from the United States Army in spring 1861. By May 1862 he had risen to major general in the Confederate army. He dubbed his command the "Light Division" for its penchant for rapid marches. At Cedar Mountain, Virginia, his movements helped win the day for STONEWALL JACKSON [20]. But Hill's greatest day came at Antietam, Maryland, where after a grueling seventeen-mile march his division arrived just in time to save the army of ROBERT E. LEE [4] from almost certain destruction.

Hill was wounded at Chancellorsville, Virginia, along with his corps commander, Jackson. Upon the latter's death, Lee carved Jackson's old command into two corps, one under Richard Ewell and the other under Hill. Though a superb division commander and ferocious fighter, Hill never mastered the larger corps. His performance at Gettysburg, Pennsylvania, and the Wilderness, Virginia, may generously be described as mediocre. He had contracted gonorrhea in early life, and his health grew progressively worse as the war went on. On April 2, 1865 just a week before Lee's surrender at Appomattox, Virginia, Hill was killed while trying to reform his men against a Union assault.

RICHARD EWELL (1817–1872)

Like Hill, Richard Ewell was thrust into command of one of the Army of Northern Virginia's three corps following the death of STONEWALL JACKSON [20]. Born in Georgetown (District of Columbia) but spending most of his youth in Virginia, he graduated from West Point in 1840, thirteenth in a class of forty-two. After frontier service with the dragoons, he won a brevet promotion during the war against Mexico. In 1859, Ewell was wounded while fighting the Apaches. As a division commander under Jackson, Ewell did splendid work in the Shenandoah Valley, Virginia, campaign and the Seven

Days' battles (Virginia). On August 28, 1862, however, a severe wound received during the fighting at Groveton, Virginia, forced the amputation of his right leg.

Ewell returned to active duty after a painful nine-month convalescence and received his new corps command. He never regained his former energy, however, alternating between riding his horse and in a buggy to ease the discomfort stemming from his old wound. During the first day's fighting at Gettysburg, Pennsylvania, LEE [4] ordered him to take strategic Culp's Hill, the eventual key to the Union right flank, "if practicable." Ignorant of the enemy's dispositions and cautious in the face of Lee's other warning—to delay a general engagement—Ewell instead halted, giving the Federals time to bring up reinforcements. As events unfolded, an opportunity had been wasted, and Ewell's piecemeal attacks over the next two days went nowhere.

Poor health made campaigning agonizingly difficult for Ewell in the next two years. At the Wilderness, Virginia, his failure to drive home an attack squandered any chance of crushing a shaken Union Army of the Potomac, and his corps very nearly broke during heavy fighting at Spotsylvania, Virginia. Eased into less strenuous duty at Richmond, he rejoined Lee's army after the evacuation of the Confederate capital, only to be badly mauled at Sayler's Creek, Virginia.

A fine division commander early in the war, as leader of a corps Ewell always suffered by comparison to his fallen predecessor, Jackson. Such an association is probably unfair, given Ewell's recurring ill-health. Yet if the Confederacy were to have won, it needed abler corps commanders than the somewhat enfeebled Ewell.

WINFIELD SCOTT HANCOCK (1824–1886)

Born in New York and graduated from West Point in 1844 (ranked an undistinguished eighteenth out of twenty-five), Winfield Scott Hancock fought in the Mexican War and had become a solid staff officer by the outbreak of the Civil War. In May 1862, during action around Williamsburg, Virginia, GEORGE McCLELLAN [7] proclaimed that "Hancock was superb today," thus leading to his flattering sobriquet, "Hancock the Superb."

As division and eventually corps commander in 1862 and 1863, Hancock was indeed superb. His greatest performance came during the three-day slugfest at Gettysburg, Pennsylvania, where his II Corps was in the thick of the fighting. Alternately leading, cajoling, and inspiring his men, Hancock was at his best when his country most needed him. The climax came on the third day, when his troops threw back Pickett's Charge. As the Confederates retreated, however, Hancock took a bullet in his right thigh.

Hancock never again achieved the greatness he had demonstrated at Gettysburg. Though the leg was saved, a painful abscess remained, making movement and activity difficult. In addition, Hancock's splendid corps, formerly the Army of the Potomac's best, suffered irreplaceable losses of veterans in the heavy fighting at the Wilderness, Spotsylvania, and Cold Harbor, Virginia. Following the war, Hancock was appointed a major general in the regular army and held a variety of department and division commands.

A lifelong Democrat, he was in 1880 his party's presidential nominee, losing a close race to Republican James A. Garfield. Although Hancock was a key military figure in the Civil War, his lack of independent command experience led me to remove him from my list of the war's most influential 100 persons, where I had originally placed him.

FRANZ SIGEL (1824–1902)

Born in Baden, Germany, Franz Sigel merits mention not for his actions as a Union general but for his ability to inspire German Americans to rally behind the Federal cause. "I fights mit Sigel" was the slogan of many a German immigrant. German loyalty to the Union was particularly important in Missouri, a slave state whose governor supported secession and whose resources might have tipped the balance in the west had they been in Confederate hands.

A graduate of a Karlsruhe military academy, Sigel had supported the German revolutions of 1848–49. Forced into exile, he emigrated to the United States in 1852 and eventually moved to St. Louis, where he became director of schools. At the threat of secession in spring and summer 1861, he organized an infantry regiment and helped keep the city under Federal control. Sigel was largely responsible for the Union loss at Wilson's Creek, Missouri, but did somewhat better in command of two divisions during the victory at Pea Ridge, Arkansas. Transferred east, Sigel fought in the Shenandoah Valley, Virginia, campaign and at Second Bull Run, Virginia. In an independent command, he lost the Battle of New Market, Virginia, and was eventually relieved for what superiors dubbed his "lack of aggression."

After the war, Sigel edited German-language newspapers in Baltimore and New York, where he continued to enjoy the support of German immigrant communities. His repeated military failures, however, made it dangerous to keep this valuable Union loyalist in a position of responsibility for very long during the Civil War. As such, Sigel ranks only in the second echelon of the period's influential persons.

JAMES B. McPHERSON (1828–1864)

Enjoying the confidence of both GRANT [2] and SHERMAN [3], James McPherson played an important supporting role in the North's western military victories. Befriended by a merchant, McPherson escaped the poverty of his boyhood and eventually secured an appointment to West Point, from which he graduated first in the class of 1853 (a group which also included JOHN SCHOFIELD [75], PHILIP SHERIDAN [18], and JOHN BELL HOOD [38]). Early in the war, he was secretly asked to verify rumors that Grant drank too heavily; McPherson stoutly denied these stories and became one of Grant's best officers. His effectiveness as commander of XVII Corps during the Vicksburg, Mississippi, campaign led Grant to name McPherson head of the Army of the Tennessee. Sherman predicted that "he'll outdistance Grant and myself" as a soldier.

In spring 1864, McPherson took a brief leave with the intention of marrying his fiancée, only to have Sherman recall his trusted comrade as the Atlanta campaign began, explaining, "Mac, it wrings my heart but you can't go now." McPherson's cautious performance in leading one of the three armies under Sherman's command has often been criticized. He was killed on July 22 by enemy skirmishers as his troops beat back John Bell Hood's attacks on the outskirts of Atlanta. Ironically, at West Point McPherson had helped the less studious Hood to pass his mathematics courses.

Handsome, congenial, and intelligent, McPherson was one of the most respected Union generals, despite his failure to exploit several advantages during the Atlanta campaign. Sherman always regretted that duty had prevented McPherson's marriage, writing the fallen general's fiancée that it was still better to be the "bride of McPherson dead than the wife of the richest merchant in Baltimore." Alas, she never married.

JOHN A. LOGAN (1826–1886)

John A. Logan was perhaps the most talented of the Union's political generals. Born in Illinois, he fought in the Mexican War and later practiced law. Elected to Congress as a Democrat in 1858, he fought at the First Battle of Bull Run, Virginia, and later raised a regiment of Illinois volunteers. Wounded at Fort Donelson, Tennessee, he was appointed brigadier and later major general. Logan led XV Corps during the Atlanta campaign and assumed command of the Army of the Tennessee after McPherson's death.

SHERMAN [3], though later acknowledging that Logan was "perfect in combat," doubted the latter's ability to master the logistical details needed to successfully lead an army. Sherman was also suspicious of Logan's continuing political interests, which often drew the latter away from the war front. Upon Sherman's recommendation, President LINCOLN [1] relieved Logan of command of the Army of the Tennessee, returning him to his old XV Corps, where he remained until war's end.

Logan attributed his reassignment to West Point prejudice against a volunteer, and upon returning to politics after the Civil War (this time as a Republican) was a vocal critic of Sherman and the regular army. Logan also helped to form the Grand Army of the Republic, a veteran's organization and lobbying group which carried a good deal of political clout during the late nineteenth century. In 1884, he was James G. Blaine's vice-presidential running mate, but the Republican ticket was defeated by the Democrats and Grover Cleveland. Consistently near but not at the center of decision-making,

Logan thus ranks only among the second tier of the most significant persons of the war.

WINSLOW HOMER (1836–1910)

Perhaps the greatest late-nineteenth-century American artist, the Boston-born Winslow Homer showed an interest in illustrations as a child, perhaps inspired by his mother's love for painting. After a short apprenticeship to a lithographer, he published several woodblock illustrations in *Ballou's Pictorial Drawing-Room Companion* and *Harper's Weekly.* Homer moved to New York in 1859, where he attended several night courses at the National Academy of Design and continued to do free-lance work for *Harper's.* His engraving of Lincoln appeared shortly before the latter's first inauguration, and he made several trips to the war fronts.

During the Civil War, Homer also took up oil painting, perhaps believing that black and white images would not effectively capture the war. He did twenty paintings of the Civil War; of these, only five showed combat and only one truly focused on a battle. Several of these wartime scenes were exhibited at the National Academy between 1863 and 1866. Probably his best work of this period was his celebrated *Prisoners From the Front.* Completed after the war had ended, this dark canvas, featuring three Confederate prisoners (one too old to care much, one still defiant, and one frightened), a sturdy Union guard, and a fresh-faced young Yankee officer, dramatically illustrates the different emotions of soldiers in conflict.

The aesthetic and financial success of his Civil War work gave Homer the confidence to devote himself entirely to his art. Of course, he moved on to other subjects, and his most famous themes often concern man's struggles against the sea. Though he had little tangible effect upon the Civil War's outcome, his wartime art did help a nation, then and now, come to grips with the human side of its most terrible war.

JUDAH P. BENJAMIN (1811–1884)

Among the most prominent American Jews of the nineteenth century, Judah P. Benjamin was the best of many cabinet officers chosen by President JEFFERSON DAVIS [5]. Born in the Virgin Islands, Benjamin came to the United States as a child with his parents. He left Yale College before graduating and moved to New Orleans, where he became a successful lawyer. Benjamin was elected to two terms in the United States Senate, first in 1852 as a Whig and then in 1858 as a Democrat.

Jefferson Davis named Benjamin his first attorney general in 1861. Having impressed the president with his hard work and sound advice, Benjamin was shifted to head the War Department later that year. Disputes with influential Confederate officers such as STONEWALL JACKSON [20] and P. G. T.

BEAUREGARD [35], however, led to his March 1862 transfer to the State Department. In this position he helped finalize for the Confederacy a fifteen million dollar loan with the Paris bankers Emile Erlanger and Company, the only significant foreign loan the government secured. After the war's close Benjamin escaped to England, where he established a successful legal practice before moving to Paris shortly prior to his death.

Benjamin, although Davis's closest adviser, found his leverage limited by the public's anti-Semitism and distrust of his close relationship with the president. "A grander rascal than this Jew Benjamin," exclaimed one Georgia congressman, "does not exist in the Confederacy." The constant fluctuations in the Confederate cabinet (six secretaries of war, five attorneys general, four secretaries of state in just over four years of the government's existence) further weakened whatever influence Davis's cabinet-level officers might have mustered.

Appendix 1

MAJOR CIVIL WAR CAMPAIGNS AND BATTLES

Battle	Alternate Name	Date	Union Commander	Confederate Commander	Union Engaged	Conf. Engaged	Union Losses°	Conf. Losses°
First Bull Run	First Manassas	21 July 1861	McDowell	Beauregard	28,500	32,200	2,645	2,000
Wilson's Creek		9 Aug 1861	Nathaniel Lyon	Ben McCulloch	5,400	11,600	1,200	1,200
Forts Henry and Donelson		6–16 Feb 1862	Grant	Floyd; Buckner	27,000	21,000	2,800	16,600
Pea Ridge	Elkhorn Tavern	7–8 March 1862	Curtis	Van Dorn	11,200	14,000	1,200	600
Shiloh	Pittsburg Landing	6–7 April 1862	Grant	A. Johnston/ Beauregard	62,800	40,300	10,200	9,700
Jackson's Valley Campaign		May–June 1862	Banks, Fremont, McDowell, Shields	Jackson	70,000	18,000	7,000	3,500
Fair Oaks and Seven Pines		31 May– 1 June 1862	McClellan	J. Johnston	41,800	41,800	5,000	6,100
Seven Days		25 June– 1 July 1862	McClellan	Lee	91,000	95,000	9,800	20,000
Second Bull Run	Second Manassas	29–30 Aug 1862	Pope	Lee	75,700	48,500	10,100	9,100
Antietam	Sharpsburg	17 Sept 1862	McClellan	Lee	75,300	51,800	11,700	11,700
Corinth		3 Oct 1862	Rosecrans	Van Dorn	21,100	22,000	2,200	2,500
Perryville	Chaplin Hills	8 Oct 1862	Buell	Bragg	37,000	16,000	3,700	3,100
Fredericksburg		13 Dec 1862	Burnside	Lee	100,000	72,500	10,900	4,700
Chickasaw Bayou and Bluffs		29 Dec 1862	Sherman	Pemberton	30,700	13,800	1,200	200
Stones River	Murfreesboro	31 Dec 1862– 2 Jan 1863	Rosecrans	Bragg	41,400	34,700	9,200	9,200
Chancellorsville		2–4 May 1863	Hooker	Lee	97,400	57,300	11,100	10,800
Champion's Hill		16 May 1863	Grant	Pemberton	30,700	20,000	2,300	2,200

° Losses include killed, wounded, missing, or taken prisoner.

Battle	Alternate Name	Date	Union Commander	Confederate Commander	Union Engaged	Conf. Engaged	Union Losses[*]	Conf. Losses[*]
Vicksburg siege		18 May–4 July 1863	Grant	Pemberton	45,000	30,000	3,000	30,000
Gettysburg		1–3 July 1863	Meade	Lee	83,300	75,000	17,700	22,600
Chickamauga		18–20 Sept 1863	Rosecrans	Bragg	58,200	66,300	17,000	11,400
Chattanooga	Orchard Knob; Lookout Mountain; Missionary Ridge	23–25 Nov 1864	Grant	Bragg	56,400	64,200	5,800	6,700
Wilderness		5–7 May 1864	Grant	Lee	102,000	61,000	17,700	7,800
Spotsylvania Campaign		8–19 May 1864	Grant	Lee	83,000	50,000	18,000	9,000
Cold Harbor		2 June 1864	Grant	Lee	100,000	60,000	12,000	2,000
Trevilian Station		11–12 June 1864	Sheridan	Hampton			700	900
Petersburg Assault		15–19 June 1864	Grant	Lee	63,800	41,500	11,400	unknown
Petersburg Campaign	Weldon Railroad; the Crater; Reams' Station; Deep Bottom; Fort Stedman	June 1864–May 1865	Grant	Lee	110,000	65,000	42,000	28,000
Kennesaw Mountain		27 July 1864	Sherman	J. Johnston	16,200	17,300	2,050	450
Atlanta Campaign, I		4 May–17 June 1864	Sherman	J. Johnston	110,000	66,000	10,500	9,200
Atlanta Campaign, II	Peach Tree Creek; Atlanta; Ezra Church	18 June–2 Sept 1864	Sherman	Hood	80,000	55,000	6,000	15,000
Winchester	Opequan	19 Sept 1864	Sheridan	Early	37,700	17,100	4,700	2,100
Cedar Creek	Belle Grove; Middleton	19 Oct 1864	Sheridan	Early	30,800	18,400	4,100	1,900
Franklin		30 Nov 1864	Schofield	Hood	27,900	26,900	1,200	5,600
Nashville		15–16 Dec 1864	Thomas	Hood	49,800	23,200	2,900	6,000
Appomattox Campaign	Five Forks; Petersburg Final Assault; Sayler's Creek; Appomattox Station	29 Mar–9 Apr 1865	Grant	Lee	112,900	49,500	10,800	23,000

[*]Losses include killed, wounded, missing, or taken prisoner.

Appendix 2

MID-NINETEENTH-CENTURY
MILITARY RANKS

ARMY	NAVY
Second Lieutenant	Ensign
First Lieutenant	Master
Captain	Lieutenant
Major	Lieutenant Commanding
Lieutenant Colonel	Master Commandant
Colonel	Captain
Brigadier General	Commodore
Major General	Rear Admiral
Lieutenant General	Vice Admiral
General	Admiral

"Brevet" rank served a bewildering variety of functions, and usually stemmed from the shortages in promotion opportunity due to the regular army's small size. During the antebellum period, the limited number of available positions forced many recent West Point graduates to accept a brevet appointment until a regular second lieutenant's slot came open. During the Mexican War, many officers received brevet rank for valor, meritorious service, or in a few cases simply for longevity of service during the Mexican War. Indian fights, however, did not qualify an officer for a brevet appointment. In some cases, brevet appointments allowed officers to assume the responsibilities, receive the pay, and wear the uniform of the higher grade, although this was by no means always the case.

Appendix 3

IN WHAT FIELDS WERE *THE CIVIL WAR 100* MOST SIGNIFICANT?

Military	41
Political and legal	26
Social reform	14
Artistic/literary	8
Economic and industrial	5
Diplomacy	3
Villains	3

All cabinet officials on both sides were included as political figures. Benjamin Butler, Nathaniel Banks, and John Breckinridge, though they commanded troops during the Civil War, were listed as political figures. Mary Todd Lincoln was included as a social reformer, but Harriet Beecher Stowe was included as an artistic/literary figure. John Wilkes Booth, Henry Wirz, and John Chivington were the "villains."

Appendix 4

WHAT REGION DID THEY REPRESENT?

North/Union	67
South/Confederacy	31
Foreigners	2

For the purposes of this book, an individual's region of contribution or allegiance seemed more important than their birthplace. Little Crow was included in the North, as were Charles Francis Adams and Gail Borden.

Appendix 5

THE SECESSION OF THE SOUTH

STATE	MONTH AND YEAR SECEDED
South Carolina	December 1860
Mississippi	January 1861
Alabama	January 1861
Florida	January 1861
Georgia	January 1861
Louisiana	January 1861
Texas	February 1861
Virginia	April 1861
Arkansas	May 1861
North Carolina	May 1861
Tennessee	June 1861

Each of the seceding states had a specially elected convention to vote on secession. The decisions of the Texas and Tennessee secession conventions were ratified by popular vote. In Texas, Governor Sam Houston refused to take an oath of allegiance to the Confederacy, and was therefore replaced.

OTHER SLAVE STATES

Kentucky	State legislature adopted a resolution of neutrality, May 1861
Missouri	Secession convention adopted resolutions favoring peace and compromise, although the governor, Claiborne Jackson, proclaimed Missouri to have seceded
Maryland	Immediate occupation by Union troops rendered the question of secession moot; Governor Thomas Hicks also opposed secession
Delaware	State legislature rejected offers by several Confederate states to leave the Union

Appendix 6

RECONSTRUCTION OF THE FORMER CONFEDERATE STATES

STATE	READMITTED TO THE UNION	REESTABLISHMENT OF CONSERVATIVE RULE
Tennessee	1866	1869
North Carolina	1868	1870
Arkansas	1868	1874
Alabama	1868	1874
South Carolina	1868	1876
Florida	1868	1877
Louisiana	1868	1877
Virginia	1870	1869
Georgia	1870	1871
Texas	1870	1873
Mississippi	1870	1876

PICTURE ACKNOWLEDGMENTS

All photographs have been reproduced from the collections of the Library of Congress, except as indicated:

Colorado Historical Society [100]

Corbis-Bettman [35, 48, 78, 91]

Chesapeake and Ohio Railroad [14]

National Archives [3, 5, 6, 7, 12, 13, 20, 27, 36, 37, 42, 52, 53, 57, 62, 63, 64, 65, 66, 68, 69, 76, 79, 80, 89, 95]

Naval Historical Center [93]

New York City Public Library [4, 7, 12, 22, 29, 30, 35, 36, 38, 58, 64, 78, 81, 98]

University of Texas at Austin, Prints and Photographs Collection [84, 92, 96]

U.S. Army Military History Institute [3, 10, 27, 33, 43, 47, 53, 69, 75, 79, 94, 99]

INDEX

Abolitionism, 33, 45, 51–52, 68–69, 109, 113
Adams, John, 3, 171
Adams, John Quincy, 3, 171, 219–20
Adams, Charles Francis, 108, 171–72
African Americans, 32, 34, 251
  colonization of, 6
  disfranchisement of, 173
  rights as citizens, 89–90, 109, 117, 119, 185
Alabama, C. S. S., 165, 172, 229–30
Alaska, 23
  purchase of, 28
American Anti-Slavery Society, 69
American Red Cross, 221–22
American Woman Suffrage Association, 113
Anaconda Plan, 102, 103
Andersonville prison camp, 224, 243–45
Anthony, Aaron, 32
Anthony, Daniel, 112–13
Anthony, Susan B., 110–14
Antietam, Battle of, 16, 26, 94–95, 108, 138, 241, 253
Anti-Semitism, 258
Apache Indians, 162
Araminta. *See* Tubman, Harriet
Arkansas, 42
Armour, Andrew, 239
Armour, Herman, 239
Armour, Philip, 238–39
Army of Northern Virginia, 14–16, 53, 60, 85, 91, 97, 105, 132, 174, 204, 241, 251, 253

Army of Tennessee, 85–86, 198
Army of Virginia, 160
Army of the Cumberland, 82, 191–92
Army of the James, 151
Army of the Mississippi, 8, 160, 167
Army of the Ohio, 188, 234–35
Army of the Potomac, 9, 16, 24–26, 39, 60, 64–65, 78, 92, 99–100, 132, 136, 204, 234, 240, 251–52, 254
  cavalry, 53–54
Army of the Shenandoah, 54
Army of the Valley, 204
Atlanta, Battle for, 12, 105
Atzerodt, George A., 71–72

Bailey, Frederick Augustus Washington. *See* Douglass, Frederick
Bailey, Harriet, 32
Bainbridge, Henry, 127
Banks, Nathaniel P., 151, 153–54, 197–98
Bartlett, Harriet, 189
Barton, Clara, 221–23
Beauregard, P. G. T., 20, 39, 96–98, 144, 149, 200, 257–58
Bee, Barnard E., 58
Beecher, Catharine, 47
Beecher, Henry Ward, 47
Beecher, Lyman, 46–47
Beecher, Roxanna Foote, 46
Belknap, William, 12
Bell, John, 156
Bellows, Henry, 202–203
Benjamin, Judah P., 257–58
Benton, Thomas Hart, 125

ABOUT THE AUTHOR

Born in Beaumont, Texas, in 1956, Robert Wooster received his Ph.D. from the University of Texas before joining the faculty at Texas A&M University–Corpus Christi in 1986. Author of several books and scholarly articles, he has also held visiting positions with the Texas State Historical Association and as Civilian Deputy Director of the USMA/ROTC Military History Fellowship.

Currently Professor of History and Chair of the Department of Humanities at Texas A&M–Corpus Christi, Wooster has won several teaching awards and is a frequent lecturer on Texas history, the wars against the Indians, and the Civil War.